STARK

FOS · BOS 12 2016

Fachabitur-Prüfungsaufgaben mit Lösungen

Englisch

Bayern

2008–2015

STARK

36. ergänzte Auflage
www.stark-verlag.de

Inhalt

Jeweils im Herbst erscheinen die neuen Ausgaben der Fachabitur-Prüfungsaufgaben mit Lösungen.

Autoren:

Günther Albrecht, Michael Albrecht

Vorwort

Liebe Schülerin, lieber Schüler,

dieser Band hilft Ihnen gezielt bei Ihrer Vorbereitung auf die **Fachabitur-Prüfung** in Englisch in der **12. Klasse** an den Beruflichen Oberschulen in Bayern.

Ausführliche **Lösungsvorschläge** der **Original-Prüfungen** der letzten Jahrgänge und **prüfungsähnliche Übungsaufgaben** geben Ihnen die Möglichkeit, Ihre eigenen Lösungen zu überprüfen, zu vergleichen und zu verbessern. **Viele Tipps** erläutern die Aufgabenstellung und zeigen Ihnen, wie Sie am besten an die Aufgaben herangehen.

In einem **umfangreichen Hinweisteil** erhalten Sie detaillierte Informationen darüber, wie die Prüfung genau abläuft, welche Aufgabenstellungen vorkommen können und welche Hilfsmittel Sie benutzen dürfen. **Tipps zur Bearbeitung aller Aufgabenarten** im ***reading***- und ***writing*-Teil** und der **mündlichen Gruppenprüfung** geben Ihnen Sicherheit für die Prüfung. Eine Sammlung von ***useful phrases*** hilft Ihnen, einen umfassenden Wortschatz für die Bearbeitung der *writing*-Aufgaben und die mündliche Prüfung aufzubauen.

Sollten nach Erscheinen dieses Bandes noch wichtige Änderungen in der Prüfung 2016 vom bayerischen Kultusministerium bekannt gegeben werden, finden Sie aktuelle Informationen dazu im Internet unter www.stark-verlag.de/pruefung-aktuell.

Wir wünschen Ihnen viel Freude bei der Arbeit mit diesem Buch und viel Erfolg in Ihrer Fachabitur-Prüfung!

Günther Albrecht
Michael Albrecht

Stichwortverzeichnis

Topics for "Argumentative writing":

Hinweise und Tipps

Vorbereitung auf die Prüfung

- Arbeiten Sie im Laufe des Schuljahres kontinuierlich mit und beteiligen Sie sich aktiv am Unterricht. Fangen Sie frühzeitig an, sich vorzubereiten.
- Machen Sie Ihre Hausaufgaben gewissenhaft und erweitern Sie Ihren Wortschatz.
- Beschäftigen Sie sich auch in Ihrer Freizeit mit Englisch. Lesen Sie englische Bücher oder sehen Sie Filme in der Originalsprache (die englischen Untertitel können meist bei Bedarf eingeblendet werden). Hören oder sehen Sie regelmäßig Nachrichten oder interessante Sendungen in Englisch. Im Internet finden Sie eine Vielzahl englischer Seiten, z. B. mit aktuellen Filmkritiken oder Podcasts zu den unterschiedlichsten Themen. Die meisten englischsprachigen Zeitungen, Radio- und Fernsehsender bieten diesen Service auf ihren Internetseiten an. Sie erweitern so Ihren Wortschatz und Sie werden feststellen, wie viel leichter Sie Englisch verstehen, wenn Sie die Sprache regelmäßig hören oder lesen.
- Suchen Sie den Kontakt zu *native speakers* und sprechen Sie möglichst oft Englisch. In vielen Städten gibt es deutsch-amerikanische Institute oder Zentren, die Stammtische und regelmäßige Treffen abhalten, und das Internet bietet weitere Möglichkeiten (per Chat, Lerntandem o. Ä.), um sich mit Muttersprachlern auszutauschen. Je mehr Sie aktiv sprechen, desto sicherer werden Sie und desto gelassener können Sie in die mündliche Prüfung gehen.
- Haben Sie keine Angst vor Fehlern, sondern lernen Sie daraus.
- *Composition* lässt sich leichter bewältigen, wenn Sie sich auf hilfreichen Wortschatz stützen, die sogenannten *useful phrases*. Eine Liste solcher Wendungen finden Sie in diesem Band.
- Üben Sie zusätzlich zu den Hausaufgaben mit den Aufgaben aus diesem Buch!
- Beziehen Sie Ihre(n) Lehrer(in) in Ihre Übungsaktivitäten ein. Lassen Sie Hausaufgaben und freiwillige Übungen korrigieren. Die Lehrer freut es in der Regel, wenn ihre Schüler sich engagieren, und Sie werden davon profitieren, denn Sie erhalten Rückmeldungen über Ihre Stärken und Schwächen.

Aufbau der Prüfung und Bewertung

Die Fachabiturprüfung besteht aus den Teilen *reading, writing* und der mündlichen Gruppenprüfung *(spoken interaction)*. Der schriftliche Teil der Prüfung zählt doppelt so viel wie die mündliche Gruppenprüfung.

- Für die schriftliche Prüfung haben Sie 150 Minuten Zeit und können 60 Bewertungseinheiten (BE) erreichen.
- Dabei entfallen auf den *reading*-Teil 90 Minuten und 30 BE.
- Zwischen *reading*- und *writing*-Teil findet eine Pause von 30 Minuten statt.

- Der *writing*-Teil dauert 60 Minuten und es gibt insgesamt 30 BE (9 BE für den Teil *descriptive writing* und 21 BE für den Teil *argumentative writing*).
- Die mündliche Gruppenprüfung dauert zwischen 20 und 30 Minuten, und Sie können 45 BE erreichen.
- Die in der mündlichen Gruppenprüfung erreichten BE werden durch 3 geteilt und ergeben die mündliche Teilnote.

Beispiel für die Errechnung der Prüfungsnote:

schriftliche Prüfung (doppelt gewertet):	2 × 10 Punkte	
mündliche Gruppenprüfung:	8 Punkte	
	28 Punkte :	3 = 9,33 Punkte (Note 3+)

Als Hilfsmittel in den schriftlichen Prüfungsteilen dürfen Sie ein nicht-elektronisches, einsprachiges Wörterbuch benutzen. Klären Sie aber in jedem Fall vorab mit Ihrem Fachlehrer, ob Ihr Exemplar zur Prüfung zugelassen ist.

Notenschlüssel für die schriftliche Prüfung

Notentendenz	**Punkteschema**	**BE**	**Notentendenz**	**Punkteschema**	**BE**
+	15	60–58	+	6	35–34
1	14	57–54	4	5	33–32
–	13	53–51	–	4	31–30
+	12	50–48	+	3	29–27
2	11	47–45	5	2	26–24
–	10	44–42	–	1	23–21
+	9	41–40	+		20–15
3	8	39–38	6	0	14–0
–	7	37–36			

Zeitmanagement

Wenn Sie sich bewusst machen, was in der Prüfung von Ihnen verlangt wird, dann werden Sie feststellen, dass ein durchdachtes Zeitmanagement ein wichtiger Punkt für eine erfolgreiche Prüfung ist. Sie sollten sich daher auf die Prüfung genau vorbereiten:

- Notieren Sie beim Bearbeiten der Übungsaufgaben, wie lange Sie für die einzelnen Aufgaben brauchen und welche Aufgabenstellung Sie besonders schnell lösen können oder welche Ihnen Schwierigkeiten bereitet.
- Machen Sie sich anhand Ihrer Erfahrungen mit den Übungsaufgaben einen Zeitplan.
- Legen Sie darin fest, wie viel Zeit Sie für welchen Aufgabentyp veranschlagen.
- Halten Sie sich während der Prüfung unbedingt an diesen Plan!
- Hören Sie mit der Bearbeitung einer Aufgabenstellung auf, wenn die veranschlagte Zeit vorüber ist. Sonst verbeißen Sie sich in Schwierigkeiten, die Sie nur Zeit kosten.
- Beginnen Sie mit der Aufgabenstellung, die die meisten Punkte gibt.

Reading-Teil

Der *reading*-Teil umfasst mehrere Aufgaben zum Leseverstehen, die sich auf einen oder mehrere Texte beziehen. Die verwendeten Texte sind Originaltexte aus Zeitschriften, Zeitungen etc.
Lesen Sie den Text und die daran anschließenden Aufgaben zuerst genau und konzentriert durch. Schlagen Sie unbekannte Wörter erst nach, wenn Sie feststellen, dass sie für die Beantwortung einer Aufgabe wichtig sind.

Aufgabentypen

- *multiple choice questions*
  Zu jeder *multiple-choice*-Aufgabe gibt es in der Regel vier Wahlmöglichkeiten, von denen genau eine zutrifft. Die Aufgaben können sich z. B. auf den Textinhalt beziehen, aber auch auf die Haltung des Autors abzielen oder Wortbedeutungen erfragen. Achten Sie darauf, dass oft angegeben ist, auf welche Passage oder Textstelle sich die Frage bezieht.
  Die Antwortmöglichkeiten scheinen auf den ersten Blick oft recht ähnlich. Daher ist es wichtig, dass Sie die Optionen genau und sorgfältig lesen und sich die Bedeutung klar machen. Denken Sie daran, dass die „*most suitable option*“, also die am besten passende Möglichkeit, gesucht ist. Vergleichen Sie die Antworten noch einmal genau mit der Frage und wählen Sie die passendste aus.
- *multiple matching*
  Beim *multiple matching* geht es darum, richtige Zuordnungen zu treffen. Sie erhalten z. B. eine Liste von Personen und eine Liste von Aussagen und müssen die Aussagen den richtigen Personen zuordnen. Achten Sie darauf, dass oft angegeben ist, auf welche Passage oder Textstelle sich die Frage bezieht.
  Markieren Sie sich im Text mit verschiedenen Farben die verschiedenen Bezugspunkte (Redner, Namen, Institutionen etc.). Sie können so die einzelnen Aussagen/Argumente leichter zuordnen.
- *gapped summary*
  Vorgegeben ist eine Zusammenfassung *(summary)* des Textes oder von Teilen des Textes. Ihre Aufgabe ist es, Lücken *(gaps)* in der Zusammenfassung mit passenden Wörtern aus dem Text zu füllen. Einen wichtigen Hinweis auf die einzusetzenden Wörter gibt Ihnen die Aufgabenstellung: Für jedes Wort (auch für *and*, *or*, *my* … oder andere kurze Wörter) ist eine eigene Lücke vorgesehen.
  Es gibt verschiedene Techniken (z. B. spontanes Einsetzen, Gliederung des Textes oder Vorgehen nach Ähnlichkeit der Phrasen oder Strukturen), wie Sie diese Aufgaben lösen können. Detaillierte Hinweise zu den einzelnen Techniken finden Sie bei den Tipps zu den Lösungen der Aufgaben.
- *short-answer questions/sentence completion*
  Hier sollen Sie Aussagen über den Inhalt des Textes auf Englisch vervollständigen bzw. bestimmte Ausdrücke aus dem Text zitieren. Besonders gefordert ist die idiomatische und strukturelle Korrektheit der Wendungen.
- Mediation
  Bei diesem Aufgabentyp sollen Sie zu einem vorgegebenen englischen Text auf Deutsch gestellte Fragen auf Deutsch beantworten. Hier kommt es darauf an zu zeigen, dass Sie den Sinn erfasst haben und ihn auf Deutsch wiedergeben können. Sie sollen die Sätze keinesfalls wörtlich übersetzen.

Writing-Teil

Der *writing*-Teil besteht aus zwei Aufgaben, dem *descriptive writing* und dem *argumentative writing*.

Im *descriptive writing* müssen Sie mit etwa 100 Wörtern ein Bild, einen Cartoon oder ein Diagramm beschreiben, analysieren oder interpretieren. Schreiben Sie dabei aber nicht weniger als ca. 80 Wörter und auch nicht mehr als ca. 120 Wörter, da andernfalls Punktabzug erfolgen kann. Es ist wichtig, neben der Beschreibung des Visuellen auch eine zusammenfassende Deutung als Kernaussage zu geben. Natürlich können Sie in der begrenzten Wortzahl nur auf die wichtigsten Aspekte eingehen. Es sind 9 Punkte zu erzielen, 3 für den Inhalt und 6 für Korrektheit und Natürlichkeit des sprachlichen Ausdrucks. Beachten Sie diesen Vorrang der Sprachkompetenz.

Im *argumentative writing* haben Sie die Wahl zwischen zwei *composition*-Themen. Der geforderte Umfang beträgt etwa 200 Wörter.

- Achten Sie darauf, dass Sie das Thema richtig und vollständig erfasst haben.
- Sammeln Sie relevante Ideen – Vor- und Nachteile, Argumente, Beispiele, Belege, Fachausdrücke – in einer Stoffsammlung bevor Sie zu schreiben beginnen.
- Führen Sie den Leser in der *composition* mit einem einleitenden Gedanken an die Thematik heran. Oft können Sie dazu die Aufgabenstellung in abgewandelter Form verwenden.
- Machen Sie Ihren Standpunkt deutlich. Beispielweise können Sie erst eine kurze Einschätzung der Problematik geben und daran anschließend die Pro- und dann die Contra-Argumente anführen. Alternativ können Sie auch auf jedes Pro sofort ein Contra folgen lassen.
- Achten Sie darauf, dass Ihr Text inhaltlich und sprachlich schlüssig, verständlich und überzeugend ist. Schreiben Sie sachlich. Gliedern Sie den Text in Absätze entsprechend der einzelnen Sinnabschnitte und verbinden Sie diese sinnvoll. Arbeiten Sie Spezialwortschatz und passende *useful phrases* ein.
- Runden Sie Ihr Werk mit einer Schlussbemerkung (z. B. Resümee) ab.

Bewertung des Bereichs *Descriptive Writing*

Punkte	Erfassen der Darstellung und Strukturierung der Beschreibung	Punkte	Korrektheit und Natürlichkeit der sprachlichen Ausgestaltung
3	– **ausschließlich** relevante Aspekte der Darstellung versprachlicht – Hauptaussage bzw. Situation **vollständig** erfasst und **durchgehend** mit geeigneten Details untermauert – logische und aufgabengerecht strukturierte Darstellung	6	– Fehler sind **seltene** Ausrutscher – Fähigkeit, sich präzise und anschaulich auszudrücken häufig erkennbar – **nahezu durchgehend** idiomatisches Englisch
		5	– Fehler kommen **bisweilen** vor, sind aber nicht systematischer Natur und nicht sinnstörend – Fähigkeit, sich präzise und anschaulich auszudrücken **häufig** erkennbar – weitgehend idiomatisches Englisch

<table>
<tr><td rowspan="2">2</td><td rowspan="2">– mehrheitlich relevante Aspekte versprachlicht
– Hauptaussage erfasst und weitgehend durch geeignete Details untermauert
– weitgehend logische und aufgabengerecht strukturierte Darstellung</td><td>4</td><td>– Fehler sind vereinzelt auch systematischer Natur, aber nicht sinnstörend
– Fähigkeit, sich präzise und anschaulich auszudrücken mehrfach erkennbar
– weitgehend idomatisches Englisch</td></tr>
<tr><td>3</td><td>– Fehler sind vereinzelt auch sinnstörender Natur; ohne jedoch die Hauptaussage zu beeinträchtigen
– Fähigkeit, sich präzise und anschaulich auszudrücken stellenweise erkennbar
– eher einfache Sprache mit vereinzelten Germanismen</td></tr>
<tr><td rowspan="2">1</td><td rowspan="2">– einige relevante Aspekte versprachlicht
– Hauptaussage nur ansatzweise erfasst und /oder durch unwesentliche / falsche Details untermauert
– wenige logische Bezüge erkennbar (Gedankensprünge und Widersprüche)</td><td>2</td><td>– Fehler kommen gehäuft vor, stören die Hauptaussage aber nur geringfügig
– umständliche und /oder monotone Ausdrucksweise
– mehrfach Germanismen</td></tr>
<tr><td>1</td><td>– Darstellung mit vielen Fehlern
– weitgehend „deutsches“ Englisch</td></tr>
<tr><td>0</td><td colspan="3">Aufgabe nicht erfüllt / Darstellung weitgehend unverständlich</td></tr>
</table>

Bewertung des Bereichs *Argumentative Writing*

Punkte	**Erfassen der Aufgabe *(relevance / depth)* und Entwicklung der Gedanken *(organisation / coherence)***	**Verständlichkeit der sprachlichen Ausgestaltung *(accuracy / cohesion)***	**Natürlichkeit der sprachlichen Ausgestaltung *(appropriacy / range)***
7	– ausschließlich relevante tiefergehende Ausführungen mit **durchgehender** Konkretisierung durch stützende Details – aufgabengerecht strukturierte, geschlossene und kohärente Darstellung	zügiges Lesen und Verstehen **absolut** gewährleistet: – Fehler sind **seltene Ausrutscher** – fast durchgehend gute Textkohäsion	**weitgehend** natürlich wirkender Text: – weitgehend angemessene Sprache – Fähigkeit sich effizient und abwechslungsreich auszudrücken **häufig** erkennbar – weitgehend idiomatisches Englisch
6	– **ausschließlich** relevante Ausführungen – **weitgehend** mit stützenden Details – aufgabengerecht strukturierte, geschlossene und kohärente Darstellung	zügiges Lesen und Verstehen **absolut** gewährleistet: – Fehler kommen vor, sind aber **nicht** systematischer Natur und **nicht** sinnstörend – **fast durchgehend** gute Textkohäsion	**weitgehend** natürlich wirkender Text: – weitgehend angemessene Sprache – Fähigkeit sich effizient und abwechslungsreich auszudrücken **mehrfach** erkennbar – **weitgehend** idiomatisches Englisch

5	– mehrheitlich relevante Ausführungen mit etlichen stützenden Details – **weitgehend** aufgabengerecht strukturierte, geschlossene und kohärente Darstellung	zügiges Lesen und Verstehen **weitgehend** gewährleistet: – Fehler sind **vereinzelt** auch systematischer Natur – allenfalls 1–2 Fehler, die den Sinn beeinträchtigen – **kleinere Schwächen** in der Textkohäsion	**im Allgemeinen** natürlich wirkender Text: – **weitgehend** angemessene Sprache – Fähigkeit sich effizient und abwechslungsreich auszudrücken **stellenweise** erkennbar – idiomatisches Englisch neben **wenigen** Germanismen klar erkennbar
4	– **mehrheitlich** relevante Ausführungen mit **etlichen** stützenden Details – Schwächen in der Strukturierung und Gedankenentwicklung (Unausgewogenheit, Plötzlichkeit), aber ohne **gravierende** logische Brüche	zügiges Lesen und Verstehen **überwiegend noch** gewährleistet: – systematische Fehler kommen **mehrfach** vor – sinnstörende Fehler kommen **vereinzelt** vor – **gelegentliche** Brüche in der Textkohäsion	**im Allgemeinen noch** natürlich wirkender Text: – um angemessene Ausgestaltung deutlich bemüht – Fähigkeit sich effizient auszudrücken **ansatzweise** erkennbar; sonst einfache Sprache, aber abwechslungsreich formuliert – **Ansätze** zu idiomatischem Englisch neben **gelegentlichen** Germanismen vorhanden
3	– einfache Ausführungen, aber **noch mehrheitlich** zum Thema – kaum stützende Details, überwiegend enumerativ – komplexere Darstellungen gelingen nicht (Gedankensprünge und Widersprüche)	zügiges Lesen und Verstehen **nicht** gewährleistet: – systematische Fehler kommen **gehäuft** vor; einfachste Strukturen werden jedoch korrekt verwendet – **wiederholt** sinnstörende Fehler – Mängel in der Textkohäsion	**zum Teil unnatürlich** wirkender Text: – angemessene Ausgestaltung kaum gegeben – einfache und monotone Ausdrucksweise – mehrfach Germanismen
2–1	– sehr banale Ausführungen – Bezug zum Thema nur in Ansätzen erkennbar – Gedankenentwicklung mit großen Sprüngen und Widersprüchen	– viele systematische Fehler – viele sinnstörende Fehler, sodass Sinn nur schwer zu entschlüsseln ist	über längere Passagen unnatürlich wirkender Text: – kurze isolierte Sätze – viele Germanismen
0	Aufgabe nicht erfüllt / Thema oder Textsorte verfehlt / Aufsatz weitgehend unverständlich		

Mündliche Gruppenprüfung

In der mündlichen Prüfung werden 4 bis 6 Schüler in einer Gruppe geprüft. Während der Vorbereitungszeit (20 bis 30 Min.) erhält jeder Teilnehmer Arbeitsanweisungen. Diese Anweisungen beziehen sich auf die individuelle Aufgabe jedes Schülers und auf die Aufgabe der Gruppe. Während der Vorbereitungszeit können die Gruppenmitglieder nicht miteinander kommunizieren (Aufsicht vorhanden), ein Wörterbuch, auch Deutsch–Englisch, steht den Prüflingen aber zur Verfügung. Zu Beginn der Prüfung stellt jeder Teilnehmer seine Rolle und seine Position vor. Dazu haben Sie etwa eine Minute Zeit. Im weiteren Prüfungsverlauf diskutieren Sie mit Ihren Mitschülern nach den Vorgaben Ihrer jeweiligen Rollen über das gegebene Thema. Dabei sollen Sie Ihr Ziel durch gute Argumente und überlegte Redestrategie erreichen. Beteiligen Sie sich am Gespräch und versuchen Sie, in die Diskussion einzugreifen. Achten Sie aber darauf, dass Sie auf die Argumente Ihrer Mitschüler eingehen und ein echtes Gespräch zustande kommt. Versuchen Sie, alle Gruppenmitglieder in die Diskussion einzubinden und spielen Sie schwächeren Mitschülern Bälle zu. Dies kann auch für Ihre eigene Bewertung nur von Vorteil sein.

Bewertung der Gruppendiskussion

Punkte	**Sprachbeherrschung** ***(fluency, accuracy, range)***	**Inhaltliche Qualität der Beiträge** ***(relevance, depth, coherence)***	**Interaktive Kompetenz** ***(strategies)***
15–13	– kann sich **fast durchweg** spontan und flüssig ausdrücken – verwendet korrekte Sprache mit wenigen Flüchtigkeitsfehlern – **weitgehend** idiomatisches Englisch und guter thematischer Wortschatz erlauben Präzision im Ausdruck	– präsentiert mit klarem Bezug auf Situation und Aufgabenstellung – liefert **breites Spektrum** an detailliert dargelegten Ideen /Aspekten / Beispielen – differenziert, problematisiert, wägt ab	– bewältigt den Sprecherwechsel **geschickt** (spontanes Reagieren, natürliches und variationsreiches *turn-taking*) und beteiligt sich **intensiv** am Gespräch – **klarer** Überblick über den gesamten Gesprächsverlauf (z. B. knüpft an, bezieht sich zurück, fasst zusammen, achtet auf Partner, trägt **besonders aktiv** zur Entscheidungsfindung bei)
12–10	– kann sich **weitgehend** fließend ausdrücken – verwendet weitgehend korrekte Sprache – Idiomatik und thematischer Wortschatz **stellenweise** vorhanden	– präsentiert **mit klarem Bezug** auf Situation und Aufgabenstellung – nennt wichtige Aspekte, legt eigene Gedanken detailliert dar – **differenziert, problematisiert, wägt ab**	– bewältigt den spontanen Sprecherwechsel und beteiligt sich in **ausgewogenem** Maß als Sprecher und Hörer – Überblick über den **gesamten** Gesprächsverlauf (knüpft an, bezieht sich zurück, fasst zusammen, achtet auf Partner, trägt zur Entscheidungsfindung bei)

9–7	– kann sich unter **gelegentlichem** Zögern insgesamt relativ fließend ausdrücken – sprachliche Fehler häufen sich – Idiomatik und thematischer Wortschatz **ansatzweise** vorhanden	– präsentiert unter Berücksichtigung der Situation und Aufgabenstellung – bringt **neue** Aspekte ein – äußert sich **weitgehend** detailliert	– wechselt angemessen zwischen Sprecher- und Hörerrolle; **leichte** Tendenz zu viel /zu wenig zu sprechen – **folgt der Entwicklung** des Gesprächs (knüpft an, trägt zur Entscheidungsfindung bei)
6–4	– Äußerungen kommen insgesamt eher zögernd – macht **vereinzelt** sinnstörende Fehler, bleibt insgesamt jedoch verständlich – einfacher, aber überwiegend korrekter Wortschatz	– präsentiert **unter Berücksichtigung** der Situation und Aufgabenstellung – bringt kaum neue Aspekte ein und beschränkt sich auf **begründetes** Zustimmen / Ablehnen – stellt Gedanken eher kurz dar	– **gelegentliches** zu starkes oder zu geringes, aber in der Regel selbstständiges Eingreifen ins Gespräch – **folgt der Entwicklung** des Gesprächs, bringt sich aber eher abrupt ein
3–1	– äußert sich mit Pausen, Abbrechen und Neuansetzen – **gelegentlich** Fehler, die den Sinn entstellen und den Gesprächspartnern das Verstehen erschweren – häufig fehlender bzw. falscher Wortschatz	– präsentiert **nur teilweise mit** Bezug zur Situation und Aufgabenstellung – bringt keine neuen Aspekte ein; beschränkt sich auf **Wiederholungen** – Gedankengänge **nicht einfach** nachvollziehbar – weicht von Situation / Thema ab	– spricht deutlich zu viel oder spricht zu wenig; bringt sich **vereinzelt noch selbstständig** in das Gespräch ein – **kennt den momentanen Stand** des Gesprächs, konzentriert sich aber auf den eigenen Beitrag
0	– kann sich nur mit langen Pausen, häufigem Abbrechen und Neuansetzen äußern – häufig Fehler, die den Sinn entstellen und den Gesprächspartnern das Verstehen sehr erschweren – häufig fehlender bzw. falscher Wortschatz	– präsentiert ohne Bezug zur Situation und Aufgabenstellung – beschränkt sich auf unbegründetes Zustimmen / Ablehnen – Gedankengänge kaum nachvollziehbar – weicht von Situation / Thema ab	– kann sich nur unter aktiver Mithilfe der anderen ins Gespräch bringen – kann der Entwicklung des Gesprächs kaum folgen
0	Beiträge zu kurz für Bewertung und /oder überwiegend unverständliche Beiträge		

Useful phrases

Composition

Time

For many years …	*Viele Jahre lang …/Seit vielen Jahren …*
In the last few years/decades/weeks/ months/days …	*In den vergangenen Jahren/Jahrzehnten/ Monaten/Wochen/Tagen …*
In recent decades/years/months/weeks …	*In den letzten Jahrzehnten/Jahren/ …*
Recently … Note: Present perfect in all these phrases	*In letzter Zeit …; Neulich …*

Opinions

Authorities /Others

Benjamin Franklin once said/wrote/claimed that …	*Benjamin Franklin hat einmal gesagt/ geschrieben/gefordert, dass …*
Many respected scholars/scientists/world leaders …	*Viele angesehene Wissenschaftler/Forscher/ Weltpolitiker …*
In the text, the author claims/expresses the belief/states that …	*Im Text fordert der Autor/drückt er seine Überzeugung aus/stellt er fest, dass …*
Many people believe that …	*Viele Menschen glauben, dass …*
It has been said that …	*Es wurde gesagt, dass …*

Your own

It is my (firm) opinion that …	*Es ist meine (feste) Meinung, dass …*
It is my belief that …	*Es ist mein Glaube, dass …*
It is my conviction that …	*Es ist meine Überzeugung, dass …*
I am firmly convinced that …	*Ich bin fest davon überzeugt, dass …*

Disbelief/Disagreement

I simply do not/cannot agree/ believe that …	*Ich kann einfach der Tatsache, dass … nicht zustimmen./Ich kann einfach nicht glauben, dass …*
It would be nonsense to say that …	*Es wäre Unsinn zu sagen, dass …*
That may be true, but …	*Das kann sein, aber …*

Order of importance

Same degree

It is also important to mention …	*Es ist ebenfalls wichtig zu erwähnen, dass …*
It is also worth mentioning that …	*Es ist ebenfalls erwähnenswert, dass …*
In the same way (= likewise) it is worth mentioning …	*Ebenso/In gleichem Maße ist erwähnenswert …*
Similarly important is the fact …	*Ähnlich wichtig ist die Tatsache …*

Equally important is the fact …	*Ebenso wichtig ist die Tatsache …*

Higher degree

More important still is the fact that …	*Wichtiger ist jedoch die Tatsache, dass …*
A more important reason is …	*Ein wichtigerer Grund ist …*
Better/worse still …	*Besser/schlimmer jedoch …*
That is better/worse …	*Das ist besser/schlimmer …*
What is more important …	*Es ist wichtiger, dass …*
More importantly …	*Wichtiger ist …*

Highest degree

The most important factor of all is the fact that …	*Der bedeutendste Faktor ist die Tatsache, dass …*
Most important of all is …	*Am wichtigsten ist …*
What is most important …	*Es ist am wichtigsten, dass …*
And/But above all …	*Und/Aber darüber hinaus …*
Most importantly …	*Am wichtigsten ist …*

Chronological contrast

at first	then	finally
at the beginning	afterwards	eventually
	after that	in the end
	later (on)	at the end of …
originally	(not so) long ago	recently
previously	in the course of	lately
in the old days	ever since	now
		today

EXAMPLES:

At first many people welcomed immigrants. Then they became afraid that immigrants would change their country. Eventually they set quotas to control immigration.
Zunächst hießen viele Leute die Einwanderer willkommen. Dann/Später befürchteten sie, dass die Einwanderer ihr Land verändern würden. Schließlich führten sie eine Quotenregelung ein, um die Einwanderung unter Kontrolle zu behalten.

Originally, no immigrants from China were allowed to enter the US. Not so long ago, there was still prejudice against the Chinese. Recently, people have realized that the Chinese succeed very well in integrating themselves into society.
Ursprünglich war es Einwanderern aus China nicht erlaubt, in die USA einzureisen. Vor gar nicht so langer Zeit gab es immer noch Vorurteile gegen Chinesen. In letzter Zeit erkannten die Menschen, dass sich die Chinesen sehr gut in die Gesellschaft integrieren.

German immigrants were among the first to arrive in the US in the old days. Ever since there have been a large number of Germans in the country. Today, 25 % of Americans are of German ancestry.
Die deutschen Einwanderer waren unter den ersten, die früher in die USA gingen. Seit dieser Zeit/Seitdem gibt es eine große Zahl Deutscher im Land. Heute/Heutzutage haben 25 % der Amerikaner deutsche Vorfahren.

Concessive contrast

however	even though	notwithstanding
but	in spite of that	unlike
still	despite the fact that	whereas
yet	nevertheless	though/although
otherwise	contrary to	on the contrary
on the one hand – on the other hand		of course

EXAMPLES:

Tom does not like spinach. Nevertheless, his mean mother makes him eat it.
Tom mag keinen Spinat. Trotzdem/Dennoch zwingt ihn seine gemeine Mutter, ihn zu essen.

Contrary to popular opinion, spinach is actually quite tasty.
Im Gegensatz zur üblichen Meinung ist (aber) Spinat tatsächlich recht schmackhaft.

In spite of that, many children still refuse to eat spinach.
Im Gegensatz dazu/Trotzdem weigern sich viele Kinder immer noch, Spinat zu essen.

On the one hand, spinach is very nutritious. On the other hand, it tastes like dirt.
Einerseits ist Spinat sehr nahrhaft; andererseits schmeckt er wie Dreck.

Of course I know spinach is healthy, but I still won't eat it.
Natürlich weiß ich, dass Spinat gesund ist, aber ich werde ihn trotzdem nicht essen.

You must finish your spinach. Otherwise you will not get any dessert.
Du musst deinen Spinat aufessen; sonst gibt es keine Nachspeise.

Notional phrases

Anmerkung: notional phrases sind idiomatische Wendungen in Dialogsituationen und für die mündliche Gruppenprüfung im kommunikativen Diskurs sehr geeignet.

Agreement

So do I.	*Sehe ich auch so.*
I think so too.	*Das denke ich auch.*
I agree with you.	*Ich stimme dir/Ihnen zu.*
I quite agree.	*Ich stimme mit dir/Ihnen überein.*
I couldn't agree more.	*Da bin ich ganz deiner/Ihrer Meinung*
Nor do I.	*Ich auch nicht.*

Disagreement

I don't think so.	*Das sehe ich nicht so.*
I couldn't agree less.	*Das sehe ich überhaupt nicht so.*

Conviction/Certainty

I am certain/sure we'll win this match.	*Ich bin mir sicher, dass wir das Spiel gewinnen werden.*
I'm convinced we'll win this match.	*Ich bin davon überzeugt, dass wir das Spiel gewinnen werden.*
There's no doubt that we'll win this match.	*Es gibt keinen Zweifel, dass wir das Spiel gewinnen werden.*

Doubt

I am not certain/sure whether we'll win this match.	*Ich bin mir nicht sicher, ob wir das Spiel gewinnen werden.*
I don't know for certain/for sure if we'll win this match.	*Ich bin mir nicht sicher, ob wir das Spiel gewinnen werden.*
I rather doubt we'll win this match.	*Ich bezweifle, dass wir dieses Spiel gewinnen werden.*

Pleasure

That's good news.	*Das sind gute Nachrichten.*
I am pleased to hear that.	*Das freut mich zu hören.*
That's great (news).	*Das ist großartig/ Das sind großartige Nachrichten.*

Disappointment

That's bad news.	*Das sind schlechte Nachrichten.*
I am sorry to hear that.	*Das tut mir leid zu hören.*
How (very) disappointing.	*Wie enttäuschend!*

Annoyance

What a nuisance.	*Was für ein Ärger!*
How (very) annoying.	*Wie ärgerlich!*

Surprise

That's surprising/amazing/astonishing	*Das ist erstaunlich/überraschend/verwunderlich.*
What a surprise!	*Was für eine Überraschung!*
Good heavens!	*Um Himmels willen!*

Sorrow/Sympathy

I'm sorry to hear that.	*Das tut mir leid zu hören.*
That's sad news.	*Das sind traurige Nachrichten.*
Oh, I am so sorry for …	*Oh, das tut mir leid für …*
That's bad luck.	*Das ist Pech/ So ein Unglück.*
That's a pity.	*Das ist schade.*
What a pity.	*Wie schade.*
That's a shame.	*Das ist eine Schande.*

Indifference

I am not really interested.	*Ich habe kein großes Interesse daran.*
I don't mind.	*Das macht mir nichts aus.*
I don't care.	*Das ist mir egal.*
That doesn't matter to me.	*Das macht mir nichts.*
I couldn't care less.	*Das berührt mich überhaupt nicht.*

Intention

I'm going to stay at home.	*Ich werde zu Hause bleiben.*
I intend to stay home.	*Ich beabsichtige, zu Hause zu bleiben.*

Determination

We're going to win the match tomorrow.	*Wir werden das Spiel morgen gewinnen.*
I've decided to win the match tomorrow.	*Ich habe mich entschieden, das Spiel morgen zu gewinnen.*
I'm determined to win the match tomorrow.	*Ich bin fest entschlossen, das Spiel morgen zu gewinnen.*
We're going to win the match tomorrow, if it's the last thing we do.	*Wir werden das Spiel morgen um jeden Preis gewinnen.*

Worry / Fear

I'm afraid I'll fail my exam.	*Ich befürchte, ich werde meine Prüfung nicht bestehen.*
I'm terrified I'll fail my exam.	*Ich habe Angst, meine Prüfung nicht zu bestehen.*

Reassurance

Don't worry, you'll pass the exam.	*Mach dir keine Sorgen, du wirst die Prüfung bestehen.*
You needn't lose any sleep over it. You'll pass it.	*Mach dir nicht zu viele Gedanken darüber. Du wirst sie schon bestehen.*
That doesn't matter.	*Das macht nichts.*

Warning

Mind what you are doing with that hammer or you'll hurt yourself.	*Pass auf was du mit dem Hammer machst, du wirst dich noch verletzen.*
Be careful with that hammer or you'll hurt yourself.	*Sei vorsichtig mit dem Hammer. Du wirst dich noch verletzen.*

Apology / Regret

I'm sorry I'm late.	*Es tut mir leid, ich habe mich verspätet.*
Sorry, I couldn't be here earlier.	*Entschuldigung, ich konnte nicht früher hier sein.*
I'm afraid I've got some bad news for you.	*Es tut mir leid, aber ich habe schlechte Nachrichten für dich/Sie.*
Unfortunately I can't help you with your homework.	*Unglücklicherweise/Leider kann ich dir nicht bei deinen Hausaufgaben helfen.*

Gratitude

Don't mention it.	*Keine Ursache.*
You're welcome.	*Gern geschehen.*
That's o.k.	*Kein Problem.*
Any time.	*Jederzeit wieder.*

Giving advice

You'd better do your homework more carefully.	*Es wäre besser, wenn du deine Hausaufgaben mit mehr Sorgfalt machtest.*
You really ought to do your homework more carefully.	*Du solltest deine Hausaufgaben wirklich mit mehr Sorgfalt erledigen.*

Übungsaufgaben und Original-Prüfungsaufgaben

Berufliche Oberschulen Bayern – Englisch 12. Klasse
Übungsaufgabe 1

Aufgabenteil: *Reading*

London's Comings and Goings

(A) The scene is quite familiar: two businessmen of different nationalities in a London restaurant being served by a waiter from a third country, all of them speaking English. But such encounters illustrate a remarkable change going on in London. Foreigners are moving in, and Britons are moving out, faster than at any time on record. The consequences are being felt across the country.

(B) Before the Second World War, London's population grew steadily, along with that of most other British cities. After the war, along with that of most other British cities, it shrank – first because of the policy of shifting people out of the slums into new towns, and second because of the decline of the heavy industries which had brought people to the cities in the first place. In the 1990s, other cities went on shrinking. Manchester's population dropped by 10 % in 1991–2001, Liverpool's by 8 %, Newcastle's by 6 % and Birmingham's by 3 %. London, however, grew by 4.8 % over the period, partly because it has a high birth rate, but mostly because foreigners started arriving.

(C) Who are these people? According to the Home Office report published in 2002, they come from everywhere, with the proportion from comparatively affluent countries being relatively high. Nevertheless, immigrants are economically polarised. Compared with the locals, more have degrees, but more have no qualifications at all (though that is partly explained by the fact that so many of them are students). White immigrants, by and large, earn quite a bit more than locals. Brown and black ones earn less. Immigrants work more in growing businesses – such as health – than locals do, and less in shrinking ones – such as manufacturing and they are more self-employed than locals – 25 % of Middle Easterners and 19 % of Eastern Europeans are self-employed, compared with 11 % of British-born people.

(D) The influx has changed London visibly. New ethnic villages have sprung up all over the place. The Arabs have long been in Bayswater, the West Indians in Brixton and the Bangladeshis in Tower Hamlets. Now the Poles are in Lambeth and Southwark, the Kosovans and Albanians in Enfield and Newham, the Iraquis in Barnet and the Congolese in Croydon. The Europeans and Americans are all over central London. The foreigners have helped drive London property prices further above those of the rest of the country. Over the past decade, according to figures from the Nationwide Building Society, prices in London have risen far more quickly than elsewhere in Britain. Rising property prices hurt those struggling to get onto the ladder. But for those already on it, they have been a boon: home-owning Londoners have found themselves sitting on large piles of cash. That has allowed them to do what Londoners, traditionally, long to do: move out. Of course, the British have always been romantic about the countryside. It's a fact that the great British 19th-century novels are either rural – Austen and Eliot – or they are about how horrible towns are – Dickens and Mrs Gaskell. In a 1997 poll, 72 % of Britons still said they would like to live outside a city. "Quietness", "escape from the rat-race", "fewer non-white people" were some of the reasons given.

(E) In many people's eyes, the high levels of immigration have increased the drawbacks to living in London. No doubt, they have put added pressure on London's stretched public services. Education is a good case in point: more immigrants mean more children with a poor command of English. They struggle at school and present an additional challenge for school staff. In Inner London, for example, 38 % of children get five or more good GCSEs; in England as a whole, 48 % do. Given these circumstances, it has become harder to recruit teachers, many of whom are unqualified or temporary. Rich people, as a result, feel condemned to send their children to expensive private schools, 16 % of secondary school children go to independent schools in London, compared with 8 % across England as a whole.

(F) Does all this mean that London will again shrink? The prognosis is that the outflow from London as well as the attraction of the capital to immigrants are likely to go on. 2004 will bring a further boost to foreign immigration, when ten new countries join the EU. The other big EU countries will not give the Union's new citizens the right to work straight away; they intend to phase it in. Britain, in contrast, gives the newcomers free access to the labour market from the start. That's unlikely to trouble the government. Immigration may be politically sensitive, but the government understands how migration has driven London's economy, and London has driven Britain's. It wants the motor to keep on running.

Adapted from The Economist, August 9th, 2000

Task I: Multiple choice questions 6 credits

Mark the most suitable option with a cross.

1. In the second part of the 20th century London's population …
   - A grew steadily over the period.
   - B shrank, because people from the slums moved into new towns.
   - C had quite a different development from those of other big British cities.
   - D had a demoscopic graphic line similar to most other British cities, but in the last decade of this century it didn't.

2. The migrants that arrived in Britain …
   - A have fewer degrees than locals.
   - B have more degrees than locals as there are more students among them.
   - C work more in the health sector than locals do.
   - D are mostly coloured people.

3. The increase of property prices in London …
   - A is due to the fact that Europeans and Americans prefer living all over central London.
   - B is because home-owning Londoners can sell their houses very expensively.
   - C is larger than elsewhere in Britain.
   - D is a result of the romantic longing of the Londoners for the countryside.

4. The great influx of immigrants …
   A has eased the demand for people working in the field of public services.
   B has resulted in more costs for London's public services.
   C means more children speak English.
   D leads to additional school staff.

5. The high levels of immigration have brought about some negative aspects to living in London:
   A Children in Inner London get fewer good GCSEs than in the rest of the country.
   B Many teachers quit their jobs.
   C Immigrants send their children to expensive private schools.
   D As many children of immigrants speak poor English, local children try to help them improve their command of English.

6. After the ten new members have entered the EU, …
   A Britain will phase in their right to employment.
   B Britain gives the newcomers free access to the labour market after they have passed a test.
   C the government is likely to be troubled by them as a workforce.
   D London's businesses will profit.

Task II: Gapped summary 6 credits

This is a summary of paragraph D. **Fill in the words or phrases from the text** (one gap, one word).

The people migrating to London have altered the city ________________. They (1)
come from almost everywhere and tend to accumulate in ________________
________________ around central London. (1)
As a consequence they have contributed towards increasing London ____________
________________ more than in other parts of the country. (1)
This boom has had very positive effects financially for ________________
________________. On the other hand, many of them have been able to (1)
do what they always wanted: ______________ __________. This longing also has (1)
a literary tradition, where the great romantic novels are either ______________ or
about how frustrating cities are. (1)

Task III: Multiple matching 6 credits

Mr Reid, father of two sons, has sent his son to Allfarthing Primary School in London's inner city. The Educational Authority Board in London is carrying out an enquiry about independent schools in London.
Mr Reid is being asked the following questions about his motives. **Match the question to the answers by adding the letter of the answer to the appropriate questions.**

1. Why do you send your son to this school? ☐
2. Was it difficult to transfer your son to this privately run school? ☐
3. How does your son get to school? ☐
4. Have you noticed changes in his behaviour or attitude? ☐
5. Are there foreign pupils in his new class? ☐
6. Are there children of different religious backgrounds in his new class? ☐

A Yes, a bit, as my son had already made friends with quite a lot of kids in his old school.

B Yes, there are, but only 3 or 4 out of 20. And they come from well-off families who are socially very much accepted.

C Well, we live in Garrat Lane quite near to this school, which is one of the 50 beacon schools for excellence.

D Yes, of course. He no longer feels bored in class. But sometimes he complains about the homework, which he has more of now.

E He takes the bus which passes by just round the corner to St. Ann's Crescent, where the school is.

F Two Muslims and one Hindu. They speak prayers in their native language when they have their red letter day. This widens the other pupils' horizons, of course.

Task IV: Short-answer questions/sentence completion 6 credits

Answer the following by providing the required information or by completing the sentences, both with words from the text (not more than three words).

In what do immigrants differ from local people? (C)

1. They have ______________________ academic grades, (1)
2. but more don't have any ______________________. (1)
3. Their income depends, ______________, on their colour of their skin. (1)
4. They work more in thriving businesses like ______________ (1)
   an not so much in ______________________ branches. (1)
5. Many more immigrants run their own businesses than ______________. (1)

Task V: Mediation 6 credits

Erklären Sie die Bedeutung des folgenden Satzes auf Deutsch (keine wörtliche Übersetzung):
"High levels of immigration have put added pressure on London's stretched public services." (l. 40/41)

Aufgabenteil: *Writing*

Task VI: Descriptive Part 6 credits

As one of 50 beacon schools in Great Britain, Allfarthing Primary School will deliver **excellence for the many, not the few**. Interpret the figures to judge whether this claim has been achieved in the three cited subjects. (Level 5 is the highest.)
Write about 60 words in English.

ENGLISH	
% of pupils achieving level 4 or above in **English**	76 %
% of pupils achieving level 5 in **English**	35 %
% of pupils absent or unable to access test in **English**	4 %
MATHEMATICS	
% of pupils achieving level 4 or above in **mathematics**	72 %
% of pupils achieving level 5 in **mathematics**	30 %
% of pupils absent or unable to access test in **mathematics**	0 %
SCIENCE	
% of pupils achieving level 4 or above in **science**	89 %
% of pupils achieving level 5 in **science**	52 %
% of pupils absent or unable to access test in **science**	0 %

http://www.dfes.gov.uk

Task VII: Argumentative Part 24 credits
Composition – Write about 200 words.

"Modern technology has minimised the drawbacks of living in the countryside." Do you agree? Give reasons for your opinion.

Lösungsvorschläge

Aufgabenteil: *Reading*

Task I: Multiple choice questions

1 D, 2 C, 3 C, 4 B, 5 A, 6 D

Hinweis: Die Fragen folgen dem Textverlauf.
zu 1: Z. 12/13 "London ... grew by 4.8 % ..., mostly because foreigners started arriving."
zu 2: Z. 19/20 "Immigrants work more in growing businesses – such as health – than locals do."
zu 3: Z. 31 „prices ... have risen ... more quickly than elsewhere in Great Britain"
zu 4: Z. 41/42 „they have put added pressure on London's stretched public services"
zu 5: Z. 44/45 "In Inner London ... 38 % of children get 5 or more good GCSEs; in England ... 48 %."
zu 6: Absatz F ist relevant. Hier muss der Zusammenhang zwischen neuen EU-Ländern (Z. 53 „when 10 new countries join the EU") und dem allgemeinen Ausdruck „Zuwanderung" (Z. 56/57 „how migration has driven London's economy") hergestellt werden.

Task II: Gapped summary

The people migrating to London have altered the city **visibly**. They come from almost everywhere and tend to accumulate in **ethnic villages** around central London. As a consequence they have contributed towards increasing London **property prices** more than in other parts of the country. This boom has had very positive effects financially for **home-owning Londoners**. On the other hand, many of them have been able to do what they always wanted: **move out**. This longing also has a literary tradition, where the great romantic novels are either **rural** or about how frustrating cities are.

Task III: Multiple matching

Hinweis: Nehmen Sie zuerst die auf Anhieb erkennbaren Zuordnungen vor. Hier also zuerst 3E / 6F, dann 5B, usw. Die weiteren Zuordnungen sind dann einfacher.

1. Why do you send your son to this school?	**C**
2. Was it difficult to transfer your son to this privately run school?	**A**
3. How does your son get to school?	**E**
4. Have you noticed changes in his behaviour or attitude?	**D**
5. Are there foreign pupils in his new class?	**B**
6. Are there children of different religious backgrounds in his new class?	**F**

Task IV: Short-answer questions

1. The have **more** academic grades,
2. but more don't have any **qualifications**.
3. Their income depends, **by and large**, on their colour of their skin.

4. They work more in thriving businesses like **health** and not so much in **manufacturing** branches.
5. Many more immigrants run their own businesses than **locals**.

Task V: Mediation

Hinweis: Die Mediation verlangt ausdrücklich keine wörtliche Übersetzung, sondern einen erläuternden Kommentar.

Die hohen Einwanderungsraten haben zusätzliche Belastungen für die öffentlichen Dienstleistungen Londons bedeutet, die schon vor solchen Einwanderungsraten den Anforderungen kaum nachkommen konnten.

Aufgabenteil: *Writing*

Task VI: Descriptive Part

Allfarthing Primary School's claim is to lead more pupils to a higher level of education than in other schools. If we look at the three subjects English, Maths, and Science, then this school has achieved this goal, as in English and Maths about 1/3 of the class has received the highest grade, and in Science even more. No one has failed the test in Maths and Science. Even the rate of failure in English is negligible. *(76 words)*

Task VII: Argumentative Part

Hinweis: Vergleichen Sie die „useful phrases" und die Hinweise zum „writing"-Teil. Das Thema kann am einfachsten bejahend behandelt werden. Orientiert man sich am Wachstum der Städte, den steigenden Pendlerzahlen, etc. kann man aber auch negativ argumentieren.

Composition

"Modern technology has minimised the drawbacks of living in the countryside." – Yes, I definitely agree with this statement. Modern technology has made it possible to live in the country without giving up many of the amenities of city life. First of all computers have opened for everyone the Internet, email and video conferencing. This enables more and more people to work at home. This is of course a great benefit not only for women who have children and want to combine having a fulfilling job with being a mother, but also for men who can live in the country with their families and have their businesses no longer in London or another big city but in their home. Modern technology has also encouraged many factories and many companies to move their plants to a rural area. Cars may not be considered modern technology anymore, but the availability of cars to (almost) all people in Britain enables people to travel to work and to go to the theatre in the larger cities should they want a whiff of city life. Life in the country no longer means being isolated and having farming as a way of making a living. Attractive jobs in rural areas are now often giving young families the chance of buying affordable houses and of having a less hectic life style. *(223 words)*

Aufgabenteil: *Reading*

Why cyclists have been forced off Britain's congested roads

It's healthy and should be safe – but two-wheelers have been squeezed out by car culture.

I

(A) Cycling is declining at such an alarming rate in Britain that a whole generation of children may never experience the health, financial and social benefits it offers. Schools and councils up and down the country routinely encourage children and adults to get off their bikes rather than onto them, senior government advisers told The Observer yesterday. Fewer people are using bikes to get to work or school than ever before: on rural roads and for primary school children the level is so low it has officially fallen to 'zero per cent of trips' in national statistics.

(B) Overall, only 2 per cent of trips are now taken by bicycle in the UK, compared with 85 per cent by car. In Switzerland, 10 per cent of children cycle to school and that rises to 11 per cent in Germany, 15 per cent in Sweden and 18 per cent in Denmark.

(C) Kevin Mayne, director of national cycling group CTC, said Britain needed a huge boost in cycling to school in order to break the 'school run' car culture and develop a generation of active adults that would not suffer the nation's current rate of 157,000 adult deaths from heart disease a year, 37 per cent of which are attributed to inactivity.

(D) A total of 136 cyclists were killed on Britain's roads last year, including 25 children – almost a halving of the annual death toll in the past decade. This is attributed to cycling's decline, but also to better road safety measures and congestion slowing down traffic in towns. However, while Britain has the lowest overall rate of road deaths in Europe, pedestrians and cyclists are more than twice as likely to be killed in the UK than in the Netherlands or Sweden, where many more cycle and walk.

(E) Experts are worried about the high proportion of cyclists being killed by lorries, with trucks involved in 26 per cent of all fatalities, and bike deaths at roundabouts, where CTC research suggests cyclists are four times more at risk than they are at traffic lights on ordinary roads. Mary Hansen, singer and guitarist with the cult Nineties band Stereolab, died earlier this month after an accident involving a lorry while she was cycling in central London.

(F) But campaigners say parents should be more worried about their children joining the 10 per cent of 10-year-olds now officially described as obese than about them being knocked off their bikes. Mayne said: 'Often there is too much fear that cycling is not safe and is part of the culture of parents being afraid to let children out on their own – giving them less of a sense of freedom and adventure as well as the health benefits and environmental education of cycling as a green form of transport.'

II

(G) As the Government admitted last week that road congestion could worsen by a fifth over the next decade – and then two days later launched a major campaign against 'couch potatoes' and child obesity – experts warned that cyclists were becoming an endangered species on Britain's roads. But that is not because people in Britain do not want to cycle. Almost half of British households own a bicycle and cycling for leisure is slowly increasing as more off-road tracks are built – but cycling as a form of transport and a way of meeting the Government's recommendation that we get 30 minutes of daily exercise is disappearing.

(H) Pro-cycling groups blame not just the 30-year legacy of road-building and car culture, but the reluctance of local and national politicians to give priority to the bicycle on the road, growing antagonism between motorists and cyclists and safety fears. One senior consultant to the Government said: 'There is a reluctance by politicians to do anything that is seen as anti-car and that translates to building cycle lanes. The commitment in most local authorities is weak compared with towns and cities on the Continent, and nationally the Government does not push things like congestion charging and speed-limit enforcements that help cyclists,' he said.

(I) 'Developers and road engineers do not account for walking or cycling until the last minute when they are planning new roads, hospitals, schools or supermarkets, and then the facilities are often token and appalling.' Cycling campaigners and consultants said that badly designed cycle lanes put in by councils paying lip service to pro-bike policies were at best useless and at worst dangerous. 'So much of what has been put in for cyclists in this country is truly awful. If you judge the record by miles of cycle lane it sometimes looks good on paper, but often it is just a white line down the middle of the pavement or a tiny green stripe squashed in the gutter that is out of the normal line of sight for a car driver and then stops abruptly as soon as you get to a junction – and in some ways that can be more dangerous,' said the consultant.

III

(J) The West Midlands, for example, has dropped the national goal of tripling cycling by 2010 to adopt its own target of merely doubling it, from a very low base and with what many observers think is little hope of achieving even that modest increase. John Grimshaw, chief executive of the Sustrans charity that is building the new National Cycle Network, said some schools had up to 70 per cent of pupils cycling in, while others had none at all. The Government is putting record levels of funding into cycling and Transport Secretary Alistair Darling has just announced a huge expansion of the 'safe routes to school' initiative. But it has only just begun a nationwide assessment of all councils' performance on cycling to find out why it is still declining.

(K) A comprehensive picture has yet to emerge but senior advisers to the Government have criticised the lacklustre, and in some cases regressive, approach of East Lothian, Carlisle, Birmingham, the London borough of Westminster, Lincolnshire, Liverpool, Norfolk, Milton Keynes, Wolverhampton, East Riding, East Sussex and Runcorn.

(L) Oxfordshire, Suffolk and cities such as Bristol, Sheffield, Cambridge, Edinburgh, Hull and the London borough of Camden were praised for showing the rest of the country that with some money, readily available knowledge and, above all, the will, cycling could be expanded.

(M) The patchy record across the country was instantly highlighted last week when The Observer was shown examples of the best and worst places to cycle in Britain. Where York leads the way as the British city closest to the best in Europe, with special facilities and priority for its thousands of cyclists, Wokingham near Reading was described as 'typically awful' and as an area with very few, badly designed provisions. As the constituency of former Tory Transport Minister John Redwood, Kevin Mayne said Wokingham was typically pro-car and the local MP was more interested in building a road bridge over the railway line to stop queues building up at the level crossing than in doing anything to encourage cycling. He demonstrated a new cycle 'path' close to Wokingham railway station that gave half the narrow pavement to cyclists, but made them give way to other traffic at each tiny side street while the motor traffic soared easily by. 'They consulted local cyclists, who wanted a lane on the road, but were ignored. There is a cycle lane nearer the town centre, but there is a mile gap between the two, where cyclists are squeezed into the side of this busy A road,' he said, above the noise of the speeding traffic. Mayne said the well-used bike rack at the station showed people wanted to cycle, but their numbers were kept down because 'all the facilities disappear within about half a mile of the centre'.

(N) York is officially recognised as Britain's top cycling city, where 5 per cent of children cycle to school and 19 per cent of people cycle to work – figures that compare respectably to many of the better Continental cities.

IV

(O) The Government is so concerned by soaring rates of heart disease and impending gridlock that Transport Minister John Spellar has called in Steven Norris, who as Tory Transport Minister spearheaded the national cycling strategy in 1996. He is heading a task force to examine every council's record on cycling and will hand out bouquets and brickbats next year to the best and worst performers. He said last week: 'There is no excuse for neglecting cycling in this country. But it is as if we are just beginning to emerge, stumbling, into the daylight of the world of the bicycle.'

(P) Even as John Spellar officially abandoned his target to reduce traffic jams last week, on the back of a revived road-building programme, he revealed that cycling had declined by 25 per cent since 1990 and walking by almost 30 per cent. Cycling groups, industry consultants and government advisers complain that as traffic levels have soared in a nation which has the longest commuting times and the highest car dependence in Europe, people who want to use bikes are increasingly marginalised on the roads.

(Q) As cycling declines while congestion and, conversely on clear roads, speeding increases, observers report that a growing number of motorists regard bikes as a nuisance and ignore or actively menace them. Meanwhile, frustrated cyclists increasingly feel the urge to reassert themselves by jumping red lights, weaving in and out of slow-moving traffic and riding on the kerb – in turn threatening pedestrians and harming the reputation of cyclists. One senior consultant to Ministers said: 'Some places are great, but the prevailing attitude in most authorities is that the car is king, money is for road-building, bikes are at best an afterthought and at worst a threat to road safety and traffic flow.'

(R) 'The Government simply has not had the balls to get to grips with this because they are afraid of the motoring lobby and now they are off spending billions widening roads again.' The Government has spectacularly missed its goal to double cycling from the level of 2 per cent of trips in 1996 to 4 per cent by the end of 2002 – the figure is stuck at 2 per cent – while driving, flying, train journeys and even bus use in some areas have increased in a growing economy.

(S) It has already downgraded its original goal of increasing cycling levels four-fold to reach 8 per cent of journeys by 2012, which would have matched the level Germany was at in 1996. Instead, it has revised the target in its 10-year plan and will now try to triple cycling by 2010 – which currently looks rather like wishful thinking.

Adapted from Joanna Walters, The Observer, December 22, 2002

Task I: Multiple choice questions 6 credits

Only passage I is relevant for questions 1 to 5.
Mark the most suitable option with a cross.

1. Cycling in Britain is becoming less common … (A)

   A as children are not allowed to experience the health, financial and social benefits it offers.

   B as schools and authorities advise adults and children to leave their bicycles at home.

   C because senior government advisers told the newspaper that parents and their children should get off their bikes instead of using them.

   D as fewer people are cycling to work or school than the previous generation did.

2. An international comparison shows that in Britain … (B)

   A the smallest number of people use a bike to make trips.

   B as many people ride a bike as in Germany.

   C five times as many people use a bike to make trips as in Switzerland.

   D 85 % don't use a bike.

3. Mayne wanted to boost cycling … (C)

   A so that the school-run car culture will be put an end to, as people later die of inactivity.

   B to develop a generation of active adults who do not suffer from heart diseases.

   C because the habit of parents of driving their children to school has to be stopped, so that later the children will be active and healthy adults.

   D as, when they are adults, 37 % of them die of heart disease due to the car culture they experienced as schoolchildren.

4. The annual death toll on roads in Britain … (D)

   A is the lowest in Europe.

   B amounted to 136 cyclists in the past decade.

   C included 25 children last year – almost half as many as in the past ten years.

   D implies that the risk of pedestrians and cyclists being killed is twice as high as in Sweden and Holland put together.

5. Cyclists are especially in danger of having fatal accidents … (E)

   A by collisions with cars and motorbikes.

   B with lorries.

   C at crossings with traffic lights.

   D in central London.

6. These are the headlines of passages I–IV. Which of the four suggestions A – D gives their correct order?

A	B	C	D	
I	IV	III	III	Cycling – a patchy record across the country
II	I	I	II	Cycling is healthy, but it goes down as it should be safe
III	III	IV	IV	Governmental cycling policy and its prospects
IV	II	II	I	Controversial views lead to marginalisation of cycling lanes

The correct order of the headlines is shown under the letter in the box.
For example: "A" would be the order "I–II–III –IV".

Task II: Multiple matching 6 credits

Only passage II is relevant for this exercise.
What did they say or which statement can be attributed to them? **Match the statements A to H by putting the letters in the boxes.** Two of them are not relevant.

1. Government and its representatives (G) ☐ ☐
2. British householders (G) ☐ ☐
3. Groups supporting cycling (H), (I) ☐ ☐
4. Politicians (H) ☐ ☐

A Traffic jams will increase by 20 % in the next ten years.
B Half an hour of cycling every day is advisable.
C Give cars priority.
D Cycling paths and footpaths come after new roads or any building of public interest.
E A cycling lane is often only a white line along the middle of the pavement.
F Cycling is on the increase as a means of transport.
G Three decades of road building are responsible for the bad state of cycling.
H Cycling for enjoyment on special bike lanes is increasing.

Task III: Gapped summary 6 credits

This is a summary of Passage III. **Fill in the words or phrases from the text** (one gap, one word).

John Grimshaw, responsible for building the new ______________________

________________ ____________________, meets with a very different state of (1)

affairs across the country. The West Midlands has also changed the national goal

of cycling to ____________________ its own goal. Nevertheless, the Government (1)

is investing a lot of money in cycling. At the same time it wants to find out why

cycling is __________________________. A nationwide report shows examples (1) of ___________ _____________ _________ ___________ places for cycling (1)

in Britain. The area around Reading was pointed out to be _______________

_______________, whereas York was praised by the government for its cycling (1)

statistics, that _____________ very well to a lot of cities with very good cycling (1)

provisions on the Continent.

Task IV: Mediation 6 credits

Passage IV is relevant for this exercise.
Formulieren Sie auf Deutsch, wobei kurze thesenhafte Sätze genügen.

1. Welche Aufgabe hat der frühere Transportminister Steven Norris übernommen? (O)

   (Vorsitzender des Prüfungsausschusses für …) _______________________

   ____

   ____ (1)

2. Wie verhalten sich motorisierte Verkehrsteilnehmer gegenüber Radfahrern? (Q)

   (Hindernis etc.) _______________________________________

   ____

   ____ (1)

3. Inwiefern sind Radfahrer eine Gefahr für Fußgänger? (Q)

   (Bürgersteig) ____

   ____

   ____ (1)

4. Weswegen verfehlte die Regierung das Ziel, die Radfahrquote zu verdoppeln? (R)

   (Lobby der Motorisierten) ______________________________

   ____

   (Straßenausbau) ______________________________________

   ____ (2)

5. Welche Ansicht äußert die Autorin des Textes über das Vorhaben der Regierung, die Radfahrquote zu verdreifachen? (S)

   (10-Jahres-Plan) ______________________________________

   ____ (1)

Task V: Sentence completion/Short-answer questions 6 credits

Answer the following questions by filling in the required words or by completing the sentence:

1. In paragraph (F) campaigners for cycling give parents two pieces of advice.
   Parents should be more concerned about their 10-year-olds, of whom 10 % are now ______________________________ (1)
   than ______________________________ (1)
2. In the same paragraph Mr Mayne talks of a certain culture of worried parents who withhold from their children a certain form of education and transport. Which two adjectives does he use? (2 words)
   ______________ ______________ (2)
3. In paragraph (P) two opposing developments have been described. Which?
   Cycling ______________________________
   ______________________________ (1)
   Car ______________________________
   ______________________________ (1)

Aufgabenteil: *Writing*

Task VI: Descriptive Part 6 credits

Explain this chart of bicycle casualties. Note that the "average" is 100.
Write between 50 and 70 words.

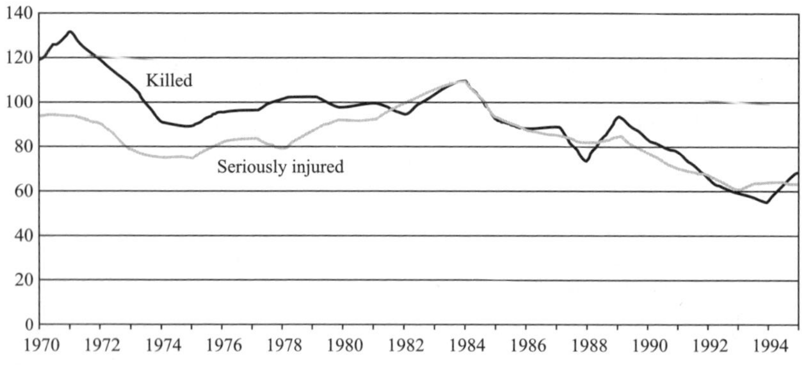

http://www.dft.gov.uk

Task VII: Argumentative Part 24 credits

Composition – Write about 200 words.

What could be done to make more people use the public transport system?

Lösungsvorschläge

Aufgabenteil: *Reading*

Hinweis: Beachten Sie, dass der Text in die Abschnitte I–IV eingeteilt ist und sich die Aufgaben nur auf die jeweils genannten Teile beziehen.

Task I: Multiple choice questions

1 B, 2 A, 3 C, 4 A, 5 A, 6 C

Hinweis:
zu 1: Z. 3–5 A gibt keinen Sinn; B Schulen („schools") und Behörden („authorities") raten dazu („to advise")– also richtige Lösung, vgl. Z. 3/4; C: Die Forderung ist zwar zutreffend, wird aber nicht von „senior government advisers" erhoben, sondern nur als Information an die Zeitung weiter gegeben. D: „the previous generation" ist viel spezifischer als „than ever before" (jemals zuvor)
zu 2: Z. 9–11 Da in GB nur 2 % aller Fahrten mit dem Fahrrad gemacht werden, wird GB von allen anderen genannten Ländern übertroffen. Richtig ist also A. D: 85 % der Fahrten, nicht der Menschen, werden mit dem Auto gemacht.
zu 3: Z. 12–15 A, B, D sind nur ungefähre Wiedergaben der relevanten Passage.
zu 4: Z. 19/20 Es geht um alle tödlichen Verkehrsunfälle in GB, also ist A richtig.
zu 5: Z. 22 ff. Die Antwort muss erschlossen werden. Da 26 % der tödlichen Unfälle mit Lastkraftwagen geschehen, muss sich der weitaus höhere Anteil mit den übrigen motorisierten Verkehrsteilnehmern ereignen, also A.
zu 6: Nach Bearbeitung von Aufgabe 1 ist klar, dass die Überschrift zu I lautet: „Cycling is healthy …". Erst bei Abschnitt III unterscheidet sich die richtige Lösung C von B.

Task II: Multiple matching

Hinweis: Unterstreichen Sie sich in Passage II die genannten Gruppen, um dann die Aussagen leichter zuordnen zu können.
- *„Government", Z. 35 „worsen by a fifth …", Z. 41/42 „30 minutes exercise recommended"*
- *„British householders", Z. 39/40 „leisure cycling increases"*
- *„Pro-cycling groups", Z. 43 „blame 30 year car culture", „cycling campaigners", Z. 53, Z. 57 „a white line …"*
- *„Politicians", Z. 44/45 „reluctance to give priority to the bicycle", Z. 46/47 „reluctance … that is seen as anti-car …"*

1. Government and its representatives	A	B
2. British householders	H	
3. Groups supporting cycling	G	E
4. Politicians	C	

Task III: Gapped summary

Hinweis: Eine Gliederung des Originaltextes zeigt die Sinnstruktur und hilft, die Fundstellen für die einzusetzenden Wörter und Wendungen einzugrenzen, wie folgende Gegenüberstellung zeigt:

Zeile	*Gliederung von Abschnitt III*	*„summary“*
61–70	*„The building of the new NCN faces difficulties, although the Government is investing a lot of money“*	*Z. 63 „adopt“, Z. 65/66 NCN* *Z. 70 „declining“*
71–78	*„List of good and bad examples“*	*(Aufzählung von Ortsnamen und Regionen)*
79–95	*„Description of the best (York) and worst (Wokingham) places to cycle“*	*Z. 80 „the best and worst places“* *Z. 83 „typically awful“*
96–99	*„York – competitive with Continental cities“*	*Z. 97 „compare“*

John Grimshaw, responsible for building the new **National Cycle Network**, meets with a very different state of affairs across the country. The West Midlands has also changed the national goal of cycling to **adopt** its own goal. Nevertheless, the Government is investing a lot of money in cycling. At the same time it wants to find out why cycling is **declining**. A nationwide report shows examples of **the best and worst** places for cycling in Britain. The area around Reading was pointed out to be **typically awful**, whereas York was praised by the government for its cycling statistics, that **compare** very well to a lot of cities with very good cycling provisions on the Continent.

Task IV: Mediation

Hinweis: Auch hier unterstreicht man am besten zunächst die Schlüsselwörter.
zu 1: Z. 103/104 „Steven Norris ... examines the records ... hands out bouquets and brickbats“
zu 2: Z. 114 „Motorists regard bikes as ...“
zu 3: Z. 115–117 „frustrated cyclists ride on the kerb“,„kerb“ = Bordstein/Bürgersteig)
zu 4: Z. 122/123 „government afraid of motoring lobby“, „spending billions widening roads“
zu 5: Z. 129/130 „ten-year-plan“, „looks like wishful thinking“

1. (Vorsitzender des Prüfungsausschusses für ...) **Als Vorsitzender eines Prüfungsausschusses hat er Berichte der Stadt- und Gemeinderäte über das Radfahrwesen zu prüfen und Lob und Tadel zu verteilen.**

2. (Hindernis etc.) **Motorisierte Verkehrsteilnehmer betrachten Radfahrer als Hindernis, übersehen sie oder bedrohen sie tätlich.**

3. (Bürgersteig) **Sie fahren auf dem Bürgersteig.**

4. (Lobby der Motorisierten) **Die Regierung fürchtet die Lobby der Motorisierten und ist dabei Milliarden für den Straßenausbau auszugeben.**

5. (10-Jahres-Plan) **Sie glaubt, dass der 10-Jahres-Plan gegenwärtig nur Wunschdenken ist.**

Task V: Sentence completion / Short-answer questions

Hinweis: *Die Absätze (F) und (P) müssen gründlich gelesen und verstanden werden.*
zu 1: Die Verfechter des Radfahrens geben den Ratschlag, dass die Eltern eher wegen des Übergewichts der 10-Jährigen („obese" = fettsüchtig) besorgt sein sollten, als darüber, dass die Kinder einen Radfahrunfall erleiden. Die Lösung insgesamt ist ein ganzer Satz mit der Struktur „... more concerned ... than" (Vergleichssatz). Ferner: „about ***them*** *being ...", als Gerund mit eigenem Subject. Sonst wären es ja die Eltern, die einen Radunfall erleiden.*
zu 2: Die begleitenden Eigenschaftswörter („adjectives") zu „education" und „transport" sind die Lösung.
zu 3: Bei „Car ..." auf die richtige Satzstellung (Subjekt, Prädikat, Ortsadverb) achten. „Car dependence" ist Subjekt. „highest" nach „is" fungiert als Prädikatsnomen.

1. Parents should be more concerned about their 10-year-olds, of whom 10 % are now **officially described as obese** than **about them being knocked off their bikes**.
2. **environmental green**
3. Cycling **had declined by 25 % since 1990**.
   Car **dependence is the highest in Europe**.

Aufgabenteil: *Writing*

Task VI: Descriptive Part

Hinweis: *Die charakteristischen Kurvenverläufe müssen hervorgehoben werden, z. B. fällt die schwarze Linie (tödliche Unfälle) überwiegend, während die graue Linie (Unfälle mit Schwerverletzten) bis 1984 steigt und dann erst stetig fällt. Bedenklich ist, dass die schwarze Linie die graue 1995 übertrifft. Der angenommene Durchschnittswert von 100 erscheint willkürlich gewählt.*

The number of fatal bike accidents from 1970 to 1995 goes down on the whole, although in between there are ups and downs.
Contrary to this the number of seriously injured, though one fifth lower, shows an upward trend until 1984 and only then drops in close proximity to the fatalities.
One reason for concern is that after 1994, the number of fatalities surpasses that of the seriously injured. Why the Index from 1981 to 1985 should be average seems to me to be deliberate. *(85 words)*

Task VII: Argumentative Part

Hinweis: *Vergleichen Sie die „useful phrases" und die Hinweise zum „writing"-Teil.*

Composition

Great Britain is the most car-dependent country in Europe with all its negative consequences. It is everyday experience that the public transport systems need improving in several ways.

Most important is a dense and extended network of trains and buses. Equally important is that they reduce the waiting time at stops as far as possible. If people have to wait twenty or more minutes for the next bus or train to arrive, they will lose their temper and decide to go by car.

Another point which should not be forgotten is that railway or tube carriages should be more comfortable and more attractive to look at. If all these measures fail, then stronger ones will have to be implemented. Great progress has been made in London, for example, by introducing congestion charge zones which car drivers may only enter if they pay a fee. This has had the effect of increasing the number of people who use public transport. However, there are some side-effects. Many car drivers have now swapped their cars for motorbikes, as these are exempt from the fees. Have they considered that this may be a case of out of the frying pan, into the fire, as they run a much higher risk of accident?

I am of the opinion that there is still a great deal to be done. I think arrangements like people working from home should also be more common, for instance, to reduce the number of people having to commute to work in the first place. *(252 words)*

Berufliche Oberschulen Bayern – Englisch 12. Klasse
Übungsaufgabe 3

Aufgabenteil: *Reading*

Text I: An ugly face of ecology

We need to be honest. Wind farms are a necessary evil, but they will not overcome the crisis of climate change

(A) The people fighting the new wind farm in Cumbria have cheated and exaggerated. They appear to possess little understanding of the dangers of global warming. They are supported by an unsavoury coalition of nuclear-power lobbyists and climate-change deniers. But it would still be wrong to dismiss them.

(B) The Whinash project on the edge of the Lake District national park will, if it goes ahead, be Europe's biggest onshore wind farm, producing, according to the developers, enough electricity for 47,000 homes. Without schemes like this, there is no chance of meeting the government's target of a 20 % cut in carbon emissions by 2010. Onshore wind turbines are currently the cheapest means of producing new power without fossil fuels, but at the moment they account for just 0.32 % of our electricity. Faced with the global emergency of climate change, it would be criminally irresponsible not to build more. The public inquiry that will decide if the Whinash farm should go ahead, and help to determine the future of energy policy, began last week.

(C) Last year the Advertising Standards Authority ruled that the No Whinash Wind Farm campaign had exaggerated the size and number of the turbines, and the impact they would have on tourism and house prices. Among those supporting the exaggerators are the organisation Country Guardians and the former environmentalist David Bellamy. Country Guardians was co-founded by Sir Bernard Ingham, Margaret Thatcher's press secretary and a consultant to the nuclear industry. Bellamy is the country's foremost climate-change denier. (He was at it again last week, claiming in a letter to New Scientist that the World Glacier Monitoring Service says 89 % of the world's glaciers are growing. Its most recent report shows that 82 of the 88 surveyed in 2003 are shrinking.) But we should try not to judge a cause by its supporters.

(D) There are several things that make me uncomfortable about wind energy and the way in which it is being promoted. Wind farms, while necessary, are a classic example of what environmentalists call an "end-of-the-pipe solution". Instead of tackling the problem – our massive demand for energy – at source, they provide less damaging means of accommodating it. Or part of it. The Whinash project, by replacing energy generation from power stations burning fossil fuel, will reduce carbon dioxide emission by 178,000 tonnes a year. This is impressive, until you discover that a single jumbo jet, flying from London to Miami and back every day, releases the climate-change equivalent of 520,000 tonnes of carbon dioxide a year. One daily connection between Britain and Florida costs three giant wind farms.

(E) Alternative technology permits us to imagine that we can build our way out of trouble. By responding to one form of overdevelopment with another, we can, we believe, continue to expand our total energy demands without destroying the planetary systems required to sustain human life. This might, for a while, be true. But it would soon require the use of the entire land surface of the UK.

(F) Consider, for example, the claims for hydrogen fuel cells. Their proponents believe that this country's vehicles could all one day be run on hydrogen produced by electricity from wind power. I am not sure if they have any idea what this involves. I haven't been able to find figures for the UK, but a rough estimate for the US suggests that the same transformation would require a doubling of the capacity of the national grid. If the ratio were the same here, that would mean a 600-fold increase in wind generation, just to keep our wheels turning. If we were to seek to compensate for the emissions produced elsewhere, there is no end to it. The government envisages a rise in British aircraft passengers from 180 million to 476 million over the next 25 years. That means a contribution to global warming that is equivalent to the carbon savings of 1,094 Whinash farms.

(G) In other words, there is no sustainable way of meeting current projections for energy demand. The only strategy in any way compatible with environmentalism is one led by a vast reduction in total use. Greenpeace and Friends of the Earth, who support the new wind farm, make this point repeatedly, but it falls on deaf ears. What is acceptable to the market, and therefore to the government, is an enhanced set of opportunities for capital, in the form of new kinds of energy generation. What is not acceptable is a reduced set of opportunities for capital, in the form of massively curtailed total energy production. It is not their fault, but however clearly the green groups articulate their priorities, what the government hears is "more wind farms", rather than "fewer flights".

(H) I would like to see the Green publish a statement about where this kind of development should stop. At what point will they say that too many wind farms are being built, and ask the government to call a halt? At what point does the switch to the decentralised, micro-generation projects they envisage take place?

(I) I would also feel happier if environmentalists dropped the pretence that wind farms are beautiful. They are merely less ugly and less destructive than most alternatives. They are a lot less ugly than climate change, which threatens to wreck the habitats anti-wind farm campaigners are so keen to preserve. We have to build them, but it would be more honest to recognise that they are a necessary evil.

(J) But these are not the only ways in which environmentalists' support for wind farms makes me squirm. The joint statement about the Whinash project published by Greenpeace and Friends of the Earth complains that "opponents of the scheme, which would be sited beside the M6 motorway, have claimed that the wind turbines will spoil the views, failing to acknowledge that the presence of a motorway has degraded the landscape". It quotes Friends of the Earth's energy campaigner Jill Perry, who says: "I'm amazed that people are claiming that the area should be designated a national park. What kind of national park has a motorway running through it?" Well the New Forest and South Downs national parks, for a start. Their creation was supported by Friends of the Earth.

(K) Elsewhere, these groups oppose the "infill" around new roads. Elsewhere, they argue that landscapes and ecosystems should be viewed holistically: that they do not stop, in other words, at an arbitrary line on the map, like the boundary of a national park. I understand that green campaigners are placed in an uncomfortable position when arguing for development rather than against it. But I do not understand why they have to sound like Wal-Mart[1] as soon as the boot is on the other foot.

(L) I believe the Whinash wind farm should be built. But I also believe that those who defend it should be a good deal more sensitive towards local objectors. Why? Because in any other circumstances they would find themselves fighting on the same side.

George Monbiot, The Guardian, April 26, 2005

---

[1] Wal-Mart: Revolutionized the retail industry by offering a wider variety of products (at lower prices) than competitors in a clean, customer-friendly environment.

Task I: Multiple choice questions 6 credits

Mark the most suitable option with a cross.

1. People opposing the wind farm in Cumbria …
   - A speak the truth.
   - B are conscious of the risks of climate change.
   - C reject the arguments of the supporters of nuclear power.
   - D should be taken seriously.

2. The building of the Whinash wind farm project …
   - A is supported by the majority of the people in the Lake District.
   - B is opposed by people in the Lake District but supported by other groups.
   - C is not important to the Government as such projects account for just 32 % of Britain's electricity.
   - D is not certain yet.

3. The organisation …
   - A "Advertising Standards Authority" is biased.
   - B "Country Guardians" has not yet made up its mind.
   - C of which Margaret Thatcher's press secretary was one of the original members is concerned about tourism and property prices.
   - D "World Glacier Monitoring Services" publishes contradictory reports.

4. According to George Monbiot, the Whinash project …
   - A replaces one third of the equivalent energy used by one daily connection of a jumbo jet between Britain and Florida over the course of a year.
   - B is a classic example of what the environmentalists call an ideal solution.
   - C tackles the problem at source.
   - D doesn't do any harm to the environment when you install it.

5. Renewable energy …
   - A like hydrogen gained from electricity by wind power could provide power for all vehicles in Britain very comfortably.
   - B like wind power is sufficient to cover US energy consumption.
   - C can compensate our ever growing energy consumption for some time.
   - D like that generated by the Whinash farm would compensate for the global warming caused by the growing number of aircraft passengers over the coming 25 years.

6. The answer to sustainable energy needs lies in …
   - A renewable energy.
   - B saving energy.
   - C more opportunities for money investors.
   - D what the government says.

Task II: Gapped summary 6 credits

This is a summary of paragraphs G – L. **Fill in the words or phrases from the text** (one gap, one word).

As ________________ energy cannot meet the projected energy demands, there is no other way than a massive reduction in total use. But this is not acceptable in a market and thus to the ____________________, where capital seeks new kinds of energy generation rather than the other way round. (1) (1)

When will the Greens say to the government that too many wind farms are being built instead of decentralised micro-generation projects as they are not ________________ but a necessary evil? (1)

The author has more scruples concerning the way "Greenpeace" and "Friends of the Earth" present their case to opponents: A wind farm cannot spoil a national park which has already been __________________ by the M 6 motorway running through them, while the creation of other national parks with motorways through it was supported by "Friends of the Earth". (1)

The author criticises the __________________ ____________________ of being hypocritical when arguing for development rather than against it. (1)

He thinks that Whinash should ________________ ________________ but local objectors should be listened to more sensitively as, when it comes down to it, both groups are fighting for the same cause. (1)

Task III: Mediation 6 credits

Formulieren Sie auf Deutsch, wobei kurze thesenhafte Sätze genügen. Das Stichwort kann dabei als Hilfestellung dienen und jeweils im Satz verwendet werden.

1. Welches Beispiel bringt der Text, um zu zeigen, dass das Windkraftwerk in Cumbria den Kohlendioxydausstoß anderer aufstrebender Bereiche nicht kompensieren kann? (D)

   (jumbo jet) ____ (1)

   ____

2. Wie kommt der Autor zu seinen Berechnungen bezüglich Wasserstoff betriebener Kraftfahrzeuge, deren Treibstoff aus der Elektrizität von Windkraftwerken gewonnen wird? (F)

   a) (USA)____ (1)

   ____

   b) (GB) ____ (1)

   ____

   c) (Flugpassagiere in den nächsten 25 Jahren) ______________________ (1)

   ____

3. Welche zwiespältige Haltung nehmen „grüne Gruppen“ ein, wenn es darum geht, Windkraftwerke gegen Gegner zu verteidigen? (J)

a) (Autobahn) ____ (1)

____

b) (New Forest and South Downs national parks) ____________________ (1)

____

Text II: Sunny side down

Britain's fledgling solar energy industry fears it is being abandoned by the government

(A) The solar energy industry is under a dark cloud. Amid growing suspicion that the government is about to pull the plug on grant money for early adopters of solar energy, the industry has openly accused Tony Blair of reneging on previous commitments.

(B) According to the Renewable Power Association (RPA), an umbrella organisation for renewable energy companies, the government plans to end its 2002–2012 programme for solar photovoltaics (PVs) – cells that convert solar radiation into electricity – prematurely in March next year. This means that the government will no longer give out grants for solar projects. The solar industry has relied on such capital grants to households and industry to build up domestic demand and hence a market for solar panels. It fears that once these grants dry up, demand will vanish and the market will collapse, and with it the UK solar industry.

(C) Since the government started its solar PV programme, the UK has seen the growth of a fledgling industry. Sharp UK has a manufacturing plant in Wrexham, Wales that employs 150 people, while firms such as Romag and BP Solar have plants in the north-east. The UK is also a world leader in the integrated solar PV market, with companies such as Marley and Solarcentury developing new solar tiles that have export as well as UK potential.

(D) But uncertainty over the government's commitment to solar is causing mounting anxiety and anger within the solar power industry. The industry first expressed its concerns last November, but recently cranked up the volume. It is now openly accusing the government of bad faith and of not living up to its rhetoric on climate change.

(E) Jonathan Bates, a director of PV-UK, a solar industry group, said "The UK PV industry has taken the government at its word and invested millions of pounds in response to the white paper commitment. This money will have been wasted and many of our members will find it hard to continue trading should the government now decide to abandon the industry as it did the nascent UK wind industry 20 years ago." Solar energy firms cite the 2003 energy white paper, which called for "2002–2012 implementation of solar PV demonstration programme in line with our competitors as set out in the Opportunities for All white paper". They also cite the principal recommendation of the government-industry PV group report of 2001, which called for a 10-year, £ 150 m programme with a target of 70–100,000 roofs. Sebastian Berry, a policy manager at the RPA, told Guardian Unlimited: "The bottom line is that the government has gone back on its previous commitments to a 10-year PV programme at a time when Tony Blair is stressing the need for more not less action on climate change."

(F) Faced with growing disgruntlement within the solar energy industry, the government insists that it remains strongly committed to long-term funding for solar power, an industry to which it has given £ 31m since 2002. The Department of Trade and Industry said in a statement: “We have reassured the solar industry that we have a long-term commitment to them, and look forward to working with them on the new arrangements.”

(G) But DTI officials have made it clear that the government favours wind and tidal power as renewable energy sources. “The climate we have does not lend itself to solar energy and the government has to decide which kind of renewable power is most viable. The government has to prioritise,” a DTI official said.

(H) So far, the UK has installed six megawatts (MW) and may have trouble meeting its target of nine megawatts – or the approximate equivalent of 3,000 domestic roofs – by this year. By contrast, Germany last year installed 300 MW of solar PV and on 12 separate occasions since 1999 the German solar programme has delivered the equivalent of the UK’s three-year target in just one month. The government has said it wants five per cent of the UK’s electricity supply to come from renewable energy sources this year, 10 % by 2010 and 20 % by 2020. Currently, the figure stands at 3.86 % of the total electricity supply. Most renewable energy experts believe that Britain will miss those targets.

Mark Tran, The Guardian, April 8, 2005

Task IV: Multiple matching

6 credits

Match the statements A to H with the source which might have voiced them.
Two of the statements are irrelevant.

Government	☐	☐
solar industry	☐	☐
director of PV-UK	☐	☐
policy manager at the RPA	☐	☐
renewable energy experts	☐	☐

A “The country won’t reach the proposed goal.”

B “The electricity supply will be four times as high in 15 years.”

C “The official policy of the government is contradictory to what it had said before.”

D “Renewable energy resources need to be given priority.”

E “If there are no further subsidies, we will gradually lose our customers.”

F “If the government no longer follows White Paper proposals, a company will have squandered a lot of money.”

G “The UK is also a world leader in integrated solar PV.”

H “Solar energy is under a dark cloud.”

Task V: Sentence completion

6 credits

Answer the following questions by filling in the required words or by completing the sentences.

1. The solar industry is worried for two reasons (A/B)
   a) The government ____ (1)
   b) Without government commitment to households the market ______________ (1)
   ____
2. What has happened since the government started its solar program? (C)
   a) In Wales ____ (1)
   b) (export) ____ (1)
3. Although the government reassures the solar industry of its long-term commitment, there might be other priorities (G) (one sentence)
   a) The government ____, (1)
   b) as the climate ______________________________ for solar energy. (1)

Aufgabenteil: *Writing*

Task VI: Descriptive Part

6 credits

Universal Press Syndicate, © 2002 The Washington Post

The cartoon "Hey, let's swim around some more" points at a crucial question concerning global warming. Answer the question of the third gentleman in the pool and interpret it. **Write between 50 and 70 words.**

Task VII: Argumentative Part 24 credits

Composition – Write about 200 words.

"We do not inherit the earth from our ancestors, we borrow it from our children."
(Slogan of the environmentalist movement)
How could the needs of future generations best be guaranteed?

Lösungsvorschläge

Aufgabenteil: *Reading*

Task I: Multiple choice questions

1 D, 2 D, 3 C, 4 A, 5 C, 6 B

Hinweis: *Die Fragen folgen dem Textverlauf.*
zu 1: Z. 4 „... still be wrong to dismiss them"
zu 2: Z. 12/13 „public enquiry ... will decide if the Whinash farm should go ahead."
zu 3: Z. 14–19 Der Zusammenhang muss gesehen werden: „No Whinash farm campaign" wird von „Country Guardians" unterstützt, die von Thatcher's press secretary, Sir Bernard Ingham, mit begründet wurde, also C.
zu 4: Z. 32/33 "One daily connection costs three giant windfarms."
zu 5: Z. 37 "This might, for a while, be true."
zu 6: Z. 51/51 "The only strategy ... a vast reduction in total use."

Task II: Gapped summary

Hinweis: *Das „summary" fasst die Gedanken der Absätze G–L zusammen. Ein Vergleich der Gliederung des Gedankengangs des Primärtextes mit den entsprechenden Passagen des „summary" erleichtert es, die fehlenden Ausdrücke aus dem Primärtext aufzufinden.*

Zeilen	***Gedankengang des Primärtextes***	***summary***
50–58	*„Saving energy is the answer in the long run, but government follows the market"*	*„sustainable" Z. 50* *„government" Z. 54*
59–67	*„Windfarms are ugly but necessary de-centralised alternatives to be proposed to the government"*	*„beautiful" Z. 64*
68–76	*„Green groups' arguments are illogical"*	*„degraded" Z. 72*
77–82	*„Green groups are in a dilemma"*	*„green campaigners" Z. 80*
83–85	*„The opposing groups have the same cause"*	*„be built" Z. 83*

As **sustainable** energy cannot meet the projected energy demands, there is no other way than a massive reduction in total use. But this is not acceptable in a market and thus to the **government**, where capital seeks new kinds of energy generation rather than the other way round. When will the Greens say to the government that too many wind farms are being built instead of decentralised micro-generation projects as they are not **beautiful** but a necessary evil?
The author has more scruples concerning the way "Greenpeace" and "Friends of the Earth" present their case to opponents: A wind farm cannot spoil a national park which has already

been **degraded** by the M 6 motorway running through it, while the creation of other national parks with motorways through them was supported by "Friends of the Earth".
The author criticises the **green campaigners** of being hypocritical when arguing for development rather than against it.
He thinks that Whinash should **be built** but local objectors should be listened to more sensitively as, when it comes down to it, both groups are fighting for the same cause.

Task III: Mediation

Hinweis: *In Text 1, Absatz D–J, markiert man sich die Stichworte. Sie folgen dem Textverlauf.*
zu 1: Z. 30–33
zu 2a: Z. 41–43 Bezug auf USA, da für UK keine entsprechenden Zahlen vorliegen
zu 2b: Z. 43 „grid" hier Netzkapazität
zu 3: Z. 73–76 nicht überlesen: die Einrichtungen der beiden genannten „national parks" (mit Autobahn) wurden von „Friends of the Earth" unterstützt, während durch die M 6 im Fall „Whinash" der Park nicht weiter schützenswert sei

1. (jumbo jet) **Ein Jumbo-Jet von London nach Miami stößt, auf das Jahr bezogen, 520 000 Tonnen Kohlendioxyd aus, was dem Einsparungspotenzial von drei Windkraftwerken der Größe des Whinash-Projekts entspricht.**

2. a) (USA) **Da für GB keine Zahlen vorliegen, überträgt er die amerikanischen vergleichbaren Werte.**

   b) (GB) **Für GB bedeutet das eine Verdoppelung der Kapazität des Netzes mit der Folge, dass die durch Windkraft erzeugte Elektrizität um das Sechshundertfache gesteigert werden müsste, nur um alle Fahrzeuge „rollen" zu lassen.**

   c) (Flugpassagiere in den nächsten 25 Jahren) **Die Zunahme der Flugpassagiere in den nächsten 25 Jahren von 180 Millionen auf 476 Millionen würde 1094 Whinash-Windkraftwerke erfordern, um den Kohlendioxydausstoß zu kompensieren.**

3. a) (Autobahn) **Da die durch den Lake District führende Autobahn M 6 die Schönheit der Landschaft beeinträchtige, könne das Windkraftwerk nichts mehr verderben.**

   b) (New Forest and South Downs national parks) **New Forest and South Downs national parks sind, obwohl Autobahnen durch sie führen, Nationalparks, deren Einrichtung von den „Friends of the Earth" unterstützt wurde.**

Task IV: Multiple matching

Hinweis: *Zweckmäßigerweise markiert man sich die Quellen („sources") dieser Aussagen und vergleicht die paraphrasierten Wendungen mit dem Ausgangstext. G, H sind Wertungen des Autors und daher nicht zuzuordnen.*

Quelle		*Paraphrase*	*Primärtext*
„solar industry" (Z. 8)	*E*	*"If there are no further subsidies, we will gradually lose our customers."*	*Z. 9–11 "It fears that once these grants dry up, demand will vanish and the market will collapse."*
„director of PV-UK" (Z. 22)	*F*	*"If the government no longer follows White Paper proposals, a company will have squandered a lot of money."*	*Z. 23/24 „... invested millions of pounds in response to the white paper ... This money will have been wasted"*

„policy manager at the RPA“ (Z. 31)	*C*	*“The official policy of the government is contradictory to what it had said before.”*	*Z. 32/33 „… the government has gone back on its previous commitments to a 10-year PV programme“*
„government“ (Z. 40)	*B*	*“Renewable energy resources need to be given priority.”*	*Z. 40/41 „… the government favours wind and tidal power as renewable energy sources. “*
„government“ (Z. 48)	*D*	*“The electricity supply from sustainable energy will be four times as high in 15 years.”*	*Z. 48/50 „it wants five per cent … to come from renewable energy sources this year, 10 % by 2010 and 20 % by 2020.“*
„experts of renewable energy“ (Z. 51)	*A*	*“The country won't reach the proposed goal.”*	*Z. 51/52 „… that Britain will miss those targets“*

Government	**B**	**D**
solar industry	**E**	
director of PV-UK	**F**	
policy manager at the RPA	**C**	
renewable energy experts	**A**	

Task V: Sentence completion

1. a) The government **is about to pull the plug on grant money for early adoption of solar energy.**

   b) Without government commitment to households the market **will collapse**.

2. a) In Wales **Sharp UK has a manufacturing plant in Wrexham that employs 150 people**.

   b) (export) **The UK is a world leader in the integrated solar PV market with companies developing new solar tiles that have export potential**.

3. a) The government **favours wind and tidal power**,

   b) as the climate **is not favourable** for solar energy.

Hinweis:
zu 1a: Z. 2
zu 1b: Z. 10
zu 2a: Z. 13/14
zu 2b: Z. 15–17
zu 3: Z. 41–43

Task VI: Descriptive Part

Hinweis: *Die einzige Frage steht im mittleren Bild in der rechten Sprechblase. Wichtig ist es, im unteren Bild wahrzunehmen, dass die drei Herren selbst in einem Topf sitzen, welcher auf lodernden Flammen steht. Sie selbst sind also (Ironie) das personifizierte Experiment mit den Fröschen, worauf auch der Titel noch einmal verweist: "... Let's swim around some more."*
Worterklärungen:
***Beats me** – etwa „geht über meine Hutschnur"*
***Go figure** – Stell dir vor*

It is absurd to believe that the frog would not jump out of water that is going to be heated up slowly when it reaches a critical temperature. The cartoon makes fun of certain scientists that pretend that a slow, but nevertheless lethal rise of global temperature can be ignored. The bottom picture shows that the pool is a pot on a fire. The three gentlemen themselves are the frogs. *(70 words)*

Task VII: Argumentative Part

Hinweis: *Vergleichen Sie die „useful phrases" und die Hinweise zum „writing"-Teil.*

Composition

This environmentalist slogan seems puzzling at first glance, but it draws your attention to the crucial point: how can this world be handed down to the next generation so that it is still worth living in?

One of the main problems is that the developed world is exploiting crude oil, coal and natural gas at such a rate that these sources will soon be exhausted forever. Consequently, attitudes must be changed and methods developed to make use of renewable forms of energy. At the same time, the devastating effects of burning fossil fuel, which is responsible for global warming, could be avoided.

However, while wind farms are being built or used, the increase in passenger flights with the large airlines, for example, means that we are continuing to increase our total energy consumption. This means that reducing carbon dioxide emissions by using sustainable forms of energy is more than cancelled out by other such developments. It is high time that market forces were organised in such a way that they resulted in a vast curtailment of our total energy consumption. Far from being a technical issue, I think this is predominantly a political challenge of the leading nations of the western world.

To sum up, a new approach towards a more conscious, ascetic lifestyle will be the price we have to pay to guarantee the future needs of our children. *(230 words)*

Berufliche Oberschulen Bayern – Englisch 12. Klasse
Beispiele für Themen der mündlichen Prüfung

Thema 1

Should students work to get some extra money? – During Sunday afternoon your family has met to discuss about taking a job to earn some extra money.

Roles:

- The father is against his children working as he gives them enough pocket money.
- The mother is also against as schoolwork is more important.
- The youngest son/daughter (15) wants to earn money through babysitting in order to buy an mp3-player (is in 10th grade of Realschule).
- The middle son/daughter (18) wants to buy fancy clothes and to have enough money to go to parties during the weekend (goes to FOS, 12th grade).
- The oldest son (22) wants to buy a car. He goes to University and wants to work during term-breaks.

Tasks:

TASK 1: At the beginning the three children explain to their parents why they want to take up a job.

TASK 2: They discuss the problem with the parents with the three children trying to support each other. At the end the discussion brings about a solution accepted by the three children.

Thema 2

Holiday trip – You and your friends are planning to go on a two-week vacation together. You have to decide which destination you will choose. You have to reach a conclusion in the end.

Roles:

- Person 1: You want to go to Mallorca. "Fun and cheap" is your motto.
- Person 2: You want to go backpacking in India. Your motto is "Keep away from the crowds".
- Person 3: You want to spend the time on a sailing boat in the Greek isles. Action is the right thing for you.
- Person 4: You want to spend your vacation in a self supplied apartment at the Baltic Sea.
- Person 5: You want to do a cultural trip to London.

Tasks:

TASK 1: Introduce yourself and tell the group why you want to go to your destination (1 minute each).

TASK 2: Talk to each other for 20 minutes and find a compromise that is satisfying to everybody.

Thema 3

Crime and punishment – The crime rate among young people has been rising dramatically over the last few years. There are several ideas to fight this negative development:

- in the USA boot camps have been introduced,
- in Sweden they prefer alternative sentences such as social work,
- the British solution is harsh prison sentences for young offenders,
- and in Singapore even corporal punishment is practised.

In a panel discussion organised by the city council in the town hall ways of appropriate punishment for juvenile delinquents are looked at.

Roles:

- Mother/Father of a criminal
- Mother/Father of a crime victim
- Young criminal who was released from prison two months ago
- Social worker who deals with young offenders every day
- Government representative who is concerned about financial and organisational aspects

Tasks:

TASK 1: At first, every single member of the group introduces himself/herself and presents his / her point of view in about 1 minute.

TASK 2: Then you start debating the issue. In the end you all have to arrive at some sort of conclusion or statement that sums up the debate.

Thema 4

After a series of severe accidents caused by drunken drivers, the mass media are discussing new laws and regulations on blood alcohol levels, tougher driving license tests, day licenses for under 21, more road checks, shorter pub opening times, higher taxes on alcohol and a number of other measures.
You are invited to take part in the television show "Youth today" as a representative of a group that is involved in the problem.

Roles:

- Mr/Mrs Right, who has been a judge in a traffic court for 16 years and has chaired lots of cases in which alcohol was the cause of the accident
- Speedy, who is a disco freak and owns a tuned Golf GTI which he/she uses to go out at night. He/she also likes drinking alcohol when he/she goes out.
- Mr/Mrs Strong, who is a delegate of the Breweries' and Distillers' Organisation and is worried about the future of his/her industry
- Mr/Mrs Clean, who is a representative of Alcoholics Anonymous
- Mr/Mrs Bocuse, who owns an expensive restaurant out in the countryside and offers exclusive French wine

Tasks:

TASK 1: Presentation stage: The different participants slip into their roles and introduce themselves. They present their personal ideas on that issue.

TASK 2: Discussion stage: You start a debate in which you try to discuss the issue in favour of your organisation and defend your position. Also try to understand and accept other views.
Try to come to some sort of conclusion or statement that shows that you have learned from the discussion.

Thema 5

The principal and staff of your school have decided that this year the organisation of all activities concerning your graduation lies with the students themselves. Therefore the members of the student board meet to talk about:

- possible activities (at school, at a restaurant ...) after sitting the last exam on Friday
- the design of a shirt: colour, logo, same shirt for all classes? etc.
- the students' paper (to be sold at the graduation ceremony): name, content
- the graduation ceremony (drinks before the beginning of the ceremony, program, music, speeches, dress code etc.) and graduation party (band/kind of music, location, program, food etc.)
- the presentation of the event in the public

Tasks:

TASK 1: Each member of your group introduces one of these points by explaining what it is all about and putting forward his/her own suggestions.

TASK 2: Then a discussion follows, in which you are supposed to come up with and agree on concrete ideas to be presented to the principal.

Roles:

Michael: Owner of a transport company
Günther: Represents the Ministry of Finance
Heidi: Member of the Green party
Anita: Single mother of two children

TASK 1: Introduction

Günther: Good morning, ladies and gentlemen. We are meeting here today in order to debate the issue of the increasing petrol prices and its consequences for the economy, the people and the state. My name is Günther Brechtal and I represent the Ministry of Finance. Our government is not yet clear about whether to increase these prices but the Ministry of Finance is clearly in favour of raising taxes for mineral oil for reasons I am sure we will be able to debate later. Would the others like to introduce themselves so we can find out a little about each other and our positions, please?

Heidi: Hello, my name is Heidi. I'm a member of the Green Party and I am strongly in favour of raising the mineral oil tax. Since the amount of traffic has increased enormously over the past few decades we must take action to reduce the amount of pollution it causes as we have to preserve the environment for future generations. I mean, why does an ordinary apple we can buy at a supermarket have to travel 10,000 kilometres by lorry, when they could be harvested right around the corner?

Michael: I completely disagree with both your points of view. My name is Michael and I am the owner of a small transport company that runs five lorries. At the moment there is fierce competition going on in the market between the transport companies all over Europe. Germany is facing the problem of millions of unemployed at the moment. If you want to increase that number any further, just increase fuel taxes and let our European competitors take over the markets.

Anita: My name is Anita and I find it very disturbing that this debate is being brought up again. As a single mother of two my budget is already tight, and on top of that I have to use the car to fetch my children or to go shopping. Have you ever noticed how many things you need to buy each week in order to feed your children properly? Does the government want me to look for an extra job to finance that so I don't see my children anymore and neglect their education?

TASK 2: Debate

Heidi: I understand the issues you are facing as a single mother. There is, however, another side to your line of argument. Don't you want your children to be able to enjoy a healthy environment without facing health risks due to the exhaust fumes emitted by cars and lorries? I am convinced that there is a solution that will satisfy both points of view. Wouldn't it be an option for you if part of the taxes were used to improve the public transport system so you and your children could use buses and trains instead of the car?

Anita: Of course, I would welcome that solution as then my children could come home from school on their own without having to wait for hours for a bus to arrive. There's still one problem, however: when I go shopping the entire boot of my 10-year-old VW Passat is filled with what we need for the week. I cannot possibly do all my shopping by bus. Since the local store closed down lately due to the competition from the discounters, the next shop is too far away and I have to carry too many things at a time. So that option would only be partly helpful. I would still need a car.

Günther: Yes, I follow you, Anita. But it can't be denied that your children also want to live in a country where they can grow up without the state being burdened by an enormous deficit. I mean, in the end it's your children or grandchildren who are going to have to pay for it. I'm sure you agree.

Anita: Yes, Günther, I do, but that doesn't help me and my kids *now*.

Günther: I can assure you that the government is aware of this problem. Since the birth rate in this country is one of the lowest in the world, we should try to find a solution that tackles the problem of the financial deficit while helping young families at the same time. And of course it's in the government's interest to improve public transport in order to reduce the traffic as a whole. Wouldn't transferring some of the money earned from higher taxation on mineral oil to increase child benefit go some way towards covering the extra fuel costs?

Anita: Well, yes, depending on how high the increase is, that could be an option.

Michael: I've never heard such rubbish! Why help families financially when there aren't going to be any jobs around when the children grow up? In Germany every seventh job depends on the automobile industry. If fuel prices go up, people will start buying those cheap Korean cars which pollute the environment even more, and German car manufacturers will have to lay people off because their cars aren't selling anymore. And what's more, most of the German transport businesses would have to shut down because of the overwhelming competition from Eastern Europe, where the wages are far lower and fuel only costs a fraction of what it does here. What these companies do is fill up with fuel, say in Poland, deliver their goods to Germany, go back, and don't spend a single cent on fuel in Germany. In my opinion this tax increase won't lead to more money for the state, it'll mean less, as the unemployment benefits will amount to more than the incoming revenue. If you care as much about the future of our companies as you do about children, we'd also have to be subsidized.

Heidi: Subsidized? Is that all you can talk about? We *must* create a sustainable economy that doesn't destroy the environment. Will subsidies lead to less pollution? Of course not, and so we're stuck with the status quo. What I suggest is that companies – OK, let's say transport companies – should receive tax relief if they invest in means of transportation which are good for the environment. In a few years the fuel cell will be ready for mass production, and natural gas could be used as a stopgap. Lorries could be refitted to be able to run on gas, and the changes to the engines would only be minor. And costs for refitting are quite low. I'm sure the government would be happy to grant tax relief for that. I just wonder why so few transport firms have switched to this form of energy considering that natural gas costs half as much per 100 km as diesel.

Michael: Of course we're aware of the advantages of natural gas, but that argument doesn't hold as far as I'm concerned. Have you ever tried looking for petrol stations that offer natural gas? OK, in Germany the network is quite dense already, and if you're lucky you can find a filling station every 400 km or so, but have you looked at the rest of Europe? There are only a few dozens around. Not to mention Eastern Europe – it's like looking for a needle in a haystack. That's why refitting our lorries wouldn't give us any advantages over our European competitors since we have to send our lorries all over Europe and sometimes all over the world.

Günther: Let me just interrupt you there for a second. So you say that if there were a network of natural gas stations all over Europe you could maybe accept a tax increase on mineral oil?

Michael: There are other issues to be considered as well, but yes, that would make a difference.

Günther: Well, that's good news for us. In the last meeting of the heads of government in Europe there was a hot debate on a long-term strategy regarding environmental policy. Part of that policy is to create a European network of petrol stations providing both natural gas and the environmentally friendly rapeseed oil. Germany is the technology leader in this field and together with some substantial funding and the investment of companies researching in this field, the network should be completed within five years. For the transition period we will have to find other solutions as lowering or maintaining the price of mineral oil is not an option at the moment. While the state needs money urgently, if steps are to be taken in the right direction concerning the issue of the environment, it would be prepared for a delay to balance the budget in order to push for a step towards a cleaner and healthier world.

Heidi: Does the government already have plans as to when the transition period should start?

Günther: We are not clear about the whole concept yet. This is part of the reason why we are here today. We would like to find a solution that benefits most of the people. Part of the plan could be to make transport by rail much cheaper if lorries have to drive small distances to and from the train stations. I'm sure that would significantly reduce the costs for transport firms. As an improvement to the public transport system has already been suggested, both sides would benefit: the new rail system on the one hand and the more frequent trains on the other. This would of course benefit private individuals as well as business.

Michael: … yeah, while I have to double my fleet in order to get to the train station. You can't be serious!

Günther: I'm not sure if you are aware that this issue was dealt with a long time ago. If you look into rail services regarding cargo deliveries it has long been common practice for lorries to be backpacked onto trains fully loaded and then to be unloaded once they reach their destination so that they can deliver their cargo as usual. Switzerland is a role model for this kind of transportation. In order to reduce congestion and pollution, every transit lorry has to use the train through Switzerland for a fixed price, which is cheaper for the firms than paying for fuel and maintenance for their trucks. I must say, it's very successful, so what's the problem with introducing such a system in Germany?

Anita: Would you mind if I raised an objection here? That idea seems good in theory, but will it work in practice? I mean, I know the rail system is used by a lot of freightliners and passenger trains, but it seems to me that there are already a lot of delays in the local transport systems because of long distance trains being late and there only being one set of tracks available in each direction. I'd hate to think of what it would be like if the train capacity were increased by 20 %. Public transport would be even more unreliable than it is now, and if you ask me, I can't imagine there being billions of euros around to extend the railway system. I don't think this system could be introduced successfully, not in a short space of time anyway. It wouldn't be any good for me – in the end I'd have to pick my children up by car anyway because I wouldn't be able to plan on their arriving at a particular time. And I wouldn't be able to count on being back home in time myself to cook and care for my kids.

Michael: I quite agree with you, Anita. In the logistics business timing is crucial. Transport companies need reliable schedules and I doubt this system could guarantee that.

Günther: On the other hand, there would be fewer traffic jams on the roads, and even if you had to use your car but you were receiving child benefit as well, it would cost you the same as before the tax increase and you would arrive faster and more safely.

In the meantime the government would make sure that the railway system was extended to meet the demand.

Heidi: But to tackle the question of rail congestion, there also has to be a fundamental change regarding the transportation of goods. I'd like to refer to the statement I made at the beginning, that the production and consumption of local goods should be encouraged. If an apple grown near Munich is cheaper than one from Spain, people are going to want to buy the local apple. This would lead to a large reduction in long distance transport, while the local transport companies would still be required to deliver goods. I doubt that European competitors could match local truck owners, as these would only have to deliver over short distances.

Anita: Well, I for one would always prefer cheaper products because I'm on a pretty tight budget.

Conclusion

Günther: So, let's try to come to a useful conclusion here, so that the government can continue its efforts in a sensible direction.

Michael: Well, I'm still quite critical concerning the tax increase. Considering the arguments raised today, I would favour the set-up of a European network of petrol stations for natural gas combined with tax relief for switching to the new technology. I would strongly oppose the system of forced rail transportation, as I don't think that on time delivery could be guaranteed.

Anita: To sum things up, I'd like to see more child benefits as compensation for the increase in petrol prices. I'd also like a better public transport system as it improves flexibility for both me and my children. Although it sounds like a good idea on the surface, I'm against the system of transporting lorries by rail as it would have a negative effect on the public transport system as a whole. But it could be a realistic option in the long run.

Heidi: The Green party are strongly in favour of anything that helps preserve the environment and supports a sustainable economy which doesn't come at the expense of future generations. So we'd like to see a European system of filling stations based on natural gas combined with more research to launch the environmentally friendly fuel cell. I also think the railway system should be improved and extended, and lorries should be forced to conduct long distance transport by rail. We encourage the increase in child allowances, and tax relief for new technology investments in order to reduce the downsides of this tax increase for certain social groups.

Günther: Well, coming to a decision on this matter will require careful consideration of all these aspects. As you know, the Ministry of Finance is currently dealing with the issue of an extensive budget deficit, and this has top priority. Certain moderations can be accepted, however, if we can achieve a cleaner environment and a reduction in traffic. To conclude, I am sure you will all agree that it won't be easy to make a decision. Considering the different points of view, it seems that if certain incentives are granted, many of the negative effects of a tax increase can be justified, and that environmental protection and balancing the budget can still be achieved at the same time.

A draft of the decision will be presented by the coalition in a few weeks. It was a pleasure to have you all here, and thank you for the interesting and lively discussion.

Anita: Thank you.

Heidi: Thanks for your time, and have a safe trip back to Berlin.

Michael: I still doubt that things are going in the right direction, but I hope that the government will find a fair solution for us truckers.

A Reading Comprehension

Text I: Pull up your pants or go to jail

(A) Jamarcus Marshall a 17-year-old high school sophomore in Mansfield, Louisiana, says he believes that no one should be able to tell him how high to wear his jeans. "It's up to the person who's wearing the pants," he said.

(B) Marshall's sagging pants, a style popularized in the early 1990s by hip-hop artists, are becoming a criminal offense in a growing number of communities, including his own. Starting in Louisiana, an intensifying push by lawmakers has decided that pants worn low enough to expose underwear pose a threat to the public, and they have enacted indecency ordinances to stop it.

(C) Since June 11, sagging pants have been against the law in Delcambre, Louisiana, a town of 2,231 that is 80 miles, or 130 kilometers, southwest of Baton Rouge. The style carries a fine of as much as $ 500 or up to a six-month sentence. "We used to wear long hair, but I don't think our trends were ever as bad as sagging," said Mayor Carol Broussard.

(D) An ordinance in Mansfield, a town of 5,496, subjects offenders to a fine of up to $ 150 plus court costs or jail time of up to 15 days. Police Chief Don English said the law, which takes effect Sept. 15, would set a good civic image.

(E) Behind the indecency laws may be the real issue – the hip-hop style itself which critics say is worn as a badge of delinquency, with its distinctive walk conveying thuggish swagger and a disrespect for authority. Also at work are the larger issue of freedom of expression and the questions raised when fashion moves from being merely objectionable to illegal.

(F) Sagging began in American prisons, where oversized uniforms were issued without belts to prevent suicide and the use of belts as weapons. The style spread by way of rappers and music videos, from the ghetto to the suburbs and around the world.

(G) Efforts to outlaw sagging in Virginia and statewide in Louisiana in 2004 failed, usually when opponents invoked a right to self-expression. But the latest legislative efforts have taken a different tack, drawing on indecency laws, and their success is inspiring other lawmakers.

(H) In the West Ward of Trenton, New Jersey, Councilwoman Annette Lartigue is drafting an ordinance to fine or enforce community service in response to what she sees as the problem of exposing private parts in public. "It's a fad like hot pants; however, I think it crosses the line when a person shows their backside," Lartigue said. "You can't legislate how people dress, but you can legislate when people begin to become indecent by exposing their body parts."

(I) The American Civil Liberties Union has been steadfast in its opposition to dress restrictions. Debbie Seagraves, the executive director of the group in Georgia, said, "I don't see any way that something constitutional could be crafted when the intention is to single out and label one style of dress that originated with the black youth culture as an unacceptable form of expression."

(J) School districts have become more aggressive in enforcing dress bans as the courts have given them greater latitude. Restrictions have been devised for jeans, miniskirts, long hair, piercing, logos with drug references and clothing suggesting gang affiliation, including "colors", hats and jewelry.

(K) Dress codes are showing up in unexpected places. The National Basketball Association now stipulates that players who are not in uniform at league-sponsored events cannot wear items like sunglasses, headgear, exposed chains or medallions. After experiencing a brawl that spilled into the stands and generated publicity headaches, the league sought to enforce a business-casual dress code, saying that hip-hop clothing projected an image that alienated middle-class audiences.

(L) According to Andrew Bolton, the curator at the Costume Institute of the Metropolitan Museum of Art in New York, fashions tend to be decried when they "challenge the conservative morality of a society." [...] Like past fashion bans, the prohibitions on sagging are seen by some as racially motivated because the wearers are young, predominantly African-American men.

(M) Yet this legislation has been proposed largely by African-American officials. It may speak to a generation gap. Michael Eric Dyson, a professor of sociology at Georgetown University and the author of *Know What I Mean?: Reflections on Hip Hop*, said, "They've bought the myth that sagging pants represents an offensive lifestyle which leads to destructive behavior." [...]

(N) But Larry Harris Jr., 28, a musician from Miami who stood in oversize gear outside a hip-hop show in Times Square in New York, said that prison style was not his inspiration. "I think what you have here is people who don't understand the language of hip-hop," he said. [...]

(O) Benjamin Chavis, a former executive director of the NAACP, said, "I think to criminalize how a person wears their clothing is more offensive than what the remedy is trying to do." Chavis, who is often pictured in an impeccable suit and tie among the baggy outfits of the hip-hop elite, is a chairman of the Hip Hop Summit Action Network. He said that the coalition would challenge the ordinances in court. "The focus should be on cleaning up the social conditions that the sagging pants come out of," he said. "That they wear their pants the way they do is a statement of the reality that they're struggling with on a day-to-day basis." *(893 words)*

Niko Koppel: U.S., a backlash against sagging jeans. The New York Times, August 30, 2007.

Task I: Mixed reading tasks 12 credits

Mediation Englisch – Deutsch (Absätze A – F) (5)

Beantworten Sie die folgenden Aufgaben **auf Deutsch**! Verwenden Sie hierfür die im Text enthaltenen Informationen!

1. Welche konkreten Strafen wurden in der Stadt Delcambre für das Tragen von herunter hängenden Hosen eingeführt? (2)

   • ______________________________

   • ______________________________

2. Erläutern Sie, welcher Vorwurf in der Formulierung „[...] worn as a badge of delinquency" (l. 18) zum Ausdruck kommt. (1)

   ____

3. Erklären Sie, wie und warum das Tragen dieser herunter hängenden Hosen ursprünglich entstanden ist. (2)

____

____

____

____

Short-answer questions/sentence completion (2)

4. Answer the following questions by providing the required information from the text:
Which civil right has so far prevented lawmakers from banning sagging trousers throughout the US? (1)

____

5. Complete the following sentence:
According to the text, ______________________ will be the population group mainly affected by the new regulations against sagging trousers. (1)

Multiple choice questions (paragraphs H–O) (5)
Mark the most suitable option with a cross.

6. In the view of Annette Lartigue, sagging pants should be banned … (1)
   A because they are just another fashion that will not last.
   B in order to ensure that people wear the right clothes.
   C because more and more people are exposing themselves.
   D in order to protect other people from offensive behavior.

7. According to paragraph J, several school districts have … (1)
   A taken some of their students to court.
   B banned crime-related items of clothing.
   C completely banned fashionable clothing.
   D expelled drug users from school.

8. According to the text, the NBA (National Basketball Association) has introduced a dress code because … (1)
   A it might lose supporters due to players' behavior.
   B gang fights have broken out between several teams.
   C some players have attacked wealthy spectators.
   D advertising revenues have decreased significantly.

9. Professor Dyson expresses the view that … (1)
   A sagging pants are offensive and can even lead to criminal behavior.
   B people's style of clothing cannot be equated with a criminal lifestyle.
   C the focus should be on addressing the underlying social problems.
   D the actual problem is the conflict between black and white Americans.

10. In this article, the author above all wants to… (1)

A compare regulations in different parts of the US.

B criticize the supporters of the new legislation.

C provide an overview of the current debate.

D warn readers about the effects of the new legislation.

Text II: Netting old friends

(A) Like millions of teenagers around the world, Sue Bloom spends several hours socializing online every day. She posts pictures, meets new friends [and] updates her blog […]. The only thing is, Bloom isn't a teenager or a twenty-something college student – she's a 58-year-old art historian. And the brand-new site where she hangs out, Eons.com, is for baby boomers (and older) only: you have to be at least 50 to join. "Social networking sites are wonderful for people of my generation," says Bloom, who lives in Maryland. "We've always been really social, and they're all about developing a community."

(B) Forget teen haunt Xanga and college student staple Facebook. Online social networking isn't just for youngsters anymore. Of course, only 1 million of the more than 215 million social networkers regularly active today are older than 50. But by the end of the year that number could explode to 20 million, says a new study from global analysts Deloitte, due out later this month. Silver surfers could prove to be an even more coveted online group than their teenage predecessors. "They're the future of social networking," says Paul Lee, director of technology research at Deloitte.

(C) The rising number of older networkers has something to do with the teenage market reaching saturation. In Ireland, for instance, 90 percent of teenagers already actively use Bebo; in the United States, it's hard to find a college student without a MySpace page. To expand, networking sites are being forced to shift their focus to older users. "Future growth has to come from older people," says Bebo founder Michael Birch. "There's no choke."

(D) Online networking took off as a phenomenon three years ago with the launch of Web 2.0 software like […] JavaScript and XML, which make online design relatively easy to do. Although MySpace was founded only in 2003, News Corp. recently shelled out $ 580 million for the company, and Google paid $ 1.65 billion for YouTube, the immensely popular video-sharing site. Neither firm, however, has posted a profit, and it's not clear if they will. Social networking's traditional bread-and-butter users, the 30-minus generation grew up on free music from Napster and are loath to pay for anything they get on the Web. Advertisers have been reluctant to have their brands displayed on unmonitored sites, which are often rife with unsavory postings. And although teens may have lots of time, they lack cash.

(E) Baby boomers, on the other hand, have both time and money. They're also more refined and restrained in the messages they post, which appeals to advertisers. Jeff Taylor, the entrepreneur who made millions off popular job-search site Monster.com, which he founded back in 1993, seems to have another hit on his hands with Eons, the social networking site for the 50-plus crowd only. Eons hit the Net in late July, backed by $ 10 million in venture capital, and now boasts more than 100,000 members and has welcomed almost a million unique visitors. In only a few months it has signed on numerous advertisers, including Hyatt Hotels, Verizon Wireless, Liberty Mutual and Fidelity. Beyond that, Deloitte's new study on the rise of older social networkers predicts that baby boomers, unlike those of the MySpace generation, will be willing to pay subscription fees for sites that offer the tech support they […] desire.

(F) The trend is happening from Tallinn to Tokyo. […] Eons […] has formed clubs around the interests of an older crowd. Among the most popular are Bookaholics, an online book club which is just starting its second book review now, and Becoming a Spiritual Adult, which encourages members to discuss moral and ethical values. […]

(G) What created this perfect networking storm for baby boomers? For one thing, the oldest boomers – who just hit 60 last year – are retiring. That means they have time to spend on networking sites that are wholly reliant on user-created content. Unlike their parents, baby boomers aren't looking for a quiet retirement. They want to stay active, social and connected during a retirement in which they're likely to live to more than 80. In the modern world, that means online as much as in person. In the United States alone, there are 44 million people over the age of 50 online. […]

(H) In some important ways, however, boomers are exactly like the teenagers and young adults who launched the online social networking phenomenon. As graduation […] keynote speakers stereotypically say to their young audiences: "The world is your oyster." But with boomers having so many healthy years to look forward to on retirement, it's just as much theirs. […] *(759 words)*

Task II: Mixed reading tasks 10 credits

1. **Gapped summary (paragraphs A to C only!)** (5)
Fill in the gaps with words taken from paragraphs A to C of the text (one word per line).

Baby boomers have always been interested in ____________________, networking and being part of a community. Therefore, online social networking is becoming more and more popular among the 50-plus generation. Until recently, it was only associated with teenagers, their ________________ as an online group. Those ________________ ________________, as the older net users are also called metaphorically, will perhaps be targeted even more intensively by online firms than teenagers, as the market for youngsters has now arrived at a state of ________________. So if ________________ in social networking is to continue, it must come from the older generation.

Mediation Englisch – Deutsch (Absätze D – H) (5)
Beantworten Sie die folgenden Fragen **auf Deutsch**!

2. Aus welchen Gründen konnten bisher weder mit MySpace noch mit YouTube Gewinne erzielt werden? (2)

a) ____

____

b) ____

____

c) Jugendliche haben wenig Geld zur Verfügung.

3. Welche Gründe werden in **Absatz G** dafür angeführt, dass die Social-Networking Angebote bei so vielen älteren Menschen auf so großes Interesse stoßen? (2)

a) ____

____

b) ____

____

4. Was bedeutet im Textzusammenhang: „it's just as much theirs" (ll. 56/57)? (1)

____

____

____

____

Text III (gapped text): Flames of hope

As for so many of us, the genocide in Darfur (Sudan) was merely an abstraction to Ashok Gadgil, a scientist at the Lawrence Berkeley National Laboratory in California. But in September 2004 he got a call from the U.S. Agency for International Development. Could Gadgil design a screw press for Darfurians, the caller asked, so they could turn their garbage into biofuel pellets? "I quickly showed him that there is not enough kitchen waste in home cooking to produce much worthwhile fuel," the physicist says, and USAID dropped the idea. [_____1_____] Eventually Gadgil decided that if he couldn't redesign the fuel, he would redesign the stove.

The violence in Darfur has not only left at least 200,000 dead but devastated the already arid landscape. [_____2_____] As they hunt farther and wider for firewood, they are denuding whole swaths of the countryside. Gathering firewood can now mean a seven-hour round trip, during which women risk rape and mutilation at the hands of the Janjaweed militias that lurk in wait. [_____3_____] A fact-finding visit to the region in late 2005 brought home the problem's urgency to Gadgil. "A huge majority of people were missing at least one meal a week because they did not have fuel to cook with," he says. [...] [_____4_____] "That's really sick, isn't it?", he added.

Gadgil, a 56-year-old Mumbai native, had experience developing simple, life-saving technology. One of his patents – a cheap method for disinfecting water using ultraviolet light – led to a successful business start-up in 1996. [_____5_____] After returning from Darfur, Gadgil worked with lab colleagues and students at UC Berkeley to modify an existing Indian stove for Darfurians' needs. "Cook stoves, although they look simple, are very complex creatures," he says. [...] While the Indian stove excelled at producing low-intensity heat for cooking rice, for instance, Darfurians needed a high-powered flame for sautéing onions, garlic and okra, ingredients in their staple dish, *mullah*. [_____6_____]

The result of their efforts is the Berkeley-Darfur stove [...], a hollow drum that looks like a cross between a lunar landing craft and a stop sign. A wind collar makes for a steady flame. Designed with smooth airflow to fuel the fire and an upper rim that fits snugly with different-size pots, the stove requires 75 percent less fuel than an open fire. [_____7_____] And those who now pay for it, Gadgil estimates, could save as much as $ 200 a year, which could be used instead for luxuries like new clothing and fresh meat.

The next step is mass production. Gadgil and his partners in Berkeley have teamed with two non-profit organisations, Engineers Without Borders and CHF International, to set up workshops in Sudan. The project is funded by USAID and individual donors. They hope ultimately to distribute stoves to nearly all 300,000 refugee families. […] Gadgil and EWB have yet to settle on a distribution plan. They won't be handing the stoves out as charity – "[______8______]," Gadgil says – but at $ 25 apiece, the devices are out of the reach of most families. Gadgil favors some sort of leasing plan, allowing families to rent the stove for about 50 cents a week. The ultimate goal is for the refugees to take over the program, from manufacturing to distribution, which would mean jobs and income for the devastated region. *(524 words)*

Task III: Multiple matching (gapped text) 8 credits

You are going to read a text on an invention making life easier for many people in the Third World. The text contains 8 gaps. Use the box below to **state which of the sentences A to L fits best into each gap**. There are **three additional sentences** which you do not need.

Gap	**1**	**2**	**3**	**4**	**5**	**6**	**7**	**8**
Sentence								

Sentences:

A The resulting company, WaterHealth International, now provides affordable clean water for more than 1 million people in the developing world.

B That means fewer risky trips outside the camp in search of firewood.

C But the problem continued to nag at him.

D Since then, the political situation in Darfur has calmed down considerably.

E They have enabled him to distribute 100,000 stoves for free.

F Men can't make the trip in their stead – They'll simply be killed.

G Giving something away turns the recipients into beggars.

H And since most families cook outside, the stove also needed to cope with the region's strong winds.

I More than 2 million people now fill groaning refugee camps.

J However, it is too expensive to be produced in great numbers.

K Many families were selling some of their food in exchange for the wood to cook it with.

B Writing

Task IV: Descriptive writing

9 credits

Choose <u>one</u> of the following two tasks (1 <u>or</u> 2) and write between 80–100 words.

1. **Describing a cartoon:**
   Describe the situation in this cartoon, which is entitled "Out of business", and state what point the cartoonist is making.

http://www.freechicago.org/freechicago/images/SmokeFree.ipg

2. **Describing statistics:**
   What do the following statistics tell you about CO_2 emissions?

Annual per capita CO_2 emissions in tonnes, 1980–2004

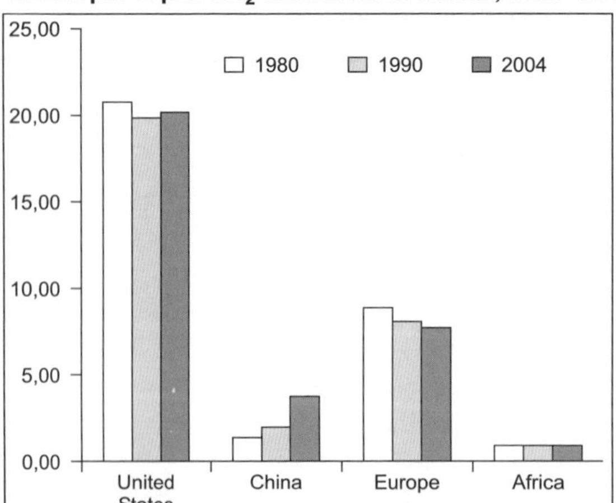

Adapted from: http://www.news.mongabay.com/2007/0508-world_bank.html

Task V: Argumentative writing 21 credits

Choose one of the following topics (1 or 2) and write at least 200 words.

1. **Composition**
   According to recent statistics, Germany has become a country with one of the highest numbers of overweight people in Europe.
   In your opinion, what are the main reasons for this development and what measures should be taken to stop this trend?

2. **Letter**
   Since you are interested in environmental issues, you want to do some voluntary work after finishing school. You have found the following advertisement on the Internet and are planning to spend four weeks in Australia.
   Write a letter to your pen-friend from London and try to persuade him or her to join you on this conservation project.

AUSTRALIA CONSERVATION PROJECT – VOLUNTARY WORK

The Conservation Volunteer Australia (CVA) package gives you the chance to get out in the fresh air and do something new and challenging.

On this Australia volunteer package, you can go to one of 10 locations in Australia for between 2 to 6 weeks and work on conservation projects (e. g. tree planting or endangered species protection).

http://www.pealgap.co.uk/Conservation-work

Lösungsvorschläge

A Reading Comprehension

Hinweis: Die Aufgaben „Mediation", „Short-answer questions" und „Multiple-choice" beziehen sich auf die verschiedenen angegebenen Textteile. Nicht übersehen: Bei „Short-answer questions" ist keine Eingrenzung angegeben, diese Aufgabe bezieht sich also auf den ganzen Text. Markieren Sie sich relevante Absätze für die jeweilige Fragestellung.

Task I: Mixed reading tasks: Pull up your pants or go to jail

Mediation Englisch – Deutsch (Absätze A – F)

1. ***Hinweis:** Das Stichwort der Frage „Delcambre" findet sich in Absatz C, Zeile 9. Die Antworten gehen aus „a fine of as much as $ 500" (Z. 11) und „or up to a six-month sentence" (Z. 11) hervor.*
   - eine Geldstrafe in Höhe von 500 $
   - oder eine Gefängnisstrafe von bis zu sechs Monaten

2. ***Hinweis:** „badge" ist ein Anstecker, ein Zeichen, „delinquency" ist straffälliges Verhalten*

   Wer diese Kleidung trägt, drückt aus, dass er die Gesetze nicht respektiert/gibt sich als Krimineller zu erkennen/Ist Erkennungszeichen von Straftätern

3. ***Hinweis:** Vgl. Absatz F: "Sagging began in American prisons, where oversized uniforms were issued without belts to prevent suicide and the use of belts as weapons." (Z. 22/23)*

   In Gefängnissen in den USA wurde an Häftlinge Kleidung in Übergröße und ohne Gürtel ausgegeben. Damit sollte verhindert werden, dass Gefangene Selbstmord begehen oder Gürtel als Waffen verwenden.

Short-answer question/sentence completion

4. ***Hinweis:** „civil rights" sind Zivilrechte, d. h. allgemeine Bürgerrechte, wie Versammlungsfreiheit und eben auch Freiheit der Meinungsäußerung. In Absatz G findet sich der Hinweis, dass in Virginia und Louisiana diese Kleidermode nicht verboten werden konnte („to outlaw sagging failed", Z. 25) Es wird auch der Grund genannt: "... opponents invoked a right to self-expression", Z. 26, ebenso „... at work (hier: betroffen ist) the larger freedom of expression ..." (Z. 19/20).*

   the right to self-expression /freedom of expression

5. ***Hinweis:** Im gesamten Text gilt es die Stellen aufzusuchen, die die Bevölkerungsgruppen beschreiben, welche am meisten von der neuen Bestimmung gegen „sagging pants" betroffen sind:*
   Z. 4: „... a style popularized ... by hip-hop artists"
   Z. 23/24: "The style spread by way of rappers and music videos ... around the world."
   Z. 38: Erst diese Wendung „... style of dress that originated with the black youth culture ..." und
   Z. 53/54: "... the wearers are young, predominantly (vor allem) African-American men." geben genaueren Aufschluss.

   young African-American men / black youth

Multiple choice questions

6 D, 7 B, 8 A, 9 B, 10 C

Hinweis:

zu 6: In Absatz H äußert sich Lartigue, weswegen hängende Hosen verboten werden sollten: „... problem of exposing private parts in public." (Z. 31) und "... people begin to become indecent by exposing their bodyparts." (Z. 33/34)

zu 7: Fundstelle im Text: "Restrictions have been devised for ... clothing suggesting gang affiliation, ..." (Z. 41/42)

zu 8: Fundstellen im Text: „NBA" (Z. 44/45); "... the league sought to enforce a business-casual dress code, saying that hip-hop clothing projected an image that alienated (be-/entfremdet) middle-class audiences." (Z. 47–49)

zu 9: Die Aussage von Prof. Dyson, "They have bought (hier: akzeptiert, übernommen) the myth (etwas Unwirkliches, Unreales) ..." (Z. 57–59), bedarf der Interpretation.

zu 10: Trotz widersprüchlicher Aufgabenstellung „In this article", beschränken Sie sich auf die Vorgabe: Absätze H – O. Lassen Sie sich nicht vom Titel in die Irre führen („a backlash against sagging jeans" = Schlag, Rückwendung gegen), der auf Lösung B hindeutet, was aber insgesamt nicht zutrifft. Lösung A – Vergleich der Regelungen in den verschiedenen Teilen der USA – trifft nicht zu, weil zu wenig systematisch vorgegangen und auch kein Ergebnis präsentiert wird; D erscheint völlig abwegig. Also bleibt nur Lösung C, denn in jedem der acht Absätze H–O wird eine andere Person oder Gruppierung benannt und deren unterschiedliche Standpunkte dargestellt.

Task II: Mixed reading tasks: Netting old friends

1. **Gapped summary**

Hinweis: *Nur Absätze A–C sind relevant. Es darf nur ein Wort pro Lücke eingesetzt werden (je Lücke 1 Punkt). Der Begriff „baby boomers" ist (mithilfe des Wörterbuchs) zu klären: Nach dem Zweiten Weltkrieg gab es den sogenannten Babyboom, einen starken Anstieg der Geburtenrate; es handelt sich also um die Generation der heute über 50-Jährigen.*

1. Lücke 1: Woran ist die Generation 50 plus laut Text interessiert?
   a) „spends several hours socialising" (Z. 1/2)
   b) „post pictures, updates her blog" (Z. 2)
   c) „social networking" (Z. 5)
   d) „been really social" (Z. 7)
   e) „developing a community" (Z. 7)
   Nach Präpositionen (hier: interested in) folgt immer ein Gerund oder ein Substantiv. c) und e) scheiden aus, da im Satz schon genannt. Es bleibt nur ein Gerund übrig.
   Lösung: socialising (Z. 1/2)

2. Lücke 2: Das possessive adjective „their" vor der Lücke bezieht sich auf „50-plus generation" und in Zusammenhang mit „until recently ... as an online group" passt nur ein Nomen in den Sinnzusammenhang aus der Phrase „... their teenage predecessors", Z. 13. Lösung: predecessors (Z. 13)

3. Lücke 3 und 4: Aufschluss gibt die Wendung „... as the older net users are also called metaphorically ..." (Metapher: bildhafte Darstellung eines Sachverhalts). Hier können nur die Ausdrücke „baby boomer" (Z. 5) oder „silver surfers" (Z. 12) in Frage kommen, aber nur der letztere ist bildhafter Natur und steht für die ergrauten, älteren Internetbenutzer. Lösung: silver surfers (Z. 12)

4. Lücke 5: „... teenage market reaching saturation", Z. 15/16 (Sättigung des Marktes). Lösung: saturation (Z. 16)

5. Lücke 6: Es ist daher logisch, dass nach der Sättigung des Marktes für Junge, nur von der „older generation" ein weiteres Wachstum kommen kann. Lösung: growth (Z. 19)

Baby boomers have always been interested in **socialising**, networking and being part of a community. Therefore, online social networking is becoming more and more popular among the 50-plus generation. Until recently, it was only associated with teenagers, their **predecessors** as an online group.
Those **silver surfers**, as the older net users are also called metaphorically, will perhaps be targeted even more intensively by online firms than teenagers, as the market for youngsters has now arrived at a state of **saturation**. So if **growth** in social networking is to continue, it must come from the older generation.

Mediation Englisch – Deutsch (Absätze D – H)

2. ***Hinweis:*** *Die Namen der genannten Firmen MySpace und YouTube finden sich in Zeilen 23/24. Die entsprechenden Textstellen lauten:*
   a) "… the 30-minus generation grew up on free music … and are loath (tun etw. nur sehr ungern) to pay for anything they get on the Web." (Z. 26 – 28)
   b) "Advertisers have been reluctant to have their brands displayed on unmonitored (unüberwacht) sites, … with unsavoury (anrüchig, abstoßend) postings." (Z. 28/29).

   a) Die unter 30-Jährigen sind mit kostenlosen Musik-Downloads aufgewachsen und deshalb nicht bereit, für Inhalte von Internetseiten Geld zu bezahlen.
   b) Werbekunden wollen ihre Produkte nicht auf Seiten präsentieren, bei denen keine Überwachung stattfindet, da diese oft abstoßende Inhalte zeigen.
   c) Jugendliche haben wenig Geld zur Verfügung.

3. ***Hinweis:*** *Die entsprechenden Textstellen lauten:*
   a) "… they have time to spend on networking sites that are wholly reliant on user-created content." (Z. 47/48)
   b) "They want to stay active, social and connected during a retirement in which they're likely to live to more than 80." (Z. 49/50).

   a) Sie haben die Zeit, sich mit Internetseiten zu beschäftigen, deren Inhalte von den Nutzern selbst erstellt werden müssen.
   b) Sie wollen die vielen Jahre des Ruhestandes, die ihnen noch bleiben, aktiv und sozial eingebunden verbringen.

4. ***Hinweis:*** *Die Wendung "The world's your oyster." (Z. 55) sollten Sie im Wörterbuch nachschlagen (to do anything or go anywhere that you want to).*
   Die relevante Textstelle "… it's just as much theirs." (Z. 56/57) bezieht sich auf diese Wendung. Ausführlich könnte man auch sagen: "it is as much their oyster"; „theirs" bezieht sich demnach auf „boomers".

   Die Welt steht älteren Menschen ebenso offen wie Jüngeren.

Task III: Multiple matching: (gapped text) Flames of hope

Gap	**1**	**2**	**3**	**4**	**5**	**6**	**7**	**8**
Sentence	C	I	F	K	A	H	B	G

Die Sätze D/E/J sind unpassend.

Hinweis: *Hier sind möglichst logische und plausible Sinnzusammenhänge herzustellen. Schlüsselwörter in der Sinnkonstellation, d. h. in der der Lücke vorausgehenden bzw. nachfolgenden Textpassage, sind unterstrichen.*

Gap	***Sinnkonstellation***	***passender Text in der Lücke***
1	*"USAID dropped the idea" (that home cooking produced enough fuel), Z. 5–7 "Eventually (schließlich) Gadgil decided … he would redesign the stove." Z. 7/8*	*C, But the problem continued to nag at him.*
2	*"The violence in Darfur not only left 200 000 dead but devastated (verwüstet) the already arid (ausgetrocknet) landscape." Z. 9/10*	*I, (weitere Folgen) More than 2 million people now fill groaning (stöhnende) refugee camps.*
3	*"… women risk rape and mutilation …" (Verstümmelung) Z. 12*	*F, Men can't make the trip in their stead (an deren Stelle) – they'll simply be killed.*
4	*"… people were missing … at least one meal a week because they did not have fuel to cook with …" Z. 14/15*	*K, Many families were selling some of their food in exchange for wood to cook it with.*
5	*"… a cheap method for disinfecting water … led to a successful business start-up …"Z. 18/19*	*A, The resulting company … now provides affordable clean water for more than 1 million people in the developing world.*
6	*"Darfurians needed a high-powered flame …" Z. 23*	*H, And since most families cook outside, the stove also needed to cope with the region's strong winds.*
7	*"… the stove requires 75 % less fuel …" Z. 28*	*B, That means fewer risky trips outside the camp in search of firewood.*
8	*"They won't be handing the stoves out as charity …"(als milde Gabe) Z. 35*	*G, Giving something away turns the recipient into beggars.*

Task IV: Descriptive writing

Hinweis: Es sind 9 Punkte zu erzielen, 3 für den Inhalt und 6 für Korrektheit und Natürlichkeit des sprachlichen Ausdrucks. Beachten Sie diesen Vorrang der Sprachkompetenz.

1. **Describing a cartoon:**

   Hinweis: Da nicht eindeutig erkennbar ist, ob der Herr der Wirt ist oder jemand, der mit der Dame die Einhaltung des Rauchverbots überprüft, sind beide Interpretationen akzeptabel. Allerdings sollte im ersteren Fall die bittere Ironie des Wirtes, gar Sarkasmus, deutlich werden. Die „Wirt-Version" ist in Klammern gesetzt.

   In this cartoon you can see an empty bar-room with tables and a counter on which there are upturned chairs. Notices indicate "No smoking" and "Out of business". In the centre there is an elderly rather stout gentleman (the landlord). He is lifting his arms – obviously (in distress) delighted– shouting (sarcastically): "Finally a smoke free environment!" He is accompanied by an elderly lady with an air of decision wearing a life-badge on her jacket. Both seem to be officials who are supervising the anti-smoking regulation. (She seems …) The point the cartoonist is making is: What is the use of a regulation for a smoke-free environment if bars and restaurants have to be closed down? *(107/112 words)*

2. **Describing statistics:**

   In the mentioned regions Unites States, Europe and Africa the CO_2 emissions have almost remained the same from 1980 until 2004, with only marginal variations in the US and Europe, but on different levels: the US emits approximately two-and-half more CO_2 than Europe and roughly ten times more than Africa, whereas China has steadily increased its output up to four tonnes in 2004; this is a fifth of that of the US or half of that of Europe. From this we can also conclude that China is in a situation completely different from those of the other three areas mentioned. *(100 words)*

Task V: Argumentative Writing

Hinweis: Für „Composition" und „personal letter" vergleiche die „Useful phrases" im Kapitel „Hinweise und Tipps". Bei Thema 1 sind Gründe anzuführen, weswegen so viele Menschen in Deutschland übergewichtig sind, ferner welche Gegenmaßnahmen ergriffen werden könnten. Auch im Brief muss der Adressat mit schlagkräftigen Argumente überzeugt werden. Hier muss inhaltlich auch auf die Anzeige Bezug genommen werden.

1. **Composition**

   If you don't believe the statistics stating that Germany has become a country with one of the highest numbers of overweight people in Europe, a quick look around the shopping centre or the crowd at football stadiums gives you enough proof. Why do people put on too much weight?

   On the one hand it may be deeply rooted within our genes. Over millions of years one had to eat every edible thing in sight. This strong inherited impulse seems to have remained. Who could therefore withstand the attractiveness of supermarket shelves filled with cheap, mass-produced, savoury food?

   On the other hand, modern technology of the last century has almost totally taken away physical exercise from the everyday lives of most people. They go by car or by public transport; hard physical labour is done by all kinds of machinery, even in the home where hard work is done by numerous household appliances, from a mixer to a vacuum cleaner.

   The consequences of these developments have a terrible effect on the human body as they increase the risk of diseases remarkably. It is urgent that measures should be taken to stop

this trend. Food experts are demanding more precise labels and more detailed information about what actually are the ingredients of food products.
Last but not least urban city planners are increasingly becoming aware that our cities and towns have to be planned in such a way that everything is within walking distance.
Summing up, there is hope that a campaign against obesity could be as successful as those against smoking and binge drinking. *(263 words)*

2. **Letter**

Dear Carole,

Thank you very much for your recent letter. You have not yet made up your mind what you really want to do in the coming months before picking up your studies in October? Can I maybe persuade you to join me on a project that sounds really fascinating?
On the internet I have come across an Australian conservation project. They offer 10 places for between 2 to 6 weeks. There is one project near Perth to protect endangered species like certain parrots and koala bears among others. You won't get money for your work, but the flight is free as well as food and accommodation. The hot climate might be a problem; temperatures of 40 degrees and more are normal. On the other hand you have the chance to make new friends, get to know faraway places and face rewarding challenges. In the reply I received from the organisation they say a pharmacist, a flight technician and a mechanic student from different nations would be on the team. Hey, doesn't this sound attractive? Come along and join this team, we'll have a great time!
Apply on the spot, but make sure you have the right papers, a passport, work permit or visa, if necessary.
Please answer as soon as possible. In the meantime give my kind regards to your parents and to your brother John.

All the best to you, and be quick,

as ever,

Toni *(238 words)*

A Reading Comprehension

Text I: Has Facebook Fatigue Arrived?

Facebook status update: Is it over already? That's the buzz in some quarters of the Web after a recent report showed the number of people logging on to the social networking site in the United Kingdom dropped by 400,000 between December and January.

The decline, a first for the Facebook-crazed British, was pounced on by critics who gleefully warned that Facebook fatigue had finally arrived. Perhaps more ominous, at least by Internet standards, is the recent appearance of a music video on YouTube that blares "I'm getting bored of Facebook," to the tune of Billy Joel's "We didn't start the fire." There's even a Facebook fatigue group on Facebook that encourages people to log off permanently. (Ironically, the group has still managed to attract 36 members to the site.)

But while Facebook's meteoric growth may indeed be slowing, experts say it's far too soon to secure a burial plot beside social networking pioneer Friendster. In the UK, for example, Facebook still boasts about 8.5 million users. That translates into about one out of every six people in the country. Globally, Facebook claims to have a user base of 67 million.

In Canada, meanwhile, Kaan Yigit, an analyst at Solutions Research Group, said his own data shows that Facebook's growth rate has slowed considerably over the past few months – a finding he attributes to the suspicion that most Canadians between 12 and 34 are already on Facebook. "The reluctance to join Facebook is primarily an older phenomenon," Yigit said. "People over the age of 40 are more likely to find Facebook time-consuming and rife with potential work-life conflicts. I don't see any fatigue in the younger, 12 to 34 age group, because with those people, it's really not an option not to have Facebook. Otherwise, you're not in the loop."

Mark Zuckerberg, the 23-year-old chief executive officer of Facebook Inc., came up with the idea for the website while attending Harvard University. Zuckerberg launched the original Facebook from his dorm room in 2004 with an eye to helping students keep track of who was dating whom. As the idea caught on, Facebook membership was gradually expanded to other U.S. colleges and universities and, in 2006, opened to the public at large. Zuckerberg, incidentally, did not bother finishing his university degree, opting instead to move to Palo Alto, Calif., with some friends to focus on developing Facebook into a business. Facebook currently employs about 500 and generates more than $ 100 million (U.S.) in annual sales.

Notwithstanding recent concerns about fatigue, Zuckerberg so far has been successful in keeping the site relevant for users by offering an open platform for software developers and, for the most part, maintaining a focus on protecting users' privacy. While Facebook's user base still trails that of News Corp.'s MySpace, which has about 110 million users globally, Facebook's rapid growth has nevertheless attracted the interest of major players who have even paid millions for the privilege of being part of the Facebook world. That even included Microsoft Corp., which last year paid $ 240 million for a 1.6 per cent stake in the company.

But even if Facebook's growth is already beginning to plateau, Info-Tech's Hickernell says, that doesn't mean people are losing interest in the site. Tens of millions of users are spending a considerable chunk of their waking hours sharing photos, sending messages and playing online games with one another. According to data supplied by U.S. firm comScore Inc., the average U.S. Facebook user spent nearly three hours on the site in December.

Still, some bloggers were quick to note that December's average usage – 169.4 minutes – was slightly less than the average length of time that visitors spent on Facebook in October, which was about 195.6 minutes. That prompted some to conclude that Facebook users were indeed "getting bored" with the site. But a spokesperson for comScore cautioned that, because the total number of new U.S. Facebook users also grew by about 2 million during the same period, one might expect to see a slight drop in the average length of time spent on the site. That's because new users need time to build a network.

With so many eyes on Facebook, Zuckerberg and his investors are betting they can transform the social network into an advertising bonanza in much the same way as Google now rakes in billions through Internet search. So far though, efforts to get big money out of Facebook proved far more difficult than building the site's sizable user base.

Zuckerberg was forced to apologize last year to subscribers for the way Facebook implemented an advertising program called Beacon, which tracks data about Facebook users when they are shopping on certain external sites and shares that information with their Facebook friends as well as advertisers. Such public relations missteps have been chalked up to an inexperienced management team, which could be why Facebook said this week it was hiring a top Google executive, 38-year-old Sheryl Sandberg, to be Facebook's chief operating officer.

Facebook's success in making the jump from hot Internet start-up to major corporate player is by no means guaranteed, but many believe that the social networking concept it helped popularize has already emerged as a key function of the Internet alongside email and instant messaging. "Everything in our research points to this as being long term," said Yigit of Solutions Research Group. "Now Facebook is just a name, as is MySpace. So will there be another social media platform? Sure. But I think the fundamentals of social media – staying connected to friends and family and, in some cases, work life – that's here to stay."

(933 words)

Task I: Multiple choice 9 credits

Mark the most suitable option by crossing the appropriate letter.

1. Find the **wrong** statement about Facebook fatigue.

   A The number of users decreased by 400,000 in Great Britain.

   B YouTube shows a music video celebrating Facebook fatigue.

   C Some people have tried to put off Facebook users.

   D Facebook will follow Friendster and disappear from the market.

2. What is the reason why Facebook is **not** much appreciated amongst the forty pluses? They …

   A fear Facebook might dominate their lives too much.

   B feel they are too old.

   C think the site is difficult to navigate.

   D are tired of social networking.

3. Which group does the "you" in l. 22 refer to?
   A Users in Canada
   B Newcomers to Facebook
   C People between 12 and 34
   D The reader of the article

4. Mark Zuckerberg …
   A founded Facebook while working as chief executive officer at Harvard.
   B turned Facebook into a business and then finished university.
   C hired some friends to help him move to California.
   D began developing Facebook in his room at university.

5. Economic data show that …
   A Facebook now is the largest social networking website.
   B other companies trusted in Facebook enough to buy their shares.
   C Facebook is in desperate need of money from investors.
   D there is not enough work for programmers in the company.

6. Which of the following statements about Facebook usage is **wrong**?
   A Some of the users are fed up with Facebook.
   B The number of users is decreasing worldwide.
   C Facebook usage is gradually levelling off.
   D More new users could mean less average using time.

7. According to M. Zuckerberg …
   A Facebook should be changed into a search engine like Google.
   B it was very difficult to attract a large number of users.
   C it will be difficult to sell Facebook.
   D Facebook can be made attractive to sponsors.

8. Why is Facebook in trouble?
   The company …
   A lost vital customer information.
   B cooperated closely with Google.
   C allowed aggressive advertising.
   D used software which violated the privacy of its customers.

9. Which statement describes the current and future situation of Facebook?
   Facebook …
   A has already become more important than electronic mail.
   B is not just a short-lived trend but meets the needs of our age.
   C is currently considering taking over MySpace in the long run.
   D is as successful as the other big companies on the market.

Text II: The Importance of Educating Girls

Who wants more poor children around the world to go to school? Raise your hand. Yep, everyone's hand is up. Education is the ultimate mom-and-apple-pie (or rice-and-beans) issue. Everyone's for it. But our best efforts to get more impoverished kids into schools aren't always effective. 73 million children worldwide don't go to primary school. Three times as many never go to secondary school. These kids are mostly doomed to a life of poverty, and so are their families.

The way out is not just to champion education generally but to focus intently on one subset of the problem: girls, who make up nearly 60 percent of the kids out of school. In parts of sub-Saharan Africa, only one in five girls gets any education at all. The waste of human capital is incalculable. Here's where to zero in on the challenge.

"The reason so many experts believe educating girls is the most important investment in the world is how much they give back to their families," says Gene Sperling, a former top economic adviser to President Bill Clinton (and currently advising Barack Obama). Sperling's book, "What Works in Girls' Education" (with Barbara Herz), is simultaneously disturbing and encouraging. It's disheartening to think of how far we have to go to get all kids into school – one of the United Nations Millennium Development Goals launched in 2000 to accelerate progress on fighting poverty, disease and other social ills. But it's also hopeful: at least we can focus on a specific solution.

When girls go to school, they marry later and have fewer, healthier children. For instance, if an African mother has five years of education, her child has a 40 percent better chance of living to age 5. A World Health Organization study in Burkina Faso showed that mothers with some education were 40 percent less likely to subject their children to the practice of genital mutilation. When girls get educated, they are three times less likely to contract HIV/AIDS.

Unfortunately, many African parents still don't know that their own lives can be greatly improved if their daughters go to school. They're often uncomfortable when their girls have to travel long distances to school (making them more subject to sexual predators). Girls themselves grow uncomfortable in school when they have no separate latrines. They fear being spied on by boys; their parents agree and withdraw them. This is the kind of everyday impediment to progress that aid organizers notice on the ground but rarely becomes part of the debate.

The biggest barrier to primary and secondary education in the developing world remains the fees that too many countries continue to charge parents for each child in school. Due to the poverty especially in rural areas, where school attendance is lowest, many families decide only to send their two oldest, healthiest boys to school with the hope that they will support their parents in their old age. This often deprives girls of the chance to go to school although they are the ones actually much more likely to help their families. Women in the developing world who have had some education share more of their earnings.

Countries like Kenya and Uganda, which have abolished fees, have seen a flood of new students, with enrolments surging by 30 percent or more. So why haven't other developing nations followed their example? It's not just the loss of fee revenue but the absence of a large enough education infrastructure to sustain the influx of new students. Five years after abolishing fees, Kenya still needs 40,000 new teachers. Officials there say they can't meet the need without more consistent funding.

Donor nations and non-governmental organisations are increasingly reaching a consensus that global education, especially for girls, is the keystone to the arch of development. The Millennium Development Goals of universal primary education with gender equity are among the hottest topics at international conferences. But Sperling calls these "the world's most ambitious and pathetic goals – ambitious because so many countries are not on track to reach them; pathetic because of the idea that five or six years of primary education will suffice when there's no real demonstrable advantage without eight."

The challenge extends beyond funding to changing the culture of the developing world. Fathers must be convinced that if their daughters go to school, they will learn enough maths to help them in the market. Mothers must learn that, while sending their daughters to school might mean one fewer pair of hands to help around the house, their families will be better off in the long run. "This is not a disease without a known cure," says Sperling. "These things work everywhere." If these become the mom-and-apple-pie values of the developing world, we'll all win. *(785 words)*

By Jonathan Alter, adapted from Newsweek, September 20, 2008.

Task II: Mixed reading tasks 11 credits

1. **Gapped summary** (7)

   Fill in the gaps with words taken from paragraphs in **line 11–38** of the text (one word per line). Note: In the summary the words do not appear in the same order as in the text.

   Children with little or no education have hardly any chance to escape ________ ________. That is why it is one of the Millennium Development Goals of the UN to enable children worldwide to attend school.

   According to experts, we should ________ on girls to address the problem. ________ in schooling for girls pays back in several ways: For one thing, girls are more likely to ________ the money they make later with their families. In addition, educated mothers more often do not accept the ________ ________ of their daughters. What is more, their children are generally ________ than others.

   But, unfortunately, things are not that simple. A lot of parents simply cannot afford to pay the school fees for all their children. Moreover, some parents ________ their daughters from school when they reach a certain age because they fear that the boys might approach them in indecent ways.

2. **Short answer questions (l. 39–58)** (4)

   Answer the following questions briefly. You may use words from the text.

   2.1 Kenya's decision to abolish school fees … (2)

   - has had an immediate consequence:

     ____

   - involves the following problems:

     – ________________________________
     – ________________________________
     – ________________________________

   2.2 How many years should all children go to school according to an expert? (1)

   ____

2.3 Which **phrase** in the last paragraph tells us that it will **take quite some time** before the advantages of educating girls become apparent? (1)

____

Text III: Growing Up Green

No way around it: your child is an environmental disaster. How eco-parenting can ease the impact

Want to wreck the environment? Have a baby. Each bundle of joy gobbles up more of the planet's food, clogs garbage dumps with diapers, churns through plastic toys and winds up a gas-guzzling, resource-consuming grown-up like the rest of us. Still, babies are awfully cute. Given that most people still intend to have them, what's an environmentally conscious parent to do?

Today's green-minded families go far beyond eco-consumerism – the buying of organic baby goodies like mohair-filled mattresses and fair-trade toys. Call it eco-parenting: it's not just buying greener but fundamentally altering the often wasteful art of child-rearing. "For us, environmental awareness and activism isn't just a question of health," says Jonathan Spalter, a 45-year-old father in eco-haven Berkeley, California. "It's a moral and ethical issue that we hope to teach our three little girls." Their kids are already on board, with one daughter telling Spalter's wife Carissa Goux, 41, "Mommy, you shouldn't waste so much."

True eco-parenting extends beyond the kitchen compost. "Parents are not just changing their behavior at home," says Deirdre Imus, author of the just published *Growing Up Green!* "They're realizing they need to get involved in greening their communities." Take actress Laura Dern, mother of two. First she hired Green Life Guru, a Los Angeles-based environmental-services company, to evaluate the eco-fitness of her house. "After they advised me on water filtration and solar paneling," Dern says, "I realized, wait a minute – I'm sending my children off to a school, which can be a toxic environment." Now she and other parents are working with the company to eliminate chemical-ridden carpeting and pesticides at their children's school and introduce composting and recycling programs there.

It turns out that the act of having kids triggers many to go green. An April 2008 Roper poll found that people identified having a child as their primary motivation for protecting the environment; 91 % said the most important reason to recycle is the impact it will have on their children's future. In fact, new parents are the leading edge of environmental awareness, says Alan Greene, a pediatrician at Packard Children's Hospital at Stanford and author of *Raising Baby Green*. "I've seen a dramatic increase in parents taking environmental responsibility for their children in the past 15 years."

Naturally, a host of new books and services have sprouted to guide the eco-parent. *Healthy Child Healthy World,* by Christopher Gavigan, offers advice on everything from having an organic pregnancy to reducing a child's carbon footprint, while Imus' book counsels parents on detoxing their sippy-cup supply and lobbying for greener legislation. A number of services focus on recycling. *Zwaggle.com* is a nationwide marketplace for used toys, children's clothing and gear. *Kidsconsignmentsales.com* lists 1,100 selling-off events across the country.

Admittedly, this emphasis on raising kids green can make some parents' heads spin. Heather Timmons, 32, a full-time mother and homeschooler of four children in Brownsville, Oregon, sticks to the doable. She tackles a different environmental challenge each month, whether it's (almost) eliminating paper towels or making her own household cleaners with vinegar and baking soda. "I believe it's important to do your part and be responsible," says Timmons, who does so by consolidating car trips, buying toys second-hand and substituting china plates for paper ones at her kids' birthday parties. "But at the same time, I don't want to be freaking out about it."

Parents have enough to freak out about already. *(565 words)*

By Pamela Paul, adapted from TIME May 8, 2008.

Task III: Mixed Reading Tasks 10 credits

1. **Multiple-matching** (7)

The following people are quoted in the text:

A Jonathan Spalter

B Deirdre Imus

C Laura Dern

D Alan Greene

E Heather Timmons

Which of the following statements describes which person? Write the appropriate letters in the boxes provided. Note that **two** persons are described **more than once**!

letter	description
	has been seeking professional help from experts.
	believes that more and more parents see problems affecting the environment more clearly than others do.
	is trying to become an eco-parent step by step.
	lives in a place full of like-minded people.
	has noticed how far-reaching the environmental consciousness of some parents is.
	can be happy about the reaction of a family member.
	is worried about his/her kids being exposed to poisonous substances.

2. **Mediation** (3)

Beantworten Sie folgende Fragen zum Textteil Z. 1–23 auf Deutsch.

Inwiefern geht „eco-parenting" über das Kaufen von grünen Produkten hinaus?

„Eco-parenting" bedeutet, …

- ______________________________
- ______________________________
- ______________________________

B Writing

Task IV: Descriptive Writing

9 credits

Choose <u>one</u> of the following two tasks (1 <u>or</u> 2) and write between 80–100 words.

1. **Describing a picture:**
   Describe the situation in the picture. Why do you think the picture has won a prize in the 2007 World Press Photo Contest?

   Tourists and refugee on a Spanish beach (Tenerife)

AP/Arturo Rodriguez

2. **Describing statistics:**
   Describe the chart and try to explain the phenomenon shown.

Most Important National Issue for the 18–24-year-olds in the US

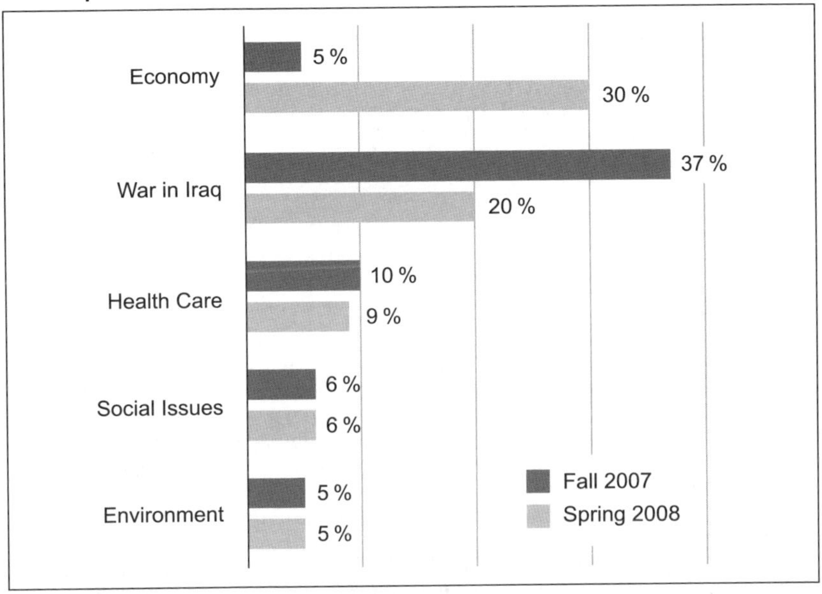

Source: Harvard University, April 2008
http://www.iop.harvard.edu/Research-Publications/Polling/Spring-2008-Survey/Executive-summary

Task V: Argumentative Writing 21 credits

Choose one of the following topics (1 or 2) and write at least 200 words.

1. **Composition 1**
   Excessive drinking has turned into a common weekend pastime of many young people. What reasons do you see for this and what can be done to tackle the problem?

2. **Composition 2**
   According to some education experts it should be common practice in schools for students to evaluate their teachers. What is your opinion on this?

Lösungsvorschläge

A Reading Comprehension

Hinweis: Es sollte bekannt sein, dass „Facebook“ eine Website zur Bildung sozialer Netzwerke ist. Nutzer legen sich ein persönliches Profil an und vernetzen sich mit anderen Menschen, mit Freunden, Arbeitskollegen, Kommilitonen, Schulfreunden, etc.
Worterklärung: „fatigue“ – ein Gefühl extremer physischer oder geistiger Ermüdung, hier: Überdruss (mit dem Medium umzugehen)
Die Aufgaben folgen dem Textverlauf. Achten Sie auf Schlüsselwörter oder -begriffe, die zum Kontext führen.

Task I: Multiple choice questions

Reading Text I: Has Facebook Fatigue Arrived?

1 D, 2 A, 3 C, 4 D, 5 B, 6 B, 7 D, 8 D, 9 B

Hinweis:

zu 1: Hier soll die falsche Aussage markiert werden, also müssen die anderen drei richtig sein und dazu Schlüsselstellen im Text gefunden werden.
A: “the social network site in the UK dropped by 400,000” (Z. 2/3).
B: „video on YouTube that blares: ‘I’m getting bored of Facebook’“ (Z. 6/7)
C: “There’s even a Facebook fatigue group … that encourages people to log off permanently.” (Z. 7–9)
Die Textstelle “it’s far too soon to secure a burial plot (= Begräbnisplatz) beside … pioneer Friendster” zeigt, dass Aussage D nicht zutrifft.

zu 2: Schlüsselwort „forty pluses“ (über 40-Jährige), “People over the age of 40 are more likely to find Facebook time-consuming and rife with potential work-life conflicts. (Z. 19/20)

zu 3: Die Wendung „otherwise“ (Z. 22 sonst, andernfalls) signalisiert, dass sich „You“ auf den Inhalt des vorhergehenden Satzes bezieht: Lösung ist also C.

zu 4: Schlüsselstelle: „… came up with the idea, for the website while attending Harvard University. Zuckerberg launched the original Facebook from his dorm room“ (Z. 23–25) (dormitory = Zimmer im Studentenwohnheim)

zu 5: Schlüsselstelle: “Facebook’s rapid growth has nevertheless attracted the interest of major players who have even paid millions for the privilege of being part of the Facebook world. That even included Microsoft Corp., which last year paid $ 240 million for a 1.6 per cent stake in the company” (Z. 36–39).

zu 6: Alle Aussagen bis auf B lassen sich am Text belegen.
A: “Facebook users were indeed ‘getting bored’ with the site”(Z. 48/49)
C: “the total number of new US Facebook users also grew by about 2 million”(Z. 50)
D: “one might expect to see a slight drop in the average length of time spent on the site. That’s because new users need time to build a network.” (Z. 51/ 52)

zu 7: Schlüsselstelle “they can transform the social network into an advertising bonanza!” (Z. 53/54) Worterklärung: bonanza – hier: ein plötzlicher großer Anstieg/Zuwachs auf einem Gebiet

zu 8: Die Tatsache, dass Facebook Probleme hatte kommt in Z. 57 zum Ausdruck: “Zuckerberg was forced to apologize.” Der Beleg für Antwort D ist “Facebook implemented an advertising program called Beacon, which tracks data about Facebook users when they are shopping on certain external sites and shares that information with their Facebook friends as well as advertisers” (Z. 57–60).

zu 9: Schlüsselstellen „has already emerged as a key function of the Internet“ (Z. 66), “Everything … points to this as being long term.” (Z. 67)

Task II: Mixed reading tasks

The Importance of Educating Girls

1. **Gapped Summary**

Hinweis: Markieren Sie die für den summary relevante Textstelle, Zeile 11 bis 38 deutlich. Beachten Sie, dass Sie pro Zeile nur ein Wort einsetzen dürfen, und dass die einzusetzenden Ausdrücke nicht dem Textverlauf folgen. Die Erfassung des Sinnzusammenhangs ist hier also besonders wichtig.

- *„poverty / disease / social ills": Das Schlüsselwort „Millenium Development Goals of the UN" aus dem ersten Absatz des gapped summary findet sich im Text in Z. 16 und beschreibt in den folgenden zwei Zeilen deren Aufgabe: „fighting poverty, disease and other social ills." Im gapped summary verweist „That's why ..." auf die möglichen Lösungswörter.*
- *„focus": Im zweiten Absatz des gapped summary fällt auf, dass nach dem Wort „children" im ersten Absatz, nur Mädchen bzw. Frauen genannt werden. Wie schon in der Überschrift aufgezeigt, findet eine Fokussierung des Themas auf Mädchen und Frauen statt: Im Text „focus on" (Z. 18).*
- *„investment": Schlüsselstelle im Text ist "The reason (why) so many experts believe (that) educating girls is the most important investment in the world is how much they give back to their families"(Z. 11/12).*
- *„share": Text: "Women ... who have had some education share more of their earnings." (Z. 37/38)*
- *„genital mutilation": bezieht sich auf die Textstelle: "... mothers with some education were ... less likely to subject their children to ... genital mutilation." (Z. 21–23)*
- *„healthier": Die relevante Textstelle ist: "When girls go to school, they ... have ... healthier children."(Z. 9)*
- *„withdraw": Die Lösung bezieht sich auf: "They (the girls) fear being spied on by boys; their parents ... withdraw them." (Z. 28/29)*

Children with little or no education have hardly any chance to escape **poverty / disease / social ills**. That is why it is one of the Millennium Development Goals of the UN to enable children worldwide to attend school.

According to experts, we should **focus** on girls to address the problem. **Investment** in schooling for girls pays back in several ways: For one thing, girls are more likely to **share** the money they make later with their families. In addition, educated mothers more often do not accept the **genital mutilation** of their daughters. What is more, their children are generally **healthier** than others. But, unfortunately, things are not that simple. A lot of parents simply cannot afford to pay the school fees for all their children. Moreover, some parents **withdraw** their daughters from school when they reach a certain age because they fear that the boys might approach them in indecent ways.

2. **Short answer questions**

Hinweis: Beachten Sie hier die Beschränkung auf die Zeilen 39–58 des Textes.

2.1 Kenya's decision to abolish school fees ...
- has had an immediate a consequence:
  - **a flood of students/surging enrolments** (Z. 39/40)
- involves the following problems:
  - **loss of fee revenue** (Z. 41) (= Verlust des Gebührenaufkommens)
  - **education infrastructure not large enough** (Z. 42) **/ not enough teachers** (Z. 43)
  - **no consistent fundings** (Z. 44)

2.2 How many years should all children go to school according to an expert?
eight (Z. 51)

Hinweis: Lesen Sie die Zeilen 48 bis 51 ganz genau, insbesondere den Satzteil „... pathetic because of the idea that five or six years of primary education will suffice when there's no real demonstrable advantage without eight.", auf Deutsch in etwa: „... aussichtslos wegen der Vorstellung, dass fünf oder sechs Jahre Grundschule genügen könnten, wenn es in der Tat keine sichtbaren Vorteile ohne eine (wenigstens) achtjährige Schulzeit gibt."

2.3 Which **phrase** in the last paragraph tells us that it will **take quite some time** before the advantages of educating become apparent?
(... their families will be better off) **in the long run** (Z. 55/56)

Task III: Mixed reading tasks

Growing up Green

1. **Multiple-matching**

Hinweis: Überlesen Sie die Anmerkung nicht, dass zwei Personen mehr als einmal erscheinen. Markieren Sie die Namen der fünf genannten Personen im Text. Dann vergleichen Sie den Kontext mit den vorgelegten „statements". Folgende Textstellen sind für die Zuordnung relevant. Jonathan Spalter und Laura Dern können je zwei Aussagen zugeordnet werden.

- *Jonathan Spalter: "... a 45-year-old father in eco-haven Berkeley, California." (Z. 10) und "Their kids are already on board, with one daughter telling Spalter's wife ... 'Mommy, you shouldn't waste so much.'"(Z. 11–13)*
- *Deidre Imus: "Parents are not just changing their behaviour at home, ... They're realizing they need to get involved in greening their communities."(Z. 14 –16)*
- *Laura Dern: "she hired Green Life Guru, a Los Angeles-based environmental-services company" (Z. 17/18) und "I'm sending my children off to a school, which can be a toxic environment." (Z. 20)*
- *Alan Greene: "I've seen a dramatic increase in parents taking environmental responsibility for their children ..." (Z. 29/30)*
- *Heather Timmons: "She tackles a different environmental challenge each month" (Z. 40/41)*

letter	description
C	has been seeking professional help from experts.
D	believes that more and more parents see problems affecting the environment more clearly than others do.
E	is trying to become an eco-parent step by step.
A	lives in a place full of like-minded people.
B	has noticed how far-reaching the environmental consciousness of some parents is.
A	can be happy about the reaction of a family member.
C	is worried about his/her kids being exposed to poisonous substances.

2. **Mediation**

Hinweis: Die Frage bezieht sich nur auf die Zeilen 1 bis 23, am besten markieren Sie sich diese Textstelle. Antworten Sie auf Deutsch, geben Sie aber keine wörtliche Übersetzung.

„Eco parenting bedeutet, …
- **Kinder so großzuziehen, dass die Umwelt geschont wird.** (Z. 8)
- **Kinder zum Umweltbewusstsein zu erziehen.** (Z. 10–13)
- **eine lebenswerte Umwelt zu schaffen.** (Z. 20–23)

B Writing

Task IV: Descriptive Writing

Hinweis: Es sind 9 Punkte zu erzielen, 3 für den Inhalt und 6 für Korrektheit und Natürlichkeit des sprachlichen Ausdrucks. Beachten Sie diesen Vorrang der Sprachkompetenz. Schreiben Sie ferner nicht weniger als ca. 80, aber auch nicht mehr als ca. 120 Wörter, damit Sie die volle Punktzahl erhalten können.

1. **Describing a picture:**

Hinweis: Es ist naheliegend, die Frage einleitend zu beantworten, womit zugleich eine wesentliche Aussage des Bildes dargelegt wird.

The photo has won the prize as it shows the clash between the rich Western world and the poverty of most African countries.
In the foreground, you see two white women in bikinis, well-nourished, kneeling before a coloured boy. He is sitting in front of them, covered over the head with a blanket, wearing shorts. All three of them are looking towards the photographer. The women show expressions of despair and commiseration whereas the boy's face is haggard, rather emaciated, obviously showing despair as he has barely survived.
In the background, several tourists are standing about with different expressions – some showing shock others no concern at all. The latter seem to feel disturbed while enjoying their holiday on Tenerife. *(119 words)*

2. **Describing statistics:**

Hinweis: Beachten Sie, dass es Daten mit relativ deutlichen Veränderungen gibt und solche, die annähernd gleich geblieben sind. Hier kann man zusammenfassen. Ein gewisses Hintergrundwissen über die wirtschaftliche Entwicklung der USA wird vorausgesetzt.

The chart shows the developments in five different areas during the period from autumn 2007 to spring 2008, in which the economy of the US suffered from a dramatic decline. The attention of the age group in question has multiplied six times regarding economy whereas it has gone back by 17 percent concerning the war in Iraq. This is due to the fact that the young are more concerned with keeping their workplaces.
For the three other fields (health-care, social problems, environment) the interest remained (nearly) the same. This lack of interest is remarkable as these are vital topics for this age group. Especially environmental concerns are menacing the world globally. *(111 words)*

Task V: Argumentative Writing

Hinweis: *Für „Composition" vergleiche die „Useful phrases" im Kapitel „Hinweise und Tipps".*
Führen Sie bei Composition 1 wenigstens zwei Gründe für die Entwicklung an und schlagen Sie mehrere Gegenmaßnahmen vor, die ergriffen werden könnten.
Bei Composition 2 können Sie entweder dafür oder dagegen Stellung beziehen. Auch eine dialektische Ausführung mit Pro und Kontra ist natürlich möglich (aber schwieriger), wobei dann Ihre eigentliche Meinung am Schluss erscheint. In der folgenden Musterlösung wurde dieser Weg gewählt.

1. **Composition**
Excessive drinking has turned into a common weekend pastime of many young people. What reasons do you see for this and what can be done to tackle the problem?

Only recently have I read in the newspaper about a 17-year-old teenager who had gone unconscious because of excessive drinking of so-called alcopops. And this is happening more and more often among young people. What might be the reasons for this irrational and health risky behaviour?
Especially young males think it is a proof of their masculinity and strength to be able to gulp down as much alcohol as possible. Sometimes this even develops into a real competition of drinking their mates under the table. Is this a consequence of the generally accepted social drinking? At any kind of celebration alcoholic drinks seem to be inevitable. The question therefore is: Does social drinking of grown-ups set an example for the young ones? I think it does.
Another equally important point is that most of the alcoholic drinks are cheaper than soft drinks, mineral water or the different kinds of juices. This must be changed by compelling the breweries, the pubs and restaurants to take this into consideration.
Most important would be to reduce the influence of advertising for alcoholic drinks. Isn't a large poster at each street corner showing young, lively people sitting together in a beautiful beer garden toasting to one another with a foaming pint of beer conveying a deceiving idyllic world?
Summing up, only in a society who feels responsible for the younger generation and where adults show the young how to enjoy oneself without drugs like alcohol, young people can be protected from binge drinking and its dramatic consequences. *(253 words)*

2. **Composition**
According to some education experts it should be common practice in schools for students to evaluate their teachers. What is your opinion on this?

Only "some" education experts suggest this kind of evaluating, which reflects a much disputed topic. This question depends on who you ask.
The great majority of students are in favour of this possibility as this enables them to exercise some power over their teachers, at least if the evaluation is made public. Quite a lot of students who have problems in this or that subject might tend to blame their teachers for insufficient results or marks. They take this as an excuse for disinterest, laziness or lack of ability. Although, this should be admitted, the more thoughtful student will come to more reliable judgments of their teachers.
On the other hand, if you interview the teachers on this issue they will be more sceptical. They know teaching and educating young people quite often means telling and making them understand that learning and acquiring knowledge needs discipline, dedication and often some considerable effort. Showing students that they are failing or not coming up to the required standards may cause anger about, or even animosity towards, the teacher. If

students are allowed to publish an evaluation of their teachers, for example online, feelings of revenge might make them try and ruin their teachers' reputation quite openly.
Coming to a conclusion, I would be against evaluating teachers as the students are not at eye-level, concerning age, experience, knowledge and professionalism. However, some kind of questionnaire now and then as a source of information for the teachers can be a helpful feedback for their work. *(251 words)*

A Reading Comprehension

Text I: Mothering as a Spectator Sport

Happy Mother's Day!

(A) Oh, I know the burnt toast and dandelion bouquet won't come until May 10. But lately, every day is Mother's Day, thanks to our relentless focus on moms (and to a lesser extent dads) and the way they parent.

(B) Parenting has become a spectator sport. We set the bar extremely high for what is "good" parenting and start judging the moment we hear someone did something that could be considered one drop dangerous.

(C) I should know. I'm the mom who let her 9-year-old ride the New York City subway by himself. Just about a year ago I made national news when my husband and I decided to take our son someplace he hadn't been before and let him try to find his way home by himself on public transport. (By day, not very far from home, with money and a map and quarters for a phone call.) The very thing he'd been begging us to let him do for months. He made it home fine, but millions of folks weighed in, often critically, on my parenting.

(D) Now I feel a little like Miss America, passing my "Bad Mom" crown and scepter to Madlyn Primoff, the Scarsdale, N.Y., lawyer who was arrested for endangering the welfare of a child a few weeks back after she left her two daughters, ages 10 and 12, in a shopping area of a New York City suburb because they were bickering in the car. (Both the girls got home safely, though one did wind up waiting for her parents at the local police station.) Primoff can have the crown, but I'm keeping the scepter for self-defense. All moms could use one. It was only when complete strangers started saying I was crazy cable-TV-fodder that I began to understand that a lot of us Americans are raising our kids in an utter state of panic. We are convinced that every day, in every way, our children are in terrible peril. We are obsessed with other parents' child-rearing decisions – and our own – because we're being told each one is of life and death importance.

(E) And it's not just about stranger danger. It begins even before birth, with the pregnancy diet books telling us "each bite" is going to determine if our kids are golden – or duds. Same goes for every other parenting decision we make: are you having natural childbirth? If not, you're traumatizing the baby! Are you breastfeeding? If not, your kid's going to be a dummy! With allergies! And extra-chunky thighs! Are you feeding your kid non-organic baby food? Did you wait too long to sign her up for music lessons? Shouldn't you get that toy that teaches multiplication? But the biggest decision of all, of course, is: can I ever leave my kids to their own devices? To climb a tree or walk to school? And lately the answer is: no. Not until their hair goes gray and they start liking bran flakes. The prevailing belief is that even one unscheduled, unsupervised childhood episode is dangerous to the point of being criminal. That kids could never possibly buck up and ask someone for help, or figure out how to use a public phone, or ask directions to the police station.

(F) But that Scarsdale lawyer's kids were not preschoolers. At age 10 or 12 in other eras, those kids would have been apprenticed already. Or working as servants in someone else's house, or picking coffee beans. Actually, in other countries, some children that age are still picking coffee beans. Why do we assume that today's American kids are the dumbest, most vulnerable, least competent generation ever – and that we are doing them a favor by treating them almost as if they are disabled? Because that's what our culture tells us to do. It tells us that kids need extra classes, extra padding and extra supervision just to make it through another day. It tells us we should always plan for the worst-case scenario.

(G) Yet, our national crime rate is back to what it was in 1970. Yes, if you grew up in the '70s or '80s, times are safer now than when you were a kid. We Americans have a very hard time believing that good news because good news is not what we are soaking in. Mostly we are soaking in 24-hour cable, bringing us the worst stories – especially child abductions – from all corners of the globe. When we pick up any parenting magazine, we find article after article, "Is your child's crib safe?" or "Is your child's food safe?" So it's in the same biz as TV News: It simply has to scare us.

(H) In short: we are being brainwashed with fear and it makes us worry that everything we do as parents may be putting our kids in danger. That's why we judge other parents so harshly, and why we keep our kids cloistered like Rapunzel. Don't get me wrong. I believe in giving kids more freedom and responsibility – not crazy freedom. Just the kind of freedom we had, back when parenting decisions were not the stuff of national news.

(848 words – abridged)

By Lennore Skenazy, adapted from Newsweek, May 7, 2009.

Task I: Multiple choice 8 credits

Mark the most suitable option by crossing the appropriate letter.

1. The author let her 9-year-old son find his way home by himself …
   - A but took the necessary precautions.
   - B because he was used to going by public transport.
   - C although he had never wanted to do it.
   - D only after equipping him with a working cellphone.

2. A New York lawyer is currently getting a lot of media attention because …
   - A attorneys can normally be expected to follow the laws precisely.
   - B she was accused of not taking proper care of her daughters.
   - C she is one of the candidates for a cable TV show.
   - D one of her daughters was arrested by the local police.

3. Which potential danger for youngsters is **not** mentioned in paragraph E?
   - A Risk of panic attacks
   - B A bad diet
   - C Lack of stimuli
   - D Child obesity

4. The phrase "one […] unsupervised childhood episode is dangerous to the point of being criminal" (ll. 33 /34) means that …
   - A youngsters are incapable of finding solutions to serious problems.
   - B the main danger for small children are strangers.
   - C there are too many offenders in many neighbourhoods.
   - D letting children go off on their own is extremely irresponsible behaviour.

5. What is the main message the author wants to convey in paragraph F?
   A most countries don't actively prevent child labour.
   B child labour should be forbidden.
   C children should shoulder responsibility at an earlier age.
   D American kids are particularly vulnerable and need extra assistance.

6. The main reason why American parents are so scared is …
   A recently released statistics about crime rates in the US.
   B warnings in magazines designed for parents.
   C reports about child kidnappings on TV news
   D a media mix that makes people believe the world is a dangerous place.

7. Which statement summarizes the author's view on child-rearing best?
   A "Reality shows should be banned from the TV screen."
   B "Children have to be given the chance to do whatever they want to."
   C "Overprotecting youngsters impedes their development."
   D "Growing up in the '70s was a lot more dangerous."

8. The meaning behind the headline "Mothering as a spectator sport" is:
   A We are extremely insecure when it comes to deciding what is good parenting.
   B We easily judge parents because of our personal standards.
   C The media are replacing real parenting.
   D We just watch what other parents do and then decide what is best for our children.

Text II: Unhappy Hour

(A) Who would buy Sir Liam Donaldson a pint these days? Not many Brits, I expect. The chief medical officer's proposal to tackle the British scourge of binge drinking – a minimum price of 75 cents per unit of alcohol – was shot down by almost everyone from 10 Downing Street to the bloke propping up the bar at the Slug and Lettuce.

(B) Yet nearly 10,000 km away, in a Southeast Asian country with roughly the same population (60 million), Sir Liam might have some sympathizers. Thailand has one of the world's highest rates of alcohol consumption, and all the burgeoning social ills that accompany it: domestic violence, sexual assault, street fights, teenage binge drinking and diseases caused by alcohol.

(C) Like Britain, Thailand has embarked upon a rocky legislative road, hoping that new laws will fix an old problem. While Brits debated minimum pricing, Thais were arguing the merits of prohibiting alcohol sales during *Songkran*, or Thai New Year, which runs April 13–15 and is the country's most important annual holiday. This is a bit like Sir Liam banning booze at Christmas. Better known among tourists as the Water Festival, *Songkran* is famous for mass water-pistol fights and – with millions of Thais visiting their families – insanely congested highways. During last year's festival, 360 people died in road accidents and 4,794 were injured. The main cause? Alcohol. Some 80 % of road accidents during long holiday periods are due to drunk driving, a senior Thai health official said recently.

(D) Thailand is a largely Buddhist country, and one of the Five Precepts of Buddhism forbids intoxication. Yet excessive drinking is deeply rooted in the culture. "Thais are fun-loving people," said a recent editorial in the newspaper Thai Rath. "We all know that a party is not complete without drinks." This perhaps explains the ban's lukewarm reception from British-educated Prime Minister Abhisit Vejjajiva's government. The Tourism Minister claimed it would drive away foreign visitors and further damage a vital industry already reeling from global recession and the shutdown of Bangkok's two airports by antigovernment protesters last year.

(E) In Britain, PM Gordon Brown rejected minimum pricing as unfair to the "responsible, sensible majority of moderate drinkers." He also knows that, in the midst of a recession and with his poor ratings, making booze more expensive is political suicide. Brown's Thai counterpart Abhisit enjoys greater popularity among his people, but still cannot afford to anger them – not when his country's unemployment rate has (like Britain's) spiked sharply. But Abhisit needn't have worried. With *Songkran* fast approaching, the ban was scrapped – not because it was unfair to the responsible majority of Thai drinkers but because, like minimum pricing, there was no guarantee it would make any difference. Thais would either stockpile booze or buy it under the counter.

(F) Thailand has an increasingly vocal anti-alcohol movement. Last November Thai Beverage PLC, the country's largest producer of alcoholic drinks, indefinitely postponed its stock listing after Buddhist monks led a blockade of the Stock Exchange of the Thailand building in Bangkok. Thais in favor of prohibition also cheered the passing of an alcohol-control act that took effect in February last year. It raised the legal drinking age from 18 to 20, banned alcohol-related advertising, and – at a time when Britain was liberalizing its licensing laws to allow for round-the-clock drinking – restricted the sale of alcohol to only two periods: 11 a.m. to 2 p.m. and 5 p.m. to midnight. But Thailand's alcohol-control act has changed little. Take *Songkran* deaths: in 2007, 361 people died on the roads during the festival; in 2008, with the act in force, 360 died – only one life saved. More people are killed by drunk driving in Thailand in two weeks than in Britain in an entire year.

(G) Thailand could learn at least two lessons from Britain's battle with the bottle. First, forget about quick-fix bans and start enforcing the laws you already have. Second, think before you legislate. If Britain has any message for Thailand, it is this: to create a nation of responsible drinkers, there's no magic elixir. *(673 words – abridged)*

By Andrew Marshall, from TIME, April 20, 2009.

Task II: Mixed reading tasks 14 credits

1. **Gapped summary** (6)

Fill in the gaps with words taken from paragraphs A, B and C of the text "Unhappy Hour" (one word per line).
Note: Do <u>not</u> use words from the gapped text.

The battle with the bottle

Thailand and Great Britain may be thousands of miles apart, but they have at least two things in common. First, in terms of size they have a similar ________ ____________ and second, both countries have to ____________ the pressing problem of binge drinking with all the social ills that go with it. While Britain's politicians were confronted with the ____________ of minimum pricing, Thais recently discussed the pros of an alcohol ban during the important and famous Thai holiday *Songkran*, the ____________ Water Festival. In Britain the suggestion was immediately ____________

______________________ by proles, press and politicians alike. In Thailand, however, there were some sympathizers, but eventually the plan was abandoned. It was just not obvious whether a ban would have any of the previously discussed ______________________.

2. **Mediation** (8)
Beantworten Sie die nachfolgenden Fragen auf Deutsch.

2.1 Welchen Widerspruch in der thailändischen Gesellschaft deckt der Autor in Absatz D auf? (2)

Einerseits ____,

andererseits ____.

2.2 Mit welchen Strategien würden die Thais vermutlich versuchen, ein Alkoholverbot während des *Songkran* zu umgehen? (2)

a) ____

b) ____

2.3 Welche Konsequenzen zog der größte Hersteller von alkoholischen Getränken in Thailand aus den Protesten der Abstinenz-Bewegung? (1)

____

____

2.4 Welche Lektionen könnte Thailand aus den britischen Erfahrungen im Kampf gegen Alkohol lernen? (3)

a) – ____ (1)

– ____ (1)

b) ____

____ (1)

c) Für die Lösung des Problems gibt es kein Patentrezept.

Text III: A 10-Year-Old Divorcée Takes Paris

In a dimly lit comer of a Paris bar a delighted young divorcée describes in a soft voice how she spent the day throwing snowballs for the first time in her life. That is not remarkable. This is: Nujood Ali is just 10 years old – and was, until recently, the youngest known divorced person in the world.

Slender with thick hair and a shy smile, Ali made headlines in Yemen last April when she walked out on a man more than three times her age, to whom her father had married her off. It was an act driven by terror and despair.

Gap A – Sentence … She first set eyes on the groom when she took her marriage vows. After spending her wedding night with her parents and 15 brothers and sisters, Nujood was taken by her new husband to his family village, where, she says, he beat and raped her every night. **Gap B – Sentence …**

Nujood finally found her moment to escape one day, when her mother gave her a few pennies and sent her out to buy bread. Instead she took a bus to the center of the capital, Sanaa – a city of 3 million people – where she hailed a taxi and asked to be taken to the courthouse. She had never been inside a courtroom but had once seen one on television, she says, and knew it was a place where people went for help. **Gap C – Sentence …** It was only once the courthouse emptied during the lunch recess that the judge noticed her and asked why she was there. "I came for a divorce," she told him. Horrified, he took her to his house to play with his 8-year-old daughter, and granted the divorce two days later.

Nujood's story might have ended there, had it not caught the attention of reporters from Sanaa's newspapers, then of journalists from the *New York Times* and the *Los Angeles Times*. Last November, New York City-based *Glamour* magazine gave Nujood its Woman of the Year award in a splashy Manhattan ceremony with fellow honorees that included Hillary Clinton and Condoleezza Rice. **Gap D – Sentence …**

Asked how she spent her week in Paris, Nujood's eyes widen as she says, "I saw the Eiffel Tower; I saw the Seine."

Shaken by the testimony of violence during her divorce trial, Yemen's lawmakers raised the minimum age of marriage from 15 to 18. Two other girls in Sanaa – one age 9, the other 12 – have since sued for divorce, while an 8-year-old in Saudi Arabia has won a divorce suit, apparently inspired by Nujood's tale. **Gap E – Sentence …**

That might be easier said than done, especially in cultures where a girl's honor is held as supremely important. Minoui, who has spent considerable time with Nujood, says the girl still risks attacks from male relatives who believe she has sullied the family's reputation. **Gap F – Sentence …**

Nujood says she thinks only about learning now. **Gap G – Sentence …** As though she has no time to lose, she cut short her stay in Paris this week – including canceling a press conference – saying she wanted to get back to school. She says she ultimately hopes to work for women's rights in Yemen; in Paris she discussed the problem of child marriage with France's Human Rights Minister, Rama Yada, and Urban Affairs Minister Fadela Amara. **Gap H – Sentence …**

Nujood's professional services would be welcome. Despite Yemen's laws against child marriage, about 52 % of Yemen's girls marry before the age of 18, often as the second or third wives of far older men.

Asked by a reporter in Paris if she hopes to meet her Prince Charming one day, Nujood sat back in her chair, crossed her arms and said bluntly, "I no longer think about marriage."

By Vivienne Walt, from TIME Feb. 3, 2009. *(603 words – abridged)*

Task III: Multiple Matching 8 credits

You are going to read the text "A 10-Year-Old Divorcée Takes Paris".
Eight sentences or paragraphs have been removed from the extract.
Choose from the sentences 1–11 the one which fits each gap (A– H). There are three extra paragraphs or sentences which you do not need to use.

GAP	A	B	C	D	E	F	G	H
SENTENCE								

Sentences:

1	He has been charged with statutory rape. Law permits marriage of women at 14 and men at 16 in Yemen.
2	Adding to their concern is the way global media have jumped on the story, with the Internet headline "Man sells 10-year-old-daughter".
3	There she sat silently on a bench, uncertain as to what to do, while crowds of people scurried past, scarcely glancing at the quiet child.
4	Now Delphine Minoui, a French reporter for *Le Figaro*, has ghost-written Nujood's autobiography.
5	Nujood's ordeal began last February, when the family gathered to celebrate her wedding to a motorcycle deliveryman in his 30s.
6	After two nightmarish months he allowed her to visit her parents, who rebuffed her pleas to end the marriage.
7	Nujood says she hopes to ignite a far broader movement of girls to quit their child marriages, adding, "They should not be scared of their fathers or their husbands."
8	A sympathetic friend reimbursed him for the dowry of about $ 250 that he had paid to Nujood's father.
9	This is hardly a typical response from a 10-year-old child, but Nujood claims to be interested in cramming.
10	And Nujood says she has already chosen her future career: "I want to be a lawyer."
11	But her fame appears to have protected her from that possibility for now.

B Writing

Task IV: Descriptive Writing 9 credits

Choose <u>one</u> of the following two tasks (1 <u>or</u> 2) and write about 100 words.

1. **Describing a cartoon:**
   Describe the situation in the cartoon and state what point the cartoonist is probably making.

http://cagle.msnbc.com/news/EnvironmentMadden/4.asp

2. **Describing statistics:**
   Describe the chart and explain what the following statistics tell you about overweight people in the US.

Overweight People in the U.S.

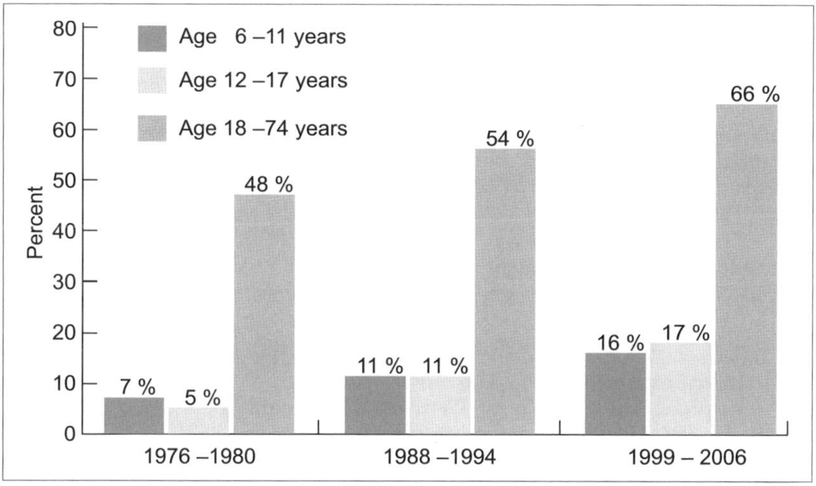

Source: CDC/NCHS, National Health and Nutrition Examination Survey 2008

Task V: Argumentative Writing 21 credits

Choose one of the following topics (1 or 2) and write at least 200 words.

1. **Composition 1**
   Lately, more and more passengers have been attacked on public transport in Germany. Can you think of measures to prevent this?

2. **Composition 2**
   "Social background determines a person's future". Do you support this view?

Lösungsvorschläge

A Reading Comprehension

Hinweis: Die Aufgaben folgen dem Textverlauf, bis auf die letzte Aufgabe, die sich auf die Überschrift bezieht. Dies ist sinnvoll, da die eigentliche Bedeutung erst durch die Kenntnis des gesamten Artikels erhellt wird. Überfliegen Sie die acht Fragen und markieren Sie sich den ausdrücklich genannten Absatz E für Frage 3, die Zeilen 33/34 für Frage 4 und den Absatz F für Frage 5. Damit strukturieren Sie Text und Aufgaben. Sie können dann davon ausgehen, dass sich Aufgaben 1 und 2 nur auf die Absätze A bis D beziehen, folglich auch Aufgaben 6 und 7 nur auf die Absätze G und H. Die unbekannten Wörter können Sie ruhig markieren – aber noch nicht im Wörterbuch nachschlagen. Tun Sie das erst, wenn die eigentliche Textstelle zur Beantwortung der Fragen gefunden ist.

Task I: Multiple choice – Mothering as a Spectator Sport

1 A, 2 B, 3 A, 4 D, 5 C, 6 D, 7 C, 8 B

***Hinweis*:**

zu 1: Das Stichwort „9-year-old" findet sich in Zeile 7, sodass ab dieser Zeile bis Absatz E die relevanten Informationen zu finden sein müssten.
- *Die Aussage: „quarters (hier: Vierteldollarmünzen/25-Cent-Stücke) for a phone call" (Z. 10/11) schließt 1 D (cellphone) aus.*
- *Der Ausdruck „begging us to let him do for months" (Z. 11) schließt 1 C aus, sodass A und B als mögliche Lösungen übrigbleiben.*
- *Zu B findet sich keine explizite Stelle im Text.*
- *„by day, not very far from home, with money and a map" (Z. 10) legt Antwort A nahe: Die genannten Punkte können als „precautions" (= Vorsichtsmaßnahmen; falls unbekannt, jetzt erst im Wörterbuch nachschlagen) gelten.*

Zu 2: Die in Frage kommende Textstelle ist auf Absatz D eingegrenzt. Das Stichwort „New York lawyer" findet sich im Text in Zeile 14.
- *Die Aussage „was arrested for endangering the welfare of a child" (Z. 14/15) ist die Paraphrase von Vorschlag 2 B.*
- *Zur Absicherung: 2 D stimmt nicht mit dem Text überein: "one did wind up waiting for her parents"(Z. 17), die Tochter hat sich also selbst zur Polizei begeben.*
- *Die Vorschläge 2 A und 2 C sind ebenso nicht kompatibel mit dem Text.*

Zu 3: Bezieht sich nur auf Absatz E. Erwähnt werden:
- *3 B (a bad diet): „pregnancy diet books", Z. 25*
- *3 C (lack of stimuli): „to sign her up for music lessons […] toy that teaches multiplication"(Z. 29/30)*
- *3 D (child obesity = Übergewichtigkeit): „And extra chunky thighs (= dicke Oberschenkel)" (Z. 28)*
- *nicht erwähnt also: 3 A (risk of panic attacks) = Lösung*

Zu 4: Die Paraphrase des Satzes in Zeile 33/34 „unsupervised (= unbeaufsichtigt, unkontrolliert) is dangerous to the point of being criminal" (= gefährlich bis kriminell) deckt sich nur mit Vorschlag 4 D.

Zu 5: Beschränkt sich auf Absatz F (to convey = vermitteln, nahe bringen).
Die Töchter der kritisierten Anwältin waren keine Vorschulkinder mehr („were not preschoolers", Z. 36). Mit 10 oder 12 wurden Kinder früher in die Lehre gegeben („apprenticed", Z. 37), in anderen Ländern müssten sie bereits arbeiten („picking coffee beans", Z. 39). In Amerika behandelt man Kinder als wären sie behindert („disabled", Z. 41). So verstanden kommt nur Vorschlag 5 C in Frage (Kinder sollten früher Verantwortung übernehmen = shoulder responsibility at an earlier age).

Zu 6: Die Antwort erhält man im Ausschlussverfahren:
- *6 A trifft nicht zu, da die Kriminalitätsrate nach aktuellen Statistiken heute niedriger ist als früher.*
- *6 B und 6 C sind zu spezifisch auf Zeitschriften und das Fernsehen bezogen, sodass nur 6 D als Lösung übrigbleibt.*

Zu 7: Das Stichwort „summarizes" (= fasst zusammen) in der Frage verweist auf „[in] short" (Z. 51) als relevante Textstelle. Zentrale Aussage ist hier der Satz "I believe in giving kids more freedom and responsibility – not crazy freedom" (Z. 53/54). Als Lösung kommt also nur 7 C in Frage.

Zu 8: Dazu sollte die Überschrift in ihrer Bedeutung klar sein: „Mothering" steht hier für „Erziehung durch die Eltern (Mutter)"; „as spectator sport": „spectator" ist der passive Zuschauer im Gegensatz zum aktiv Handelnden. Damit scheiden Vorschläge 8 C und 8 D aus. Es bleiben daher Vorschläge 8 A und 8 B. Bei 8 A vermisst man den Aspekt des Zuschauers (spectator sport), sodass 8 B die Lösung sein muss.

Task II: Mixed reading tasks – Unhappy Hour

1. Gapped Summary – The battle with the bottle

***Hinweis:** Beachten Sie die Arbeitsanweisungen, wie z. B. nur ein Wort pro Lücke zu verwenden. Markieren Sie sich die Absätze A, B, C, denn nur diese Textstellen sind relevant. Sie sollten sich den Inhalt der drei Absätze klarmachen. Worum geht es hier? Benutzen Sie das Wörterbuch, wenn Wörter unbekannt sind, z. B. „scourge" (= Plage, Geißel). Achten Sie aber immer auch auf den Kontext, bei „Slug and Lettuce" hilft es Ihnen beispielsweise nicht, die Bedeutung der Wörter (Schnecke und Kopfsalat) nachzuschauen, hier müssen Sie erkennen, dass es sich um den Namen einer Kneipe handeln muss.*

Beide Länder, Großbritannien und Thailand mit einer etwa gleichgroßen Bevölkerung, kämpfen mit einem ähnlichen Problem, nämlich dem des Alkoholmissbrauchs mit all seinen Folgen. Gesetze sollen hier Abhilfe schaffen, in GB durch die Preisgestaltung („minimum pricing", Z. 11), in Thailand durch ein Verbot des Alkoholverkaufs („prohibiting alcohol sales", Z. 12) über die Neujahrsfesttage vom 13. bis 15. April.

Wenn wir nun die Lücken des gapped summary aus diesem Textverständnis heraus, frei mit sinnvollen Lösungen auffüllen und dann mit Wörtern gleicher oder ähnlicher Bedeutung aus den Absätzen A, B, C ersetzen, ist die Aufgabe gelöst. Beachten Sie bitte, dass keine Ausdrücke, die im gapped summary vorkommen, verwendet werden dürfen.

In einem ersten Arbeitsgang könnten sich für die sechs Lücken folgende sinnvolle Lösungen ergeben:
- *Lücke 1: population (Z. 5/6)*
- *Lücke 2: (have to) solve; entsprechendes Wort aus dem Text: „tackle" (Z. 2) oder "fix" (Z. 11).*
- *Lücke 3: introduction; Textabgleich ergibt: „proposal" (Z. 2).*
- *Lücke 4: well-known, popular; Textabgleich ergibt: „annual" (Z. 13).*
- *Lücke 5: rejected, attacked; Textabgleich: „shot down" (Z. 3)*
- *Lücke 6: results, effects; Textabgleich: „merits" (= Erfolge, Verdienste; Z. 11)*

Thailand and Great Britain may be thousands of miles apart, but they have at least two things in common. First, in terms of size they have a similar **population** and second, both countries have to **tackle** the pressing problem of binge drinking with all the social ills that go with it. While Britain's politicians were confronted with the **proposal** of minimum pricing, Thais recently discussed the pros of an alcohol ban during the important and famous Thai holiday *Songkran*, the **annual** Water Festival. In Britain the suggestion was immediately **shot down** by proles, press and politicians alike. In Thailand, however, there were some sympathizers, but eventually the plan was abandoned. It was just not obvious whether a ban would have any of the previously discussed **merits**.

2. **Mediation**

Hinweis:

- *Zu 2.1: Das Wort „Widerspruch" in der Aufgabenstellung weist auf folgende Textstelle hin: „Yet", (Z. 20; = jedoch).*
- *Zu 2.2: Stichwort „Songkran" (Z. 32 ff.); relevante Textstelle: „stockpile booze or buy it under the counter" (Z. 35; „booze" = ugs. für Alkohol).*
- *Zu 2.3: Stichwort „größter Hersteller von alkoholischen Getränken", siehe Zeile 37: „largest producer of alcoholic drinks"; Konsequenz aus der Entwicklung: „postponed its stock listing" (Z. 37/38).*
  Worterklärungen: „postponed" (Z. 37) = verschob, „Stock Exchange" (Z. 38) = Börse, „a stock list(ing)" (Z. 38) = Börsennotierung
- *Zu 2.4: Vgl. Absatz G „Thailand could learn at least two lessons" (Z. 47)*
  Worterklärungen: „quick-fix bans" (Z. 48) = überhastete Verbote, to enforce a law (vgl. Z. 48) = ein Gesetz durchsetzen, to legislate (vgl. Z. 49) = ein Gesetz beschließen.

2.1 Einerseits **verbietet der Buddhismus (übermäßigen) Alkoholkonsum**, andererseits **ist der Genuss von Alkohol ein Bestandteil thailändischer Kultur.**

2.2 a) **Alkoholvorräte anlegen**
    b) **Alkohol illegal beschaffen**

2.3 **Der Börsengang wurde (auf unbestimmte Zeit) verschoben.**

2.4 a) – **Unüberlegte Verbote sind nicht die Lösung des Problems.**
    – **Stattdessen gilt es, bestehende Gesetze durchzusetzen.**
    b) **Bevor man Gesetze einführt, sollte man sie gründlich überdenken.**
    c) Für die Lösung des Problems gibt es kein Patentrezept.

Task III: Multiple Matching – A 10-Year-Old Divorcée Takes Paris

Hinweis: *Diese Aufgabe stellt hohe Anforderungen an das Textverständnis und die Fähigkeit, einen Gedankengang mit vorgegebenen Sätzen zu ergänzen. Es werden hier nur 8 Punkte vergeben. Strategisch sollte man sich deshalb überlegen, ob nicht Aufgaben wie „descriptive" oder „argumentative writing", die mehr Punkte ergeben, zuerst zu bearbeiten sind. Beachten Sie auch, dass von den elf vorgegebenen Sätzen nur acht eine sinnvolle Ergänzung ergeben. Wenn Sie sich nicht sicher sind, verwenden Sie die Ziffern doppelt und entscheiden Sie sich erst am Schluss. Auch hier werden Sie das Wörterbuch wohl häufiger verwenden, um Begriffe und Bedeutungen abzusichern.*

Vorgehensweise: Verfolgen Sie die Zeitachse im Text und in den Sätzen, die Sie einsetzen sollen: Die Geschichte hat einen Anfang (Hochzeit) und einen Verlauf (Klage bei den Eltern, Flucht, Gerichtsverhandlung, Reaktion der Presse etc.).

- *Satz 5 beschreibt den Beginn: "Nujood's ordeal (= Albtraum, schwere Prüfung) began last February": Gap A.*
- *Satz 6: "After two nightmarish months (= im April) […][her parents] rebuffed (= wiesen zurück) her pleas to end the marriage.": Gap B.*
- *Es folgt die Flucht des Mädchens, es gelangt mit dem Taxi in den Gerichtshof, wo es wartet, also Satz 3 ("There she sat silently on a bench."): Gap C.*
- *Der Richter nimmt sie mit nach Hause und löst die Ehe auf („granted the divorce two days later", Z. 19) und dann gelangte die Geschichte an die Presse („caught the attention of reporters", Z. 20) folglich Satz 4 („a French reporter for ‚Le Figaro'"): Gap D.*
- *Der Schluss des Artikels erwähnt Nujoods Berufswahl ("[her] professional services would be welcome", Z. 41) also Satz 10 („has already chosen her future career"): Gap H*
- *Satz 9 ist eindeutig: "interested in cramming (= pauken, lernen)" verweist auf Zeile 35:*

"she thinks only about learning now": Gap G

– *Es gilt nun noch, die Lücken E und F entlang der Zeitachse zu ergänzen, was zu folgenden Lösungen führt: Satz 7: Gap E, Satz 11: Gap F*

GAP	A	B	C	D	E	F	G	H
SENTENCE	**5**	**6**	**3**	**4**	**7**	**11**	**9**	**10**

Die Sätze 1, 2, 8 sind unpassend.

B Writing

Task IV: Descriptive Writing

***Hinweis:** Halten Sie sich an die vorgegebene Anzahl der Wörter. Auch deutlich mehr Wörter können zu Punktabzügen führen.*

1. **Describing a cartoon:**

***Hinweis:** Die Aufgabe ist klar gegliedert:*
- *Beschreibung der Situation*
- *Was möchte der Karikaturist aufzeigen?*

Two gentleman from a refrigerator company, dressed like businessmen in dark jackets and ties, are sitting around a large table covered with diagrams obviously showing statistics of successful sales. On the wall there is also a diagram with rising profit curves. The elderly bald, rather stout gentleman, apparently the boss, tells his partner that the production of their refrigerators contributes to global warming. His partner replies that the warmer the planet the more refrigerators will be sold.
The cartoonist wants to show the absurd situation of how unrestricted profit-making on the part of the economy destroys the world and itself, if it does not follow ecological rules.

(107 words)

2. **Describing statistics: Overweight people in the U.S.**

***Hinweis:** Halten Sie auch hier folgende Gliederung ein:*
- *Beschreibung der Darstellungsmethode*
- *Darstellung, welche Schlussfolgerungen daraus gezogen werden können*

Three age groups are represented on a bar chart showing the development of obesity in the US population in the course of 30 years from 1976 to 2006: Children aged 6 to 11, teenagers aged 12 to 17 and grown-ups aged 18 to 74. Each group shows a steady increase of overweight people. The largest rise happens within the group of teenagers which more than triples from 5 % to 17 %; the children's age group more than doubles from 7 % to 16 %, whereas the group of adults rises only by more than a third, meaning that in 2006 two in three adults were overweight. *(107 words)*

Task V: Argumentative Writing

Hinweis: *Halten Sie sich an die vorgegebene Anzahl der Wörter. Composition 1 ist steigernd zu bearbeiten, Composition 2 dialektisch mit Pro und Kontra.*

1. **Composition**
   Lately, more and more passengers have been attacked on public transport in Germany. Can you think of measures to prevent this?

   I remember two incidents and both of them were on the suburban railway in Munich. Otherwise I don't know of any other occurrences of this kind in Germany. On the contrary, according to statistics public transport in Germany is safer than anywhere else in the world.
   Nevertheless, what could be done by Munich Transport (MVG) to prevent such tragic assaults?
   Firstly, the infrastructure within the communication systems of trains, suburban railway or underground should be improved. Until recently it has been impossible to use a mobile phone on the underground to activate an emergency call to the police. I think the authorities have now installed some technical device to make up for this kind of deficiency.
   Secondly, security guards should be present on each train or at least at every other station. The mere presence of people in uniform might deter potential offenders.
   In addition, people should be informed and taught how to react in case of transgression or violence, so that fellow passengers feel encouraged to come to help in such situations.
   Last but not least, this is also part of the responsibility of the media. They shouldn't report on such incidents in order to scare us by spectacular headlines but rather stimulate civil courage of how fellow passengers can help each other. *(214 words)*

2. **Composition**
   "Social background determines a person's future". Do you support this view?

   The results of the last PISA study have shown that Bavarian pupils are excellent but there is substantial criticism as to equal chances for pupils coming from disadvantaged families.
   On the one hand, that does not mean that the future of children from favourable backgrounds is guaranteed. I know very sad examples of people who failed in their profession later because it had been too easy for them to reach their A-levels at school or their degrees at university. They had all the support imaginable, extra lessons from private teachers at home or maybe their parents, on account of their reputation, used some very helpful connections to guide their children through "special" situations. What these children hardly acquire is stamina, self-discipline and self-responsibility, which is indispensable for a satisfying and rewarding career and life.
   On the other hand, let me give you my own example as a son of a poor farmer from a faraway village. Nobody cared much for my education but as soon as I found out how to complete my education at evening schools for adults I took my O-levels and now hope to pass the exam at this vocational college to be able to continue my studies at the University of Applied Sciences.
   From these two examples you can conclude that social background contributes to a large extent to a person's future but does not determine it completely. *(233 words)*

Berufliche Oberschulen Bayern – Englisch 12. Klasse
Fachabiturprüfung 2011

A Reading Comprehension

Text I: Teenage Trips: That First Parent-Free Holiday

Five writers recount the adventures – and mishaps – of their first holiday without mum and dad:

Person A (Hilary Bradt: Staying with a German pen pal)

When I was 15 I went to stay with my pen friend in north Germany. It was my first trip abroad and the first without my parents and I hated every minute of it. From the moment we met, Christina and I disliked each other and, in hindsight, I can only feel sorry for this normal teenager who liked boys and pop music. I only liked horses and was shamefully retarded on the emotional front. It's hard to pick out the low point from a trough of tearful gloom but it was probably when I was alone in the house and there was a persistent ringing at the bell which I ignored. Then, to my alarm, I could see the visitor walking around the house looking through the windows. I hid under the dining room table. That afternoon Dr Schmidt, Christina's very frightening mother, came home from work and told me she'd left her key behind and had needed to pick up some papers from the house. "But you didn't hear me," she said. "Oh, I must have been in my room. Sorry!" I said, blushing crimson, with the awful knowledge that she'd seen me.

Person B (Sam Wollaston: Hitchhiking to the Lakes)

I come from a strange family whose approach to parenting was that we should learn to fend for ourselves from an early age. That included holidays. I remember my poor brother being sent off to canoe down the entire length of the Thames with a friend, when they were both just 12 years old. They had a miserable time, were almost murdered by some hooligans from Maidenhead, and neither has ever really recovered from the experience. I was allowed to wait until I was 15 for my first adventure. What are your plans for half term, I was asked. Dunno, I'll probably sit around watching TV and picking my spots, I said. Oh no, you're not, you're going to hitchhike to the Lake District with a tent, you're going to camp, up in the mountains, for a week; and then – if you're still alive – you're going to hitchhike back again. The only consolation was that I too was allowed to take a friend with me. And that's what we did. We hitchhiked the length of England, we camped, we got cold and wet and scared, and couldn't afford to buy enough food. But, against the odds, we survived. I don't recommend it at all. If your parents try it, make sure you steal some money from them and at least stay in a Travelodge.

Person C (Emma Kennedy: Campsite)

In fact, my first holiday without my parents was a school trip when I was seven to Cuffley Camp Outdoor Centre, near Potters Bar. I was stuck in a tent with four other girls, one of whom wet herself with anxiety within the first 10 minutes. I was unable to open my suitcase and decided that, rather than ask for help, I would just spend the week in the clothes I was standing in. It was pure hell and I even earned the nickname "Emma, the skunk".

Person D (Kevin Rushby: Walking the South West Coast Path)

Although my parents were quite worried, I hitched down to Cornwall with a friend and walked the path at the age of 16. I'm surprised that no one asked if we were runaways since neither of us looked more than 12. One night we slept rough in Plymouth, but apart from that it was straightforward camping and walking. The weather was superb, the sea aquamarine. We had almost no money and lived on sandwiches and tea. In fact, one of the first things I learned was that a fire and a mug of tea can make the world seem right. Second thing: the amount of money spent does not alter the amount of fun to be had. What really counted was talking to people. I had to do lots of chatting, negotiating, entertaining, discussing and questioning. Travelling forced me to engage with strangers in a way that I had never done before, and I learnt to be far more self-reliant. Strangers, I discovered, could be very helpful and endlessly fascinating. They could also be dangerous, boring and stupid, or any combination of those three – it was up to me to evaluate and decide. I wrote it all down, which was a very good idea, but subsequently lost the notebook – which was not so clever. My advice is simple: avoid travel agents, tour groups and rabid animals, embrace the unexpected and enjoy the unplanned.

Person E (Marcus Sedgewick: Camping in the Ardennes)
Having an older brother that I was really close to meant we could drive somewhere when I was about 16. We took a cross-channel ferry and went camping in the Ardennes: a beautiful wooded part of Europe. We cooked badly, but it was then I realised that everything tastes wonderful under canvas, thanks to the fresh air … and starvation. We walked a bit, but what we mainly did was drive around in circles playing music loudly. We didn't even mind that we were in deeply unexciting Belgium.

(about 860 words – adapted and abridged)

By The Guardian, June 12, 2010.

Task I: Multiple Matching (Teenage Trips: That First Parent-Free Holiday) 9 credits

You are going to read the text "Teenage Trips".
Find out which sentence describes which person (A–E) best.
Please note that some persons are described **twice**! *Fill in one letter per box.*

A Hilary Bradt

B Sam Wollaston

C Emma Kennedy

D Kevin Rushby

E Marcus Sedgewick

Person (one letter only)	
	plays down the importance of financial resources.
	wasn't suffering from overprotective parents.
	was better off with a family member.
	was caught lying.
	lacked comfort and cleanliness due to their own incapability.
	refrains from organized tourism.
	was better off than a family member.
	was in the company of someone who lacked self-assurance.
	seemed to feel different from his/her peers.

Text II: Feminism of the Future Relies on Men
By Katrin Bennhold

(A) In 1965, my mother was the only female engineering student in her class in Germany. There were no ladies' toilets except in the basement, where the cleaners had their lockers, and her professor urged her to find a husband quickly so she wouldn't fail the exams.

(B) Feminism in those days was pretty clear-cut: It was about women closing ranks to battle blatant sexism, get an education and go to work. It was, as my mother said recently, "about women pushing into the world of men."

(C) The feminism of the future is shaping up to be about pulling men into women's universe – as involved dads, equal partners at home and ambassadors for gender equality from the cabinet office to the boardroom.

(D) In the early 21st century, women in the developed world find themselves in a peculiar place. With boys failing in school and working-class men losing their jobs due to the economic crisis, some recently published articles predict not just *The Death of Macho* but *The End of Men.* Reality is more nuanced. Women earn more doctorates, but less money. They are overtaking men in the work force, but still do most housework. They make the consumer decisions, but run only 3 percent of *Fortune 500*[1] companies.

(E) In the Western world, motherhood remains the barrier to gender equality. Until they have children, young women now earn nearly the same as men and climb the career ladder at a similar pace. With the babies often come career breaks, part-time work and a rushed two-shift existence that means sacrificing informal networks like the after hours beer-and-bonding experience often crucial at promotion time.

(F) So far, the instinct of politicians, companies and women themselves has generally been to sharpen their focus on, well, women. Many Western countries legally protect female jobs during maternity leave, and several offer mothers a right to cut back their hours. In the corporate world, (female) human resource officers lobby for flexible work time, and (female) diversity officers[2] organize female mentoring programs. Female executive networks where the ladies can bond are booming. At countless women's conferences, women debate with women about women and bond some more.

(G) At best, those initiatives are good for tips and morale. At worst, they trap women in their role as primary carers. What they're not doing is getting more women into leadership positions. "We've got to wake up," said Avivah Wittenberg-Cox, a gender management consultant. "We've got to start focusing on the guys."

(H) The only thing that can level the playing field at work is a level playing field at home. And that requires a major shift in public policy and corporate culture. In the few countries where fathers take paternity leave on a significant scale, that leave is highly paid and not transferable to the mother. Predictably, the Nordics have led the way. Iceland, which comes closest to reaching gender equality, has gone furthest, reserving three months – a full third – of its leave for fathers.

(I) It took a male prime minister to sell the legislation to the country, and it took male leaders in Sweden and Norway to pass similar laws. It was a man who championed Norway's boardroom quota obliging companies to fill at least 40 percent of the seats with women.

(J) Would a female Spanish prime minister have been able to appoint a cabinet that is 50 percent female in 2004? Unlikely, thinks Celia de Anca, of IE Business School in Madrid. "When you want to change a culture," she said, "it's easier for a representative of that culture to sell the change." Basically, guys are the more effective feminists because other guys are more likely to listen to them. That's also true in business. Role models of female leaders matter, Ms. de Anca said. But male role models who take time off with their children, leave the office at a decent time, promote women and spread the word with male colleagues matter perhaps even more.

(K) The message is filtering through. Jean-Michel Monnot, head of the European diversity program, says his gender is his greatest asset in convincing male colleagues of the business case for promoting women: "You need to speak the language of the guys. Few men are overtly sexist these days," he said. "But they don't think twice about scheduling late meetings. Some who give the promotion to the guy instead of the recent mother think of themselves as considerate."

(L) Giving the next generation strong father figures would not only help explode the glass ceiling, it might also be the best hope for those failing boys in school who lack male role models. Men have a lot to gain from the rise of women. Put another way: The last frontier of women's liberation may well be men's liberation. *(786 words – abridged)*

1 A ranking list of America's largest corporations

2 A diversity officer's major responsibilities are to promote cooperation of employees from different backgrounds and both sexes.

Adapted from New York Times, June 22, 2010

Task II: Mixed reading tasks (Feminism of the Future Relies on Men) 13 credits

1. **Mediation**

Beantworten Sie die folgenden Fragen auf Deutsch mit Hilfe der Absätze A–G.

1.1 Anhand welcher drei Gegensätze will die Autorin in Paragraf D belegen, dass trotz mancher Fortschritte Frauen auch heute noch nicht wirklich gleichberechtigt sind? (3)

– ______

– ______

– ______

1.2 Weshalb stellt es für junge Mütter ein so schwerwiegendes Problem dar, wenn sie keine Zeit mehr für die Pflege informeller Netzwerke haben? (1)

______

______

1.3 Welche rechtlichen Grundlagen sollen die berufliche Gleichstellung von Müttern in vielen westlichen Ländern fördern? (2)

– ______

______

– ______

______

1.4 Was kritisiert die Autorin an den Maßnahmen zur Verbesserung der beruflichen Gleichstellung weiblicher Arbeitskräfte? (2)

– ____

____

– ____

____

2. **Short Answer Questions or Sentence Completion**
Answer the following questions or complete the sentences by providing the required information from the text (paragraphs H–L).

2.1 According to paragraph H, huge transformations are required in

____________ and ____________ to increase male commitment at home. (2)

2.2 When men, for example, go on paternity leave or spend more time with

their children they act as ______________ for their own sex. (1)

2.3 Which expression in paragraph K indicates that men are <u>of highest value</u>, for example when it comes to changing certain male attitudes? (1)

____

2.4 According to paragraph L, what – apart from the glass ceiling – is the final barrier for women before they can rise and reach true equality? (1)

____

Text III: Big Brother is Getting Bigger
By Philip Hunter

(A) It is four years since Britain's then information commissioner, Richard Thomas, warned we were slipping almost imperceptibly into a surveillance society. He singled out CCTV, in which Britain is the world leader, with 10 per cent of all the world's cameras (about one for every 12 people) covering large swathes of our cities.

(B) The countless anecdotal reports of CCTV's growing intrusion into the fabric of everyday existence made my own experience, on Christmas Day last year, hardly unique. I had just crossed the local railway line via a public right of way, taking me briefly onto the platform, when a voice boomed from the station speaker system: "What are you doing here, there are no trains today?" "I'm just walking by," I muttered (I assume there was a microphone somewhere, though I didn't see one). Grudgingly, the person in a central control room miles away allowed me to continue.

(C) CCTV footage used to be pretty useless because it was such poor quality and time-consuming to analyse. Police often failed to arrest criminals even when they were caught, supposedly red-handed, on camera. But new technology has made it possible to detect incidents as they occur or even before. Researchers at Reading University have developed CCTV monitoring software capable of identifying, say, an abandoned package, and following the person who left it while they are still within range of a camera. Using technology first developed 20 years ago for burglar alarms, these systems are programmed to distinguish between different types of movement, and identify those defined as unusual.

(D) Such a system is capable of many useful things, like sounding the alarm when a parked car is being broken into, or when a senior citizen has a fall in sheltered housing. And it could play a major role in policing the London Olympics, providing a powerful tool in the otherwise near-impossible task of monitoring public areas for signs of an impending terrorist attack.

(E) Meanwhile, another development promises to reinforce intelligent CCTV surveillance by generating images of suspects from DNA profiles derived from crime-scene samples. These images could in principle be used either to sift through CCTV pictures as they are taken in "real time" or to search through recorded footage to find a suspect, and perhaps even reconstructing their actions leading up to a crime. Researchers at Arizona University have discovered that the identifying characteristics of hair, skin and eye colour are determined by variants in a handful of critical genes, and can be derived from DNA samples. From this, they believe it is possible to build up a profile that could be more accurate than E-Fit pictures generated from eyewitnesses.

(F) Although these discoveries are some way from being put into practice, their investigative potential is obvious. But so are the dangers of wrongful suspicion. Early versions of the technology would almost certainly need to be refined, perhaps by taking extra genes into account. Even then, variations caused by environmental or lifestyle factors, such as diet and exposure to the sun, could render images little more useful than rough tools. And at what point would we judge DNA-generated likenesses accurate enough to be admissible in court?

(G) There is also the issue of balancing sophisticated surveillance against concerns about civil liberties. The latest intelligent CCTV provides yet more scope for intrusion into our private lives – from governments monitoring political dissidents to people hacking into the system to spy on suspected cheating partners.

(H) Yet there is little point attempting to inhibit the technology itself, for once it is out there it will be used. The answer must lie in stringent controls over its use and availability. This is no different in many ways from the situation with current systems of identification, like fingerprint records and vehicle registration databases. It's just that as the scope for intrusion becomes more pervasive, we need to be ever more careful about how and why surveillance is carried out – and by whom. *(659 words – abridged)*

Adapted from: Prospect, Issue 170, April 26, 2010

Task III: Multiple Choice (Big Brother is Getting Bigger) 8 credits

Mark the most suitable option by crossing the appropriate letter.

1. Four years ago, the former information Commissioner Richard Thomas warned us …

   A of monitoring systems which would manipulate our daily lives.

   B of monitoring systems which would spread unexpectedly.

   C of monitoring and intrusion into our lives which was happening almost unnoticed.

   D of a growing number of reports which proved CCTV's intrusion into our lives.

2. The author's experience on Christmas Day was …

   A unprecedented.

   B one incident among few examples.

   C one incident among a few examples.

   D an incident among numerous examples.

3. On Christmas Day the author was watched …
   - A and finally, but reluctantly, allowed to continue his way.
   - B and the person in charge instantly allowed him to continue his way.
   - C while talking to passers-by and continued his way.
   - D while arguing with the person in charge.

4. Some years ago CCTV footage could not be used efficiently because …
   - A the equipment was too expensive.
   - B people were hardly recognisable.
   - C the police failed to apply adequate software.
   - D the police failed to catch criminals red-handed.

5. But new technology has made it possible to detect suspicious or dangerous incidents. Which example is not mentioned in paragraphs C and D?
   - A Car theft or burglary
   - B Accident in a home for the elderly
   - C Monitoring hooligans at a sporting event
   - D Identifying the owner of unattended items

6. In paragraph F the author …
   - A mentions specific drawbacks of the new technology.
   - B criticises some people's lifestyles.
   - C describes the current misuse of genetic material in court.
   - D illustrates cases in which the new technology could be useful.

7. The "issue of balancing sophisticated surveillance against concerns about civil liberties" in paragraph G means:
   - A The use of surveillance technology in big companies should respect people's privacy.
   - B The opportunities of the new technologies may not outweigh the infringement of people's rights.
   - C Personal freedom should be limited in certain exceptional cases.
   - D Governments are justified to use the new technology freely to fight political opponents.

8. Which statement summarizes the article best?
   - A Experience with less sophisticated software has shown that we should concentrate on crime prevention.
   - B Intrusion into our private lives has to be forbidden by all means.
   - C There are numerous reasons why we should inhibit the technology itself.
   - D Intelligent CCTV software may have improved, but the basic problems have not been solved yet.

Task IV: Descriptive Writing 9 credits

Choose <u>one</u> of the following tasks (1 <u>or</u> 2) and write about 100 words.

1. **Describing a cartoon:**
   Describe the situation in the cartoon and state what point the cartoonist is probably making.

"Cell phone...must...have... cell...phone."

2. **Describing statistics:**
   Describe the chart and explain what the following statistics tell you about typical US media habits in 2009.

Time Spent with Each Medium by Age

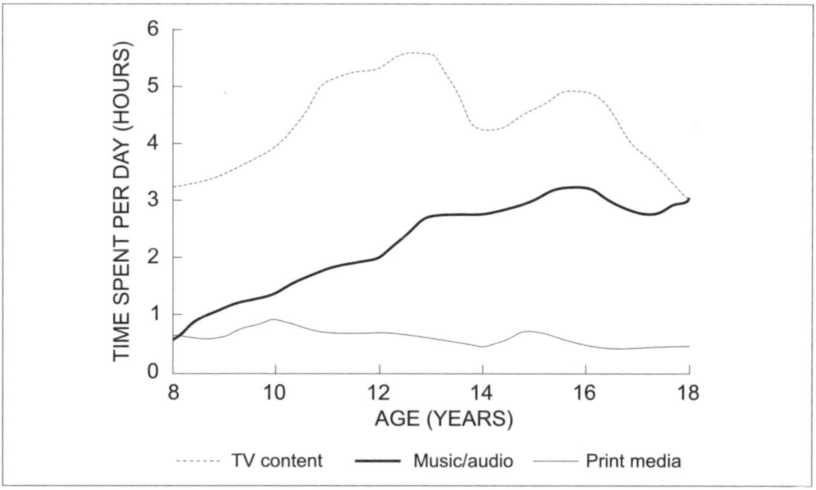

Source: http://www.frankwbaker.com/mediause.htm (adapted)

Task V: Argumentative Writing 21 credits

Choose <u>one</u> of the following topics (1 <u>or</u> 2) and write at least 200 words.

1. **Composition 1**
   Some politicians and environmentalists are demanding the introduction of a speed limit of 30 km/h in German inner city areas. Discuss the advantages and disadvantages of such a speed limit.

2. **Composition 2**
   In the US, more and more schools are sponsored by fast food and soft drink companies. Do you think that similar sponsorships should be allowed at German schools, too? Discuss the advantages and disadvantages of such a sponsorship.

Lösungsvorschläge

A Reading Comprehension

Task I: Multiple Matching (Teenage Trips: That First Parent-Free Holiday)

Hinweis: *Den fünf Personen A bis E sollen die über sie gefällten neun Aussagen zugeordnet werden. Beachten Sie den Hinweis „twice", d. h. vier Personen müssen Sie zwei Sätze zuordnen. Es ist empfehlenswert schrittweise vorzugehen. Lesen Sie jeweils den Text zu einer Person und notieren Sie welche Statements Ihnen dazu am zutreffendsten erscheinen. Überprüfen Sie Ihr Ergebnis, indem Sie die betreffenden Aussagen des Textes markieren und mit den vorgegebenen Typisierungen vergleichen.*

Person A

- *Wortschatz: pen pal (Z. 1) = pen friend; in hindsight (Z. 4) = im Nachhinein; retarded (Z. 6) = zurückgeblieben; trough (Z. 6) = hier: Talsohle; trough of tearful gloom (Z. 6/7) = etwa: düsteres Tränental; persistent (Z. 7) = hartnäckig, andauernd; blushing crimson (Z. 12) = feuerrot werden*
- *Lösung: „seemed to feel different from his/her peers" (Textnachweis: „was shamefully retarded on the emotional front", Z. 5/6) und „was caught lying" (Textnachweis: „I said, blushing crimson, with the awful knowledge that she had seen me", Z. 12/13)*

Person B

- *Wortschatz: hitchhiking (Z. 14) = per Anhalter fahren; approach (Z. 15) = Haltung, Einstellung; to fend for oneself (Z. 16) = sich alleine durchschlagen; half term (Z. 20/21) = hier: Ferien nach der Hälfte des Trimesters; Dunno (Z. 21) = I don't know; against the odds (Z. 26/27) = trotz aller Erwartungen, allen Widrigkeiten zum Trotz; to recommend (Z. 27) = empfehlen; Travelodge (Z. 28) = günstige Übernachtungsmöglichkeit (wie Jugendherberge)*
- *Lösung: „wasn't suffering from overprotective parents" (Textnachweis: "we should learn to fend for ourselves from an early age", Z. 15/16) und „was better off than a family member" (Textnachweis: „my poor brother being sent off […] when they were both just twelve years old", Z. 16/17; "I was allowed to wait until I was fifteen.", Z. 19/20)*

Person C

- *Wortschatz: to wet oneself (Z. 32) = sich in die Hosen machen; skunk (Z. 35) = Stinktier*
- *Lösung: „lacked comfort and cleanliness due to their own incapability" (Textnachweis: "I was unable to open my suitcase and decided that […] I would spend the week in the clothes I was standing in", Z. 32–34) und „was in the company of someone who lacked self-assurance" (Textnachweis: „one of whom wet herself with anxiety", Z. 31/32)*

Person D

- *Wortschatz: to sleep rough (Z. 39) = unter freiem Himmel schlafen; a mug of tea (Z. 42) = ein Becher/eine große Tasse Tee; subsequently (adv., Z. 49) = hier: danach; rabid (Z. 50) = tollwütig; to embrace (Z. 51) = umarmen, hier: zugehen auf*
- *Lösung: „plays down the importance of financial resources" (Textnachweis: "the amount of money spent does not alter the amount of fun to be had", Z. 43) und „refrains from (= Abstand nehmen von) organized tourism" (Textnachweis: „my advice […]: avoid travel agents, tour groups", Z. 50)*

Person E

- *Wortschatz: … that I was really close to (defining relative clause, Z. 53) = dem ich wirklich nahestand; ferry (Z. 54) = Fähre*
- *Lösung: „was better off with a family member" (Textnachweis: "having an older brother […] meant we could drive somewhere when I was about 16", Z. 53/54)*

Person (one letter only)	
D	plays down the importance of financial resources.
B	wasn't suffering from overprotective parents.
E	was better off with a family member.
A	was caught lying.
C	lacked comfort and cleanliness due to their own incapability.
D	refrains from organized tourism.
B	was better off than a family member.
C	was in the company of someone who lacked self-assurance.
A	seemed to feel different from his/her peers.

Task II: Mixed reading tasks (Feminism of the Future Relies on Men)

1. **Mediation**

Hinweis: Markieren Sie sich für diese Aufgabe den Textbereich A–G. Da die Fragen im allgemeinen dem Textverlauf folgen und für die erste Frage ausdrücklich Absatz D genannt wird, kann man davon ausgehen, dass sich die folgenden Fragen jeweils auf die darauffolgenden Absätze beziehen.
- *1.1 (Absatz D): Die drei Gegensatzpaare finden sich in den Zeilen 13–15.*
- *1.2 (Absatz E): Wortschatz: beer-and-bonding experience (Z. 19/20) = nach der Arbeit bei einem Glas Bier soziale Kontakte mit Kollegen pflegen; crucial (Z. 20) = entscheidend; at promotion time (Z. 20) = Zeit, in der Beförderungen anstehen*
- *1.3 (Absatz F): Um „rechtliche Grundlagen" geht es ab Zeile 22: „legally protect". Beachten Sie, dass nur die Möglichkeit zu Teilzeitarbeit gesetzlich geregelt ist, nicht die flexible Einteilung der Arbeitszeit.*
- *1.4 (Absatz G): Wortschatz: to trap (Z. 28) = einfangen, einschließen, hier: festlegen; carers (Z. 29) = im Sinne von „child-carers" (Kinderbetreuerinnen)*

1.1 – Frauen werden häufiger Doktortitel verliehen, sie verdienen aber weniger als Männer.
– Frauen überholen Männer bei der Anzahl der Erwerbstätigen, übernehmen aber immer noch den größten Teil der Hausarbeit.
– Frauen treffen die Kaufentscheidungen, leiten aber nur 3 % der größten Firmen (in den USA).

1.2 Dies wäre für Beförderungen äußerst wichtig.

1.3 – Es besteht Arbeitsplatzgarantie während der Elternzeit.
– Es gibt ein Recht auf Teilzeitarbeit.

1.4 – Sie zementieren die Rolle der Frau als Hauptbetreuungsperson der Kinder.
– Sie bringen keine Frauen in Führungspositionen.

2. **Short Answer Questions or Sentence Completion**

Hinweis: Für diese Aufgabe sind die Absätze H bis L relevant.
- *Zu 2.1 (Absatz H): Wortschatz: to level (Z. 32) = glätten, einebnen; corporate culture (Z. 33) = Unternehmenskultur; commitment (Aufgabenstellung bei 2.1) = Verpflichtung, Bereitschaft, sich einzubringen*
- *Zu 2.2 (Absatz J): "male role models who take time off with their children […] promote*

women and spread the word with male colleagues", (Z. 47–49)
- *Zu 2.3 (Absatz K): Wortschatz: asset (Z. 51) = value (Wert, Bereicherung)*
- *Zu 2.4 (Absatz L): „final barrier" (Aufgabenstellung 2.4) verweist auf „last frontier" (Z. 58)*

2.1 According to paragraph H, huge transformations are required in **public policy** and **corporate culture** to increase male commitment at home.

2.2 When men, for example, go on paternity leave or spend more time with their children they act as **role models** for their own sex.

2.3 Which expression in paragraph K indicates that men are of highest value, for example when it comes to changing certain male attitudes?
greatest asset

2.4 According to paragraph L, what – apart from the glass ceiling – is the final barrier for women before they can rise and reach true equality?
men's liberation

Task III: Multiple Choice (Big Brother is Getting Bigger)

1 C, 2 D, 3 A, 4 B, 5 C, 6 A, 7 B, 8 D

Hinweis: *Auch hier folgen die Aufgaben dem Textverlauf. Entweder verweisen Schlüsselbegriffe in den Aufgaben auf einen bestimmten Absatz oder die Aufgaben werden ausdrücklich begrenzt: „information commissoner Richard Thomas" in Aufgabe 1 verweist auf Absatz A (Z. 1), „Christmas Day" in Aufgabe 2 und 3 auf Absatz B (Z. 6) und „CCTV footage" auf Absatz C (Z. 12).*
- *Zu 1 (Absatz A) – Wortschatz: information commissioner (Z. 1) = Datenschutzbeauftragter; imperceptibly (Z. 2) = unmerklich; surveillance (Z. 2) = Überwachung; CCTV (Z. 3) = closed circuit television, Videoüberwachung; swathe (Z. 4) = Streifen, Gebiet*
  Lösung: C (Textnachweis: „slipping [...] imperceptibly into a surveillance society", Z. 2)
- *Zu 2 (Absatz B) – Wortschatz: fabric (Z. 5) = Struktur, Gewebe; hardly (Z. 6) = kaum; unique (Z. 6) = einmalig, einzigartig*
  Lösung: D (Textnachweis: "intrusions into the fabric of everyday existence [...] made my own experience hardly unique", Z. 5/6)
- *Zu 3 (Absatz B) – Wortschatz: grudgingly (Z. 19) = widerwillig*
  Lösung: A (Textnachweis: "Grudgingly, the person [...] allowed me to continue", Z. 10/11)
- *Zu 4 (Absatz C) – Wortschatz: CCTV footage (Z. 12) = Aufnahmen der Überwachungskamera; to catch red-handed (Z. 13/14) = auf frischer Tat ertappen*
  Lösung: B (Textnachweis: "CCTV footage used to be [...] useless because it was such poor quality", Z. 12)
- *Zu 5 (Absatz C und D) – Wortschatz: abandoned package (Z. 16) = herrenloses Gepäckstück; impending attack (Z. 23/24) = drohender Angriff*
  Lösung: C (Es gibt Textnachweise für alle anderen Auswahlmöglichkeiten. A: Z. 18, 20/21; B: Z. 21; D: Z. 16. Hooligans kommen nicht im Text vor und somit ist C die richtige Antwort.)
- *Zu 6 (Absatz F) – Wortschatz: wrongful suspicion (Z. 35) = falscher Verdacht; admissible (Z. 40) = zulässig*
  Lösung: A (Textnachweis: „are some way from being put into practice", Z. 34; „wrongful suspicion", Z. 35; „admissible in court", Z. 40)
- *Zu 7 (Absatz G) – Wortschatz: sophisticated (Z. 41) = hochentwickelt; civil liberties (Z. 42) = (freiheitliche) Bürgerrechte*
  Lösung: B (Auch bei A geht es um den Schutz von Bürgerrechten, aber in Bezug auf Überwachungskameras in Unternehmen, was im Zitat nicht enthalten ist.)

- *Zu 8 (bezieht sich auf Absatz H, in dem der Text nochmals zusammengefasst wird) – Wortschatz: to inhibit (Z. 45) = verbieten, verhindern; stringent (Z. 46) = streng, straff; pervasive (Z. 49) = weit verbreitet, überall vorhanden*
  Lösung: D (Textnachweis: "Yet there is little point attempting to inhibit the technology itself", Z. 45; "we need to be ever more careful", Z. 49)

B Writing

Task IV: Descriptive Writing

Hinweis: *Es sind neun Punkte zu erzielen, drei für den Inhalt und sechs für Natürlichkeit und Korrektheit des sprachlichen Ausdrucks. Beachten Sie diesen Vorrang der Sprachkompetenz. Schreiben Sie nicht weniger als ca. 80, aber auch nicht mehr als ca. 120 Wörter, damit Sie die volle Punktzahl erhalten können.*

1. **Describing a cartoon:**

   Hinweis: *Beginnen Sie mit einer möglichst detaillierten Beschreibung des Cartoon und fassen Sie dann eine mögliche Deutung knapp zusammen.*

   A man crawling on all fours has reached the boundary of a desert or an oasis where another man wearing a broad-brimmed hat is standing in front of a house next to a large water barrel. The man on all fours is wearing ragged trousers and a tie and is stretching out one arm towards the gentleman, obviously desperate for help. Quite unexpectedly he asks him not for water but for a cell phone.
   The cartoonist probably wants to show the estrangement of modern people expecting help from sophisticated technology like a cell phone rather than looking for a solution themselves, which – like the water barrel in the cartoon – is sometimes right in front of their eyes. *(117 words)*

2. **Describing statistics: Time Spent with Each Medium by Age**

   Hinweis: *Erklären Sie zu Beginn, was das Diagramm abbildet, nämlich die Zeit, die Kinder und Jugendliche unterschiedlicher Altersstufen mit verschiedenen Medien verbringen. Beschreiben Sie danach die drei Kurven für die Benutzung der Medien Fernsehen, Musik und Print genauer.*

   The chart shows how much time young people spend with different kinds of media at different ages. Up to the age of 18 they spend the most time watching TV with peaks of 5 ½ hours at 13 years and 5 hours at about 16, before it decreases to 3 hours daily at 18, the same amount of time as at the age of 8 (and the same time youngsters spend listening to music at 18). Listening to music starts with about half an hour and increases constantly up to three hours daily at 18, whereas reading is always far behind the other media. Although it is half an hour at 8 – about the same time 8-year-olds spend listening to music – it sinks almost continuously below half an hour at 18. *(120 words)*

Task V: Argumentative Writing

Hinweis: *Vergleichen Sie hierzu die „useful phrases" im Kapitel „Hinweise und Tipps". Beide Themen sind dialektisch mit Vor- und Nachteilen zu behandeln. Es empfiehlt sich, der Einfachheit halber, blockweise vorzugehen, d. h. die Vor- und Nachteile (in der Rangfolge der Wichtigkeit) jeweils nacheinander aufzuführen. Das, wofür Sie eintreten, sollte am Schluss er-*

scheinen. Vergessen Sie nicht, einen eigenen Schlussgedanken zu formulieren, z. B. einen Kompromissvorschlag oder eine begründete Entscheidung dafür oder dagegen.

1. **Composition 1**
Some politicians and environmentalists are demanding the introduction of a speed limit of 30 km/h in German inner city areas. Discuss the advantages and disadvantages of such a speed limit.

Inner city areas are almost suffocating by the fumes of the dense traffic in all larger European cities. In London, for example, they charge you a fee for driving into the inner city area by car. In Germany some politicians and environmentalists are now demanding a speed limit of 30 km/h. Is this a reasonable demand?
On the one hand, people fear that going into the city centre would become too time-consuming. With a speed limit of 30 km/h there would be endless traffic jams. Moreover, the longer one drives in those areas, the more exhaust fumes would be released, thus polluting the air even more.
On the other hand, reducing the speed limit means reducing the consumption of fuel, and therefore, the emission of poisonous gases considerably. Likewise, the noise and the amount of serious traffic accidents would go down.
What really seems to be a remaining drawback is that one spends much more time when going into town. It is, thus, the responsibility of the government to provide compensation for this negative aftermath. More park and ride places should be provided, and public transport systems should be improved, so that people use them more often. Thus, the number of cars in inner cities could be reduced considerably.
Coming to a conclusion I believe that introducing a speed limit of 30 km/h is really worth considering, as the advantages outweigh the disadvantages. *(234 words)*

2. **Composition 2**
In the US, more and more schools are sponsored by fast food and soft drink companies. Do you think that similar sponsorships should be allowed at German schools, too? Discuss the advantages and disadvantages of such a sponsorship.

More and more schools in Germany are extending lessons into the afternoon with the consequence of having to provide meals on the premises. This means costs for schools and local authorities. No wonder that they are looking for financial relief like those sponsorships that are already quite common in the United States. Is this really an alternative worth considering?
At first sight the financial aspects are very tempting. The schools do not have to provide adequate kitchen equipment, nor the personnel for cooking, for serving and washing up, nor the whole catering management. The sponsor would be ready to bear these costs.
On the other hand, those companies do not offer their services because of charitable reasons. On the contrary, they are profit-oriented, which means the food they provide must not cost them a lot, with the consequence of cheap, mostly fattening and, therefore, unhealthy food. Additionally, the drinks may contain too much sugar, so that sales among the kids increase. Again, this has negative consequences for their health. The problem of obesity among youths in the US should be a warning example for German schools.
Summing up, unless German schools find a reasonable compromise with those companies between healthy, nourishing food and maybe sharing the costs, sponsoring by fast food and soft drink companies should not be taken into account. *(221 words)*

A Reading Comprehension

Text I: What I wish I'd known when I graduated

Person A (Emma Lee Moss, musician)

"I got very depressed when I left university because I felt like I needed to know what I was going to do. I'd had those first three years to think about it, but still hadn't found it. What I've discovered over the past five or six years is that a lot of people don't know what they're doing. They just appear to you as if they do.

"I wish I'd known that you didn't have to have it all figured out straight away. The job that you do straight after university isn't going to define you for your whole life. Nobody gets it right immediately. There are people in their 40s who are starting something brand new and they're OK with that. So it's OK to be 21 without any definite plans.

"I wish I'd known not to be anxious about the future. I would like to go back in time and tell myself to relax, and just to do all of the work I did without the concern over where it would take me.

Person B (Kira Cochrane, journalist)

After leaving Sussex University in 1999, I stayed on in Brighton, with my then-boyfriend, in a bedsit. I was taking a postgraduate course in magazine journalism, working at a call centre, running a cafe at a windsurfing club, and writing stories for local papers. It was a 90-hour work week, minimum. I had five pounds a week after bills, maximum. I was too broke to spend £ 300 on the optional shorthand course. I was scared of debt. But stinting here was a mistake. It was a fair price, a necessary skill, and a loan would have saved time and trouble later.

It would have been good if I'd presented myself professionally from the start. I wanted to write for national publications, but I didn't have any contacts or a clue how people behaved. So I guessed. I figured that the people who worked at style magazines were hipsters, and I should therefore email them in hip talk, with a hip idea. My subject line read: "Dudes who drink their own piss." Weirdly, they never replied.

At the end of my course, I sent my CV to all the newspaper sections I liked, asking if they had any short-term research jobs. It reached an editor at the Sunday Times who needed a full-time administrator. I landed the job. I was soon writing regularly. Starting a new job is hard, and starting your first is hardest. But you will settle in.

Person C (Martin Lewis, website entrepreneur)

I'd say: "Don't expect to run before you can walk." It's a difficult thing to learn. In my first job, I had to make the occasional cup of coffee for people and stick newspapers up on the wall. I'd just come from being president of my student union with a big ego and thinking I was the bee's knees, and I was in effect back to doing an apprenticeship. I think we all have to do an apprenticeship in life. Think about it this way: if you've been working for two years and the person sitting next to you has been there 20 years, they've been in the working world 10 times as long as you. I wish I'd known at the time to take a deep breath, to bide my time and understand that, actually, it was great.

I'm glad I did the job I did – it taught me a lot about work and I gained skills. One of the greatest lessons you can learn in life is this: don't gain jobs as much as gain skills. If you're not learning extra skills, then you probably need to move on. It's what I did at 25 – I knew I was in the wrong job.

Person D (Chuka Umunna MP, politician)

I didn't use email properly until I went to university in 1997. The proliferation of social media and the internet into our lives was still at a fairly early stage then. I really wish I'd learned more about it then, and perhaps pursued a net-based commercial venture at that time. I've got friends who now run online-based firms and what they do is incredibly dynamic and innovative. I feel like I missed a trick there, and that's one of the reasons I love my role as shadow minister for small business and enterprise.

I adore my job. But the one thing I find difficult is managing the many demands on my time – I literally work a seven-day week. If I'd known I would be so short of time now, I would have made a lot more of the spare time that I had then.

(786 words – adapted and abridged)

Task I: Multiple Matching (What I wish I'd known when I graduated) 9 credits

Four people reflect on leaving university and starting a job.
Find out what each person has said.
Please note that some people have made more than one statement.
Fill in all the boxes – one letter per box!

A Emma Lee Moss, musician

B Kira Cochrane, journalist

C Martin Lewis, website entrepreneur

D Chuka Umunna, politician

Person (one letter only)	
	The right tone is important when looking for a job.
	I felt terrible about my lack of orientation after graduating.
	Start at the bottom and work your way up.
	I wish I had used my leisure more wisely.
	Somebody should have told me that there are many people with similar experiences.
	Once you are lucky enough to get your foot in the door things will turn out alright.
	It's time for a change if you are not developing your abilities.
	Investing at the right time means less bother later.
	Why should I be concerned when there are older people than me starting afresh?

Text II: Ensuring Petty Crimes Don't Lead to Big Ones

(A) The 16-year-old defendant seemed annoyed and a bit confused. Seated in the witness box in a courthouse in Staten Island, her answers were curt and short on detail. The inquiry into her crime – stealing a shirt in April at the Staten Island Mall – had just begun. Could she describe what happened? "Well, basically, it was stupid and I did it and whatever," the defendant said. "I got grounded for it, and I'm sorry." More than a dozen questions followed, intended not so much to elicit information about the theft, but rather to engage the defendant on a personal level. It was more self-help seminar than traditional prosecutorial grilling. Did she have any future goals? Did she know how to achieve those goals? Did she have a role model? The defendant relaxed a little. Yes, she explained, she would like to study at the Fashion Institute of Technology and work in the industry.

(B) Such questions go a long way in distinguishing the Staten Island Youth Justice Center – where the 16-year-old girl's case was recently heard – from the traditional criminal justice system. Each question was posed not by a hard-bitten prosecutor, but by 14- to 18-year-old members of the youth court tasked with a simple yet challenging goal: to provide offenders with a transformative experience, one that might keep them from disappearing down the drain of the criminal justice system. "We're not here to punish them," said Edwin Saunders, an 18-year-old youth court member. "We're here to help them out."

(C) Almost all the roughly 300 cases the Staten Island youth court has heard since it was started last year began as real crimes with real arrests. Cases are referred by local criminal courts, the police and probation officers seeking to divert youngsters who have committed petty crimes: shoplifting, vandalism and possession of marijuana are a constant at youth court. "We'd never take a case like armed robbery or murder," said Melissa Gelber, of the Center for Court Innovation, which runs the Staten Island youth court along with three similar ones in New York City. "That's not appropriate for our model."

(D) The 20 or so teenagers who are part of the court act as judge, jury, prosecutor and defense lawyer for defendants who have already admitted to their crimes. Though their backgrounds vary – some already know they want to be lawyers and they can use the court as a résumé builder, while others are former defendants recruited by the court's administrators – they approach their tasks in the same way. After two months of training, they begin hearing cases and are paid $ 80 to $ 110 per month.

(E) Instead of putting defendants on probation for six months and to pay a small fine, as a criminal judge might, the court issues sanctions. What the 16-year-old defendant who admitted to shoplifting received, for instance, was fairly standard: performing three hours of community service and writing an essay focused on her career. "This benefits them way more than a criminal court because they're around people their own age," Mr. Saunders said. "In a criminal court, it's a whole bunch of adults and just that kid. It might be kind of awkward, as opposed to here, where we can relate to what they're talking about."

(F) Mr. Saunders could be right. Nancy Fishman, a project director with the Center for Court Innovation, said 85 percent of the teenagers who were processed through the organization's youth courts successfully completed their sanctions. (Besides the ones in New York, the group also runs a youth court in Newark.) After that, their criminal records are scrubbed clean. "It's a really great early intervention," Ms. Fishman said. "It's a way of getting to kids who are just starting to get into trouble."

(G) She also said the number of youth courts across the country doubled in the past decade to more than 1,000. And the New York State Bar Association has begun a campaign to promote the courts and help towns and cities set up their own. The association's president, Stephen P. Younger, said every community in the state should have a youth court. "The courts are viewed as legitimate, but they're not as well known as they should be," Mr. Younger said. "These kids buy into the process. Instead of an outside authority telling them to do something, it's their peers." At the Staten Island youth court, nowhere is that more apparent than among the five teenagers who started as defendants, completed their sanctions and went on to be part of the court. *(756 words – adapted and abridged)*

Task II: Mixed reading tasks (Ensuring Petty Crimes Don't Lead to Big Ones) 11 credits

1. **Gapped Summary** (6)

Fill in the gaps with the most suitable words taken from paragraphs A–D of the text – only one word per line! Please note: the missing words do not necessarily appear in the same order as in the text.

The Staten Island Youth Justice Center is pursuing a difficult ____________: in order to fight low level crimes among juveniles more effectively it has changed how it deals with offenders' cases at ____________.

During the ____________ into their offences, culprits are not interrogated by the state prosecutor but by people of their own age, some of whom are ____________ ____________ and can therefore understand the youngsters' situations. This initiative does not want to ____________ such delinquents but confront them with a ____________ ____________ that prevents them from getting into deeper trouble with the law.

2. **Mediation** (3)

Beantworten Sie die folgende Frage stichpunktartig auf Deutsch! (Abschnitte A–E)

Worin unterscheidet sich die Arbeit des Staten Island Jugendgerichts von herkömmlichen Strafgerichten?

	Staten Island Jugendgericht	herkömmliche Strafgerichte
Ziel der Befragung während des Prozesses	*Angeklagte zum Nachdenken über ihre persönliche Situation anregen*	
Art der Bestrafung (Beispiele)	– –	– –

3. **Short-answer questions** (2)

Answer the following questions with words from the text by providing the required information. (paragraphs D–F)

How can the new type of youth justice system be beneficial for the professional future of those youngsters who …

3.1 function as judge, jury or prosecutors in the case hearings? (1)

____

3.2 have served the penalty issued by the youth tribunal? (1)

____

Text III: How Steve Jobs rescued old media

(A) It seems strange to think of Steve Jobs as the man who saved traditional media. After all, everywhere you look, his products are wreaking havoc on old media formats: people are watching TV shows on their iPads instead of staying home to watch them live; people are reading e-books instead of lugging around paper; bookstores and record stores replace much of their shelf space with iPhone and iPod sections. But never mind the shakeups that are occurring in businesses like music: if it hadn't been for Jobs and iTunes, there might not be a music business to shake up. Jobs's fellow corporate tycoon, Viacom's Sumner Redstone, put it very simply in a 2007 speech at Boston University: iTunes "resurrected the music industry."

(B) Think back to 2000, before the iPod and iTunes existed. Napster had cut deeply into music sales, and while the service itself was shut down, there was no shutting down the concept of music piracy. The '80s and '90s compact disc boom, when people ran out to buy physical albums in little plastic jewel cases, was over, and music companies couldn't accept that Michael Geist, a law professor at the University of Ottawa who specializes in technology issues, told *Maclean's* that "they sought to sue the MP3 player out of existence. Any sort of innovation that left someone other than the industry with control was something to be feared and stopped." But no lawsuit could change the fact that people wanted music that they didn't have to stuff into suitcases and carry from place to place, and they wanted it for free.

(C) *Computer Weekly* proclaimed in 2000 that "the battle against piracy may be lost completely," and that "mass copyright infringement over the Internet" would be the future. The music companies countered by trying to create their own music services, which bombed because, as Geist puts it, "They were label-specific, they only played on a limited number of MP3s. It was just so consumer-unfriendly." Jobs realized that no one was going to sign up and pay for only the music that Sony or Universal was willing to give them. "People don't want to buy music as a subscription," he told *Rolling Stone* in 2003. "They want to own their music."

(D) Jobs's alternative was the iTunes store, which many music corporations were initially reluctant to go along with. It was a counterintuitive idea in the post-Napster era: it was based on the notion that people still wanted to pay for music, even though they could get it for free on some other part of the internet. Talking with Jobs the day the store was launched, CNN interviewer Miles O'Brien was incredulous that anyone could try to put that genie back in the bottle: "What makes you so certain," O'Brien said, "that people are going to actually pay for music they see online?"

(E) But Jobs had a plan, and that plan revolved around the number 99. "You can just buy music at 99 cents a song," he enthused to O'Brien in explaining why people would go for his legal service. With the price of many individual tracks kept below $ 1 – a price point that hardly seems like a major investment, no matter how many you wind up buying overall – Jobs realized that purchasing a song would seem like a much more casual decision than buying a CD. Moreover with iTunes, you were free from the guilt of breaking the law. And you could be pretty sure the hit you downloaded would be the actual song, and not some bootlegger holding a recording device up to the radio.

(F) Perhaps most importantly, it was more convenient and faster to go to iTunes than to search everywhere for a pirated version; as Jobs put it, illegal downloaders were "spending an hour to download four songs that you could buy for under $ 4 from Apple, which means you're working for under minimum wage." Jobs realized that people will pay extra money if it saves time and trouble.

(G) But iTunes didn't just revive the idea of paying for content; it helped expand the amount of content people were able to pay for. In the CD era, a lot of obscure music didn't make it into the format, and if it was released, most stores didn't stock it. In the era of online-only music, free from the necessity to package and distribute a physical copy, companies were able to release all sorts of uncommercial music.

(H) Of course, while Jobs helped save music sales and music profits, he also left them a little different than before he came along. The 99-cent song has "shifted us from a CD world to a singles world," Geist says, and the labels still haven't come to terms with the fact that we can buy only the song we want: But even that is a return to an older model, a very old model – thanks to Steve Jobs, the single is king, just like it was before albums took over the music world. Whatever happens, Jobs will be known as the man whose company, as he put it, "brought music back into people's lives." *(860 words – adapted and abridged)*

Task III: Mixed reading tasks (How Steve Jobs rescued old media) 10 credits

1. **Multiple Choice Questions** (6)

Mark the most suitable option by crossing the appropriate letter.

1. According to Sumner Redstone, iTunes …
   - A posed a threat to the music industry.
   - B has become part of the music industry.
   - C led to a revival of the music industry.
   - D devastated the music industry.

2. Which statement is made by Professor Geist in paragraph B?
   - A Apple tried to make the MP3 player smaller and smaller.
   - B The music industry tried to have the MP3 player forbidden by law.
   - C We should fear and stop new technologies that cannot be controlled.
   - D Innovations not monitored by the music industry should be banned.

3. The author refers to the year 2000 twice in order to …
   - A give details of the launch of iTunes.
   - B criticize the continuous violation of copyright laws.
   - C prove that Jobs was a genius.
   - D illustrate the tough situation of the music industry.

4. Early commercial Internet music services failed because they …
   - A were too expensive.
   - B did not satisfy customers' needs.
   - C did not own the music they sold.
   - D offered music nobody wanted.

5. Which of the reasons for the success of iTunes is <u>not</u> mentioned in the text?
   - A It offers a wide range of music.
   - B It provides good sound quality.
   - C It is customer-friendly.
   - D It is considered trendy.

6. In paragraph H, Professor Geist …
   A thinks the music companies' concepts are not up-to-date.
   B praises Steve Jobs for his completely new ideas.
   C claims that the music industry has to face losses.
   D regrets that there have been changes on the music market.

2. **Short-answer questions / Sentence completion** (4)
   Answer the following questions or complete the sentences by providing the required information with words from the text. (paragraphs D–H)

2.1 Which word in paragraph D expresses that in its time the concept of iTunes did not seem likely to work out? (1)

It seemed ______________________________

2.2 Which metaphorical expression is used to describe attempts to stop music piracy? (1)

____

2.3 A person who commits music piracy is a … *(one word only!)* (1)

____

2.4 iTunes has revived the antiquated format of the … *(one word only!)* (1)

____

B Writing

Task IV: Descriptive Writing 9 credits

Choose <u>one</u> of the following tasks (1 <u>or</u> 2) and write about 100 words.

1. **Describing a cartoon:**
   Describe the situation in the cartoon and state what point the cartoonist is making.

© *INKCINCT Cartoons, www.inkcinct.com.au*

2. **Describing statistics:**
   What do the following statistics tell you about the situation in Ireland?

Unemployment rate in Ireland – Irish emigrants

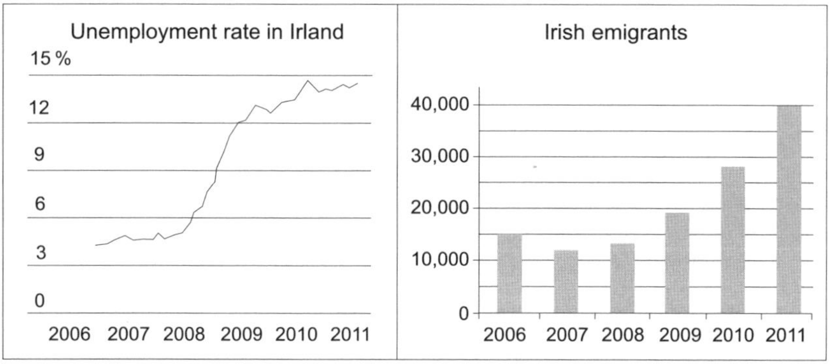

Source: Eurostat *Central Statistics Office Ireland, CSO*

Task V: Argumentative Writing 21 credits

Choose <u>one</u> of the following topics (1 <u>or</u> 2) and write at least 200 words.

1. **Composition 1: Flash mobs**
   Flash mobs are becoming more and more popular these days. Why do you think they are so fascinating, particularly for young people, and which dangers do you see in this trend?

2. **Composition 2: Young people in debt**
   More and more young people have difficulties in managing the money they receive and run into huge debt. In your opinion, what are the reasons for this trend and what could be done about it?

Lösungsvorschläge

A Reading Comprehension

Task I: Multiple Matching (What I wish I'd known when I graduated)

Hinweis: *Lesen Sie die Texte A–D der Reihe nach durch. Suchen Sie nach der Lektüre des Textes von Person A alle vorgegebenen Aussagen nach einer passenden Paraphrasierung ab. Verfahren Sie ebenso bei Person B usw.*
Es ergeben sich folgende Lösungen:

Person A: *I felt terrible about my lack of orientation after graduating. (Satz 2)*
Siehe Z. 1–2: "I got very depressed when I left university because I felt like I needed to know what I was going to do."

Person A: *Somebody should have told me that there are many people with similar experiences. (Satz 5)*
Siehe Z. 2–5: "What I've discovered over the past five or six years is that a lot of people don't know what they're doing."

Person A: *Why should I be concerned when there are older people than me starting afresh? (Satz 9)*
Siehe Z. 8–9: "There are people in their 40s who are starting something brand new and they're OK with that. So it's OK to be 21 without any definite plans."

Person B: *The right tone is important when looking for a job. (Satz 1)*
Siehe Z. 21–24: "It would have been good if I'd presented myself professionally from the start. … I figured that the people who worked at style magazines were hipsters, and I should therefore email them in hip talk, with a hip idea. … Weirdly, they never replied."

Person B: *Once you are lucky enough to get your foot in the door things will turn out alright. (Satz 6)*
Siehe Z. 27–28: "It (the application) reached an editor at the Sunday Times who needed a full-time administrator. I landed the job. I was soon writing regularly."

Person B: *Investing at the right time means less bother later. (Satz 8)*
Siehe Z. 18–20: "But stinting here was a mistake. It was a fair price, a necessary skill, and a loan would have saved time and trouble later."

Person C: *Start at the bottom and work your way up. (Satz 3)*
Siehe Z. 36–38: "… they've been in the working world 10 times as long as you. I wish I'd known at the time to take a deep breath, to bide my time and understand that, actually, it was great."

Person C: *It's time for a change if you are not developing your abilities. (Satz 7)*
Siehe Z. 40–41: "If you're not learning extra skills, then you probably need to move on."

Person D: *I wish I had used my leisure more wisely. (Satz 4)*
Siehe Z. 51–52: "If I'd known I would be so short of time now, I would have made a lot more of the spare time that I had then."

Person (one letter only)	
B	The right tone is important when looking for a job.
A	I felt terrible about my lack of orientation after graduating.
C	Start at the bottom and work your way up.

D	I wish I had used my leisure more wisely.
A	Somebody should have told me that there are many people with similar experiences.
B	Once you are lucky enough to get your foot in the door things will turn out alright.
C	It's time for a change if you are not developing your abilities.
B	Investing at the right time means less bother later.
A	Why should I be concerned when there are older people than me starting afresh?

Task II: Mixed reading tasks (Text II: Ensuring Petty Crimes Don't Lead to Big Ones)

Hinweis: *Verwenden Sie in den folgenden Absätzen jeweils eine unterschiedliche Farbe, um die relevanten Stellen zu markieren.*
1. Gapped Summary: Absätze A – D
2. Mediation: Absätze A – E
3. Short-Answer-Questions: Absätze D – F

1. **Gapped Summary**

Hinweis: *Lesen Sie sich in den Text der Absätze A – D ein und verschaffen Sie sich einen Überblick über den Sinnzusammenhang, ggf. mit Hilfe des einsprachigen Lexikons.*

*Lücke 1: a difficult _______ – es muss ein Substantiv folgen; „case" (Fall) ist denkbar, aber zu wenig allgemein, auch erscheint zwei Zeilen weiter „cases" in der Mehrzahl. Ein passender Oberbegriff wäre „**goal**", Z. 14, (Ziel) oder auch „**model**", Z. 24.*

*Lücke 2: ... how it deals with offenders' cases at _______ – strafrechtliche Fälle werden bei Gericht verhandelt, also ist „**court**", Z. 14 und Z. 18, die richtige Lösung.*

*Lücke 3: During the _______ into their offences – die Lösung muss wieder ein Substantiv sein: „**inquiry**", Z. 2, (Ermittlung)*

*Doppellücke 4: some of whom are _______ _______ – „**former defendants**", Z. 28; diese können die Lage der jungen Straftäter beurteilen.*

*Lücke 5: ... does not want to _______ – es muss ein Infinitiv folgen: „**punish**", Z. 16*

*Doppellücke 6: ... but confront them with a _______ _______ – legt ein Attribut (Adjektiv oder Partizip Präsens) plus Substantiv nahe; es bieten sich, wiederum im Sinnzusammenhang, „challenging goal", Z. 14, und „**transformative experience**", Z. 15, an; das „fordernde Ziel" erscheint zu abstrakt, „goal" kam außerdem schon für Lücke 1 in Betracht; die Lösung ist also „transformative experience" (die das Leben verändernde Erfahrung).*

The Staten Island Youth Justice Center is pursuing a difficult **goal/model**: in order to fight low level crimes among juveniles more effectively it has changed how it deals with offenders' cases at **court**. During the **inquiry** into their offences, culprits are not interrogated by the state prosecutor but by people of their own age, some of whom are **former defendants** and can therefore understand the youngsters' situations. This initiative does not want to **punish** such delinquents but confront them with a **transformative experience** that prevents them from getting into deeper trouble with the law.

2. **Mediation**

	Staten Island Jugendgericht	herkömmliche Strafgerichte
Ziel der Befragung während des Prozesses	*Angeklagte zum Nachdenken über ihre persönliche Situation anregen*	**Erkenntnisse / Informationen zur Straftat zu gewinnen** *Hinweis: Die objektive (unpersönliche) Ebene wird sichtbar: Z. 6, „... to elicit (gewinnen, herauslocken) information about the theft“, Z. 7: „traditional prosecutional grilling“ (Kreuzverhör durch den Staatsanwalt)*
Art der Bestrafung (Beispiele)	– **Sozial- / Gemeinschaftsdienst** *Hinweis: Z. 34, „community service“* – **Verfassen eines Aufsatzes über die berufliche Zukunft** *Hinweis: Z. 34, „writing an essay focused on her career“*	– **Bewährungsstrafe** *Hinweis: Z. 31, „putting defendants on probation“* – **kleinere Geldstrafe** *Hinweis: Z. 31, „to pay a small fine“*

3. **Short Answer Questions or Sentence Completion**

Hinweis: Absatz D – F: Hier sollen Sie Fragen mit Wendungen aus dem Text beantworten. Lesen Sie die Fragestellung genau durch, damit Sie die richtige Stelle im Text finden. Die Fragestellung ist für die Lösung ins Deutsche übertragen worden.

Wie kann der neue Typ des Jugendgerichtsystems sich günstig auf die berufliche Zukunft der jungen Leute auswirken, die

3.1 als Richter, Geschworene oder Strafverfolger (Staatsanwälte) in den Anhörungsverfahren fungieren?
Lösung, vgl. Z. 28: **as a résumé builder** (für den Lebenslauf)

3.2 ihre vom Jugendgericht auferlegte Strafe abgeleistet haben?
Lösung, vgl. Z. 41–42: (**their**) **criminal records are scrubbed clean**

Task III: Mixed reading tasks (How Steve Jobs rescued old media)

Hinweis: Einzelne Stichworte in den jeweiligen Teilaufgaben geben Ihnen bereits einen Hinweis, an welcher Stelle im Text sich die richtige Antwort verbirgt. In den Hinweisen sind die Stichworte jeweils unterstrichen.

1. **Multiple Choice**

1 C

Hinweis: siehe Z. 7–9: “... Sumner Redstone ... put it very simply ...: iTunes ‘resurrected’ the music industry.’”; to resurrect: hier: wieder zum Leben erwecken

2 B

Hinweis: siehe Z. 14–16: “... Michael Geist, a law professor ... told Maclean’s that ‘they sought to sue the MP3 player out of existence.’”

3 D

Hinweis: *siehe Z. 10–11: "Think back to 2000 … Napster had cut deeply into music sales …";*
siehe Z. 20–22: "Computer Weekly proclaimed in 2000 that 'the battle against piracy may be lost completely,' and that 'mass copyright infringement over the Internet' would be the future. … their own (the music companies') music services … bombed …"

4 B

Hinweis: *siehe Z. 22–24: "… music services … were label-specific, they only played a limited number of MP3s … consumer-unfriendly."*

5 D

Hinweis: *Im Text werden erwähnt:*
Z. 40–41: "free from the guilt of breaking the law", "hit you downloaded would be the actual song" (good quality)
Z. 47: "… saves time and trouble" (customer-friendly)

6 A

Hinweis: *siehe Z. 55–56: "… Geist (in paragraph H) says … the labels still haven't come to terms with the fact that we can buy only the song we want …";*
to come to terms with sth.: sich mit etw. abfinden

2. Short-answer questions / Sentence completion

Hinweis: *Beachten Sie, dass sich die passenden Wörter bzw. Wendungen nur in den Abschnitten D bis H finden lassen.*

2.1 It seemed **counterintuitive**.

Hinweis: *Z. 29: "counterintuitive idea" („eine kontraproduktive, der Intuition zuwiderlaufende Idee")*

2.2 T**o put that genie back in the bottle**.

Hinweis: *Z. 32–33; „metaphorical expression" bezeichnet eine bildhafte Ausdrucksweise; "to put the genie back in the bottle" hier in etwa: „eine Entwicklung umkehren (das weit verbreitete illegale Downloaden von Musik)."*

2.3 **bootlegger**

Hinweis: *Z. 42; bootlegger: jemand, der etwas illegal herstellt oder verbreitet*

2.4 **single**

Hinweis: *Z. 57; früher: Einzeltitel auf einer Schallplatte*

B Writing

Task IV: Descriptive Writing

Hinweis: *Bearbeiten Sie nur eine der beiden Aufgaben. Die Vergabe von 9 Punkten erfolgt im Verhältnis von 3 : 6 (Inhalt : Sprache). Halten Sie sich auch an die empfohlene Länge von etwa 100 Wörtern. Deutliche Unter- oder Überschreitungen können zu Punktabzügen führen.*

1. **Describing a cartoon:**

Hinweis:
Beschreiben Sie zuerst das Bild:
a) ein Paar in einem reichen Land im Wohnzimmer (huge TV set)
b) die Frau beschäftigt sich mit einer Rechnung („Bill"), der Mann liest den Wirtschaftsteil der Zeitung („Economy down")
c) sie ignorieren eine Fernsehsendung, die einen hungernden Mann in einem Kriegsgebiet zeigt
d) Bildunterschrift: sie besagt sinngemäß, dass die Probleme in reichen Ländern relativ sind („relative" hier nicht verwechseln mit Verwandte/Verwandter)
Kernaussage: viele Menschen in den reichen Ländern sorgen sich nur um ihre eigenen Probleme, die, verglichen mit der lebensbedrohenden Situation vieler Menschen in armen Ländern, vergleichsweise unbedeutend sind.

The cartoon shows the gap between rich and poor countries. A couple from a wealthy country is sitting on the sofa in their living-room ignoring the TV programme on their huge TV set. The programme shows a hungry person in a devastated war zone. The woman is studying a bill whereas her husband is reading the business section of a newspaper showing a diagram with an "economy down" tendency. The caption, commenting on this scene, reads "our relative problems".
The message is that many people in rich countries only worry about their own problems, which are relatively unimportant compared to the life-threatening situation of many people in poor countries. *(109 words)*

2. **Describing Statistics:**

Hinweis:
- *Hier geht es um die jüngsten Entwicklungen in Irland hinsichtlich Arbeitslosigkeit und Auswanderung („emigration"; nicht verwechseln mit „immigration" = „Einwanderung")*
- *Beschreiben Sie die beiden Diagramme: das **Liniendiagramm** zeichnet die Entwicklung der Arbeitslosenquote nach, die zwischen 2006 und 2008 stabil war und dann von 4 % auf beinahe 15 % im Jahr 2011 kletterte. Das **Balkendiagramm** zeigt die Anzahl der Iren, die auswanderten. Gibt es 2007 noch eine geringfügige Abnahme, steigt die Zahl von etwa 12 000 im Jahr 2007 auf 40 000 im Jahr 2011 steil an.*
- *Zusammenhang zwischen den beiden Diagrammen: die Wirtschaftskrise in Irland zeigt sich in zunehmender Arbeitslosigkeit und führt zu einer starken Zunahme der Auswanderung.*

The two graphs show the developments in Ireland in the years 2006 until 2011 concerning the unemployment rate and the number of Irish people leaving their country.

The line graph shows that the unemployment rate remained stable between 2006 and 2008 before it soared from about 4 % to almost 15 % in 2011.

The bar graph depicts the number of emigrants. There is a slight decrease in 2007, with the numbers afterwards rising from 12 000 in 2007 to 40 000 in 2011.

The connection between the two graphs is that the economic crisis in Ireland with a sharp rise of the unemployment rate has lead to a significant increase in emigration. *(113 words)*

Task V: Argumentative Writing

Hinweis: *Wählen Sie hier wiederum nur eine der beiden Aufgaben. Sie sollten nicht weniger als 200 Wörter schreiben, um unnötige Punktabzüge vermeiden. Für einen gut durchdachten Aufsatz brauchen Sie hier auch wesentlich mehr Wörter. Die 21 Punkte werden nach den Kriterien Inhalt/Sprache/Stil (3×7 Punkte) verteilt (siehe auch Seiten V und VI). Grundsätzlich sollten neben dem Einleitungs- und Schlussgedanken wenigstens zwei Argumente ausgeführt werden. Vergleichen Sie hierzu auch die „useful phrases" im Kapitel „Hinweise und Tipps".*

1. **Composition 1**

Hinweis: *„Flashmob" (flash = Blitz; mob = aufgewiegelte Volksmenge, Pöbel) bezeichnet einen kurzen, scheinbar spontanen Menschenauflauf an öffentlichen oder halböffentlichen Orten. Die Teilnehmer, die sich nicht persönlich kennen, veranstalten dort dann ungewöhnliche Aktionen. Flashmobs werden über Online-Communitys, Weblogs, Newsgroups, E-Mail-Kettenbriefe oder per Mobiltelefon organisiert.*
Vergessen Sie in Ihrem Aufsatz nicht, auf beide Teilfragen einzugehen ("Why do you think are they so fascinating?" und "… which dangers do you see in this trend?")

Flash mobs
Since social media platforms such as Facebook have become popular, especially with the younger generation, a new phenomenon can be observed: flash mob activities have reached a high level of popularity. So why are they so fascinating?
If you watch flash mob recordings you can see and understand why many people take part in them. First of all, doing the same things the other participants do that have joined the same flash mob event you picked creates a sense of community. In addition you meet people who share the same views as you do. Finally, although flash mobs used to have no political intention when first introduced, they are a way of raising awareness for some issues you and the other participants care about.
Fascinating as they may be, there are also dangers that come with flash mobs. Since most of the flash mobs seem to have no real intention, and a lot of people take part in such events just for fun, their good intentions could be misused and exploited. Of utmost importance, however, is: Since no one can estimate the amount of people attending, security and safety issues arise. Everyone remembers the horrible events of the Love Parade in Duisburg when a huge crowd of people panicked. Although the event was planned and a lot of police was present people died.
To sum up one can say that flash mobs are a great way to express yourself, but you should always take into account personal risks or dangers to your health. *(255 words)*

2. **Composition 2**

Hinweis: *Vergessen Sie in Ihrem Aufsatz nicht, auf beide Teilfragen einzugehen ("… what are the reasons for this trend?" und "… what could be done about it?")*

Young people in debt
In Britain, a recent survey showed that almost 200 000 young Britons are in debt – 7 % are over-indebted with about € 3 000 of debts. Why is this the case and what can be done about it?
One major issue is that society and the media teach young people that it is OK to live off credit and to buy things at once even if you actually cannot afford them. Take, for example, telecommunications. Young adults often sign expensive contracts which run over two years in order to get the newest and coolest mobile phone.
Furthermore, banks make it easy for young adults to spend more money than they have. When you turn 18, usually it is easy for you to get a bank card and a credit card. Since credit card bills are only charged the following month you can easily step into the debt

trap. What can be done to prevent this? As most young people get pocket money parents can train their kids. When the pocket money has been spent or wasted, children should have to wait for the next month's allowance and not be given extra money and so learn to plan ahead. Additionally, there should be classes at school which inform young people about the risks of taking credit and which in general inform them about sensible ways of dealing with money.

To sum up one can say that parents and schools should address the issue of debt. If the children and teenagers of today grow up to use common sense when making decisions about money, then the measures mentioned above will have been successful. *(275 words)*

A Reading Comprehension

Text I: Pedal Push

(A) Jeff Frings has a talent for attracting trouble. Soda bottles have been hurled at his head without warning. He's been called unprintable names by people who don't know his actual name. He's been sideswiped and rear-ended and run off the road more times than he can count. Red Sox fans wandering through Yankee Stadium have been subject to less abuse from complete strangers than Frings has on the streets of his hometown, Milwaukee.

(B) So what's his problem? It's simple: he's an avid bicyclist. Over the past few years, Frings – a 46-year-old photographer who bikes well over 100 miles a week – has suffered more than a few injuries in scrapes with cars, but what really stands out is the gratuitous hostility. It's not just that inattentive drivers fail to give him the three feet of space required by law. It's that they're annoyed by his very presence.

(C) In many ways, there's never been a better time to be a bicyclist in the US. After decades of postwar decline – matched by the rise of the car – the number of Americans biking regularly has been increasing steadily over several years. More and more people are using bikes to commute to work and just to get around, in cities such as Washington D.C. and Minneapolis, which have some of the country's highest cycling rates. Progressive mayors in Chicago, San Francisco and elsewhere have been laying down bike lanes and replacing car parking spaces with bike racks. Bike shares, which lend out two-wheelers for short trips at low fees, are blossoming around the US, with a 10,000-bike program sponsored by Citibank launching in New York City this month.

(D) But even in the most pedal-friendly cities, cyclists can still feel they're biking against traffic, legally and culturally. It's as if just enough Americans have started cycling to prompt a backlash – call it a bikelash – as drivers and pedestrians ally against these rebels usurping precious traffic space. Is there room on the road for everyone?

(E) There's no more contested space to explore that question than New York, which almost certainly has the most crowded streets in the US. Though New Yorkers ride the nation's most extensive transit system, more than 600,000 cars crawl into lower Manhattan each day, leading to miserable congestion. "All that traffic has a major economic cost," says transport analyst Charles Komanoff.

(F) One way to relieve some of that congestion – while improving public health and cutting greenhouse-gas emissions – is to take people out of cars and put them onto bikes. So over the past several years, Mayor Michael Bloomberg's department of transportation has set about trying to make New York into a bike-friendly city. It hasn't been easy. For years, only semi-psychotic bike messengers and minimum-wage-earning deliverymen would brave the asphalt jungle on two wheels. But what Mayor Mike wants, Mayor Mike usually gets. More than 290 miles of bike paths have appeared under Bloomberg's administration, including segregated protected lanes on major streets like Manhattan's Ninth Avenue. The new Citi Bike system, with 600 stations around town, is modeled after successful programs like the Capital Bikeshare in Washington D.C. and the Velib in Paris, which have significantly boosted cycling rates. A recent survey estimated that the Washington D.C. program has reduced driving miles per year by nearly 5 million.

(G) Bloomberg's policies have produced results. More than twice as many New Yorkers commuted to work by bike in 2011 as in 2006 (rising to nearly 19,000 from 8,300). But drivers have pushed back against the bike lanes in a city where parking can be an exercise in frustration. And many pedestrians have complained about a plague of cyclists whizzing over sidewalks and through stop signs. Even cyclists admit that some of their kind can be maddeningly mercurial, blowing through intersections and weaving through traffic. But it should be pretty clear that a 20-lb. bike is considerably less dangerous than a half-ton car.

(H) So why are cyclists so despised? To a driver, a cyclist is an unpredictable outsider, someone implicitly less worthy of respect – or for that matter, of space on the road. And if one biker blows a red light, that's evidence that all these outsiders are careless, whereas a law-breaking driver isn't held up as proof that all drivers are thoughtless. It's not that drivers are unusually susceptible to this kind of confirmation bias. There are simply far more drivers than bikers operating in towns and cities designed for cars.

(I) The brains of the US's more than 200 million licensed drivers can't be rewired. But there are ways to ensure that bikes, cars and pedestrians can all safely use the street. In the Netherlands, for example, drivers are drilled early to watch out for cyclists on the road, and bikers enjoy physically separated lanes. Those rules and regulations have helped make cycling ubiquitous and safe in the Netherlands, where 26 % of daily trips are by bike. But more than any law, it's that sheer number of cyclists – men and women, kids and the elderly – that really makes the difference. No US city is anywhere near Amsterdam when it comes to pro-cycling policies; (Portland, Oregon, where nearly 6 % of people commute to work by bike, comes closest.) But as biking gathers speed across the US, the out group could become the in group. And maybe poor Jeff Frings will be able to ride in peace. *(901 words – adapted)*

adapted from: Bryan Walsh: Pedal Push. In: TIME Magazine, July 16, 2012.

Task I: Mixed Reading Tasks (Pedal Push) 10 credits

1. **Multiple Choice Questions** (7)
   Mark the most suitable option with a cross.

   1. Which of the following has Jeff Frings not experienced when cycling in Milwaukee?
      He has been …

      A insulted by strangers.

      B deliberately attacked by several other road users.

      C hit by careless motorists frequently.

      D involved in accidents due to his careless cycling.

   2. What surprises Jeff Frings most is the fact that …

      A cyclists are disliked so much for no obvious reason.

      B so many car drivers do not abide by the law.

      C there is so little space for cyclists on the road.

      D despite cycling every day he has remained relatively unharmed.

   3. According to paragraph D, …

      A bikers in the United States have never had it so good.

      B biking is becoming widely accepted throughout the US.

      C cyclists are being regarded as an obstacle by other road-users.

      D cyclists' lives are hardly endangered in inner-city traffic.

4. According to the text, New York holds the US record for the …
   A largest public transport network.
   B best developed network of roads.
   C most expensive traffic system.
   D easiest access by car into the city center.

5. Find the **false** statement about cycling in New York (paragraphs F and G):
   A Cycling can help to ease the city's traffic problems.
   B Cycling on some of New York's main roads is safer today than it used to be.
   C Creating a new cycling infrastructure means that less parking space is needed.
   D Within five years the number of people cycling to work more than doubled.

6. When "cyclists admit that some of their kind can be maddeningly mercurial" (lines 45–46) they agree that …
   A some cyclists are annoying because of their reckless behavior.
   B it is still risky for some cyclists to bike through US cities.
   C in American cities they can travel more quickly by bike than by car.
   D there are too many cyclists sharing the road with cars.

7. Choose the most suitable heading for paragraph H.
   A No offence without evidence.
   B Unfair generalisations.
   C Inattentive motorists.
   D Bikers are to blame.

2. **Mediation Englisch-Deutsch** (3)
Beantworten Sie die folgende Frage stichpunktartig auf Deutsch. Keine wortwörtliche Übersetzung!

2.1. Welche Maßnahmen wurden in den Niederlanden ergriffen, um die Sicherheit von Radfahrern zu erhöhen? (2)

- ______________________________
  ____
- ______________________________
  ____

2.2 Wie könnte laut Text die Akzeptanz von Radfahrern in den USA erhöht werden? (1)

____
____

Text II: Risky Rise of the Good-Grade Pill

(A) He steered into the high school parking lot, clicked off the ignition and scanned the scraps of his recent weeks. Crinkled chip bags on the dashboard. Soda cups at his feet. And on the passenger seat, a rumpled SAT[1] practice book whose owner had been told since elementary school that he was headed to one of the best universities in the country. Pencils up in 20 minutes. The boy exhaled. Before opening the car door, he recalled recently, he twisted open a capsule of orange powder and arranged it in a neat line on the armrest. He leaned over, closed one nostril and snorted it. Throughout the school parking lot, he said, eight of his friends did the same thing.

(B) The drug was not cocaine or heroin, but Adderall, an amphetamine prescribed for attention deficit hyperactivity disorder (ADHD), which the boy said he and his friends routinely shared to study late into the night, focus during tests and ultimately get the grades worthy of their prestigious high school in an affluent suburb of New York City. The drug did more than just jolt them awake for the 8 a.m. SAT. It gave them a tunnel focus for the marathon of tests long known to make or break college applications. "Everyone in school either has a prescription or has a friend who does," the boy said.

(C) At high schools across the United States, pressure over grades and competition for college admissions are encouraging students to abuse prescription stimulants, according to interviews with students, parents and doctors. Pills that have been common in university circles are going from rare to routine in many competitive high schools, where teenagers say they get them from friends, buy them from dealers or fake symptoms to their parents and doctors to get prescriptions.

(D) Observed Gary Boggs, a special agent for the Drug Enforcement Administration (D. E. A.), "We're seeing it all across the United States." The D. E. A. lists prescription stimulants like Adderall and Ritalin as Class 2 controlled substances – the same as cocaine and morphine – because they rank among the most addictive substances that have a medical use. So they carry high legal risks, too, as few teenagers appreciate that merely giving a friend such a pill is the same as selling it illegally and can be prosecuted as a felony.

(E) Students taking these drugs find that just one pill can jolt them with the energy to push through all-night homework binges and stay awake during exams afterward. But abuse of prescription stimulants can lead to depression and mood swings (from sleep deprivation), heart irregularities and acute exhaustion or psychosis during withdrawal, doctors say. Little is known about the long-term effects of abuse of stimulants among the young.

(F) Drug counselors say that for some teenagers, the pills eventually become an entry to the abuse of painkillers and sleeping pills. "Once you break the seal on using pills, or any of that stuff, it's not scary anymore – especially when you're getting good marks," said the boy who snorted Adderall in the parking lot. He spoke from the couch of his drug counselor, detailing how he later became addicted to painkillers and eventually heroin.

(G) Paul L. Hokemeyer, a family therapist in Manhattan, said: "Children have prefrontal cortexes that are not fully developed, and we're changing the chemistry of the brain. That's what these drugs do. It's one thing if you have a real deficiency – the medicine is really important for those people – but not if your deficiency is not getting into the best universities."

(H) The number of prescriptions for A. D. H. D. medications dispensed for young people ages 10 to 19 has risen dramatically since 2007, to almost 21 million yearly, according to IMS Health, a health care information company – a number that experts estimate corresponds to more than two million individuals. But there is no reliable research on how many high school students take stimulants as a study aid. Doctors and teenagers from more than 15 schools across the nation with high academic standards estimated that the portion of students who do so ranges from 15 percent to 40 percent. *(687 words – adapted)*

1 SAT: an examination that American high-school students take in order to get a place at university or college.

Task II: Multiple Matching (Risky Rise of the Good-Grade Pill) 8 credits

Match the paragraphs of the text (A–H) with the most suitable heading.
Fill in one number per box.
Please note: There are two more headings than needed.

Paragraph	A	B	C	D	E	F	G	H
Heading								

Headings	
1)	Drugs help to concentrate
2)	Negative side-effects
3)	Gateway drugs
4)	No exact figures available
5)	Mostly male students affected
6)	Students behaving like drug addicts
7)	Headed for the emergency room
8)	Widespread in colleges and high schools
9)	Young people as potential criminals
10)	Drugs intended to help ill people

Text III: Gadgets go to Class

(A) Even though the vast majority of students own cell phones – something like 80 % by eighth grade – more than half of schools prohibit the use of any mobile device. And yet a few pioneering administrators are considering a new approach called BYOT – bring your own technology. BYOT solves an old problem elegantly. Instead of outlawing kids' devices, BYOT policies allow kids to take their phones or tablets to class and use them not just to post stupid photos from Friday night but also to engage with one another in classroom lessons.

(B) To many parents who use a call phone to juggle the obligations of work and family and stay in touch, school bans on phones can seem ridiculous. Even a first-generation iPhone is more powerful than some computer labs' ancient desktops. Putting a new laptop at every desk can cost hundreds of dollars per student, so tapping into the tech that kids already have seems like a no-brainer.

(C) That is why a small but growing number of schools are trying to turn these devices into learning tools. Some districts have developed BYOT policies that allow kids not only to take their mobile devices to school but also to access school networks. The districts – all in relatively wealthy enclaves where a new iPad causes no stir – enforce strict rules. Kids can use devices only with a teacher's permission; activating a screen during tests can be grounds for expulsion.

(D) Companies like Avaya and HP, as well as many smaller players, are racing to develop in-classroom apps for mobile devices. One idea is that a teacher presenting a math problem can ensure that all students have responded to the assignment. It's not as complicated as it sounds. At many colleges, professors are using clickers – remote-control-like devices that let students answer questions from their seats – to gather real-time information about whether students have comprehended lessons.

(E) Cell phones are the easiest fit for BYOT. Even for kids from poor neighborhoods, cell phones have become nearly biological appendages. Ask 10th-graders about, say, mitochondria, and they can deploy a phone to give an answer in seconds. Do you really expect them to walk over to that dusty shelf with the Encyclopedia Britannica?

(F) Many parents want their kids constantly connected for safety reasons, and, of course, teachers and administrators have their own devices. Teachers look away when kids pull phones from backpacks during lunch, but the classroom remains a contested arena. That's partly because school officials fear getting caught up in lawsuits. "The technology has great promise, but it has created huge legal issues for school districts," says Daniel Domenech, executive director of the American Association of School Administrators. "Some kids use their phones to bully students or to make inappropriate phone calls."

(G) One concern is that schools could run afoul of the Children's Internet Protection Act (CIPA), which President Bill Clinton signed in 2000. The law says schools can lose federal funding if they don't adequately monitor the online activities of minors. CIPA predated smart phones and social networking, but administrators must hold to its letter. If, say, a student tweets something from a locker room that is gross and compromising, cops could arrive.

(H) BYOT also raises equality issues. It's true that most kids have cell phones, but they aren't necessarily carrying smart phones that are capable of running elaborate apps. Some families can't afford a cell phone of any type. School districts can lend devices to students who have less money. But the choice may create a high-tech version of who's on the free lunch list in the cafeteria.

(I) Tech advocates are convinced that it's worth the trouble."Parents are desperate for kids to be prepared for the jobs of the future," says Julie Evans, executive director of Project Tomorrow, a nonprofit that studies how to use mobile tech in schools and is partly funded by HP. "We have to create a classroom experience with the tools they already own. If we do that, they won't wander off into Facebook or play a game." When Project Tomorrow studied a pilot project in North Carolina, it found that students who had used the mobile devices to collaborate on school projects scored better on tests than kids who hadn't.

(K) Those test scores are at once encouraging and dispiriting. Any parent knows that mobile devices erase the idea of separation between work and home. Kids may be right that using their mobiles at school will be fun – but they might feel a little less fun when deployed to do homework. *(766 words – adapted)*

adapted from: John Cloud: 9 Gadgets Go To Class. In: TIME Magazine, Aug. 27, 2012.

Task III: Mixed reading tasks (Gadgets go to Class) 12 credits

1. **Gapped summary** (6)
Fill in the most appropriate words or expressions from the corresponding sections of the text – only one word per line. The words needed are to be found in paragraphs A–C and I–K.

What is the best way of dealing with the use of mobile devices in an educational environment? So far most US schools have answered that question by ________________ cell phones on their premises. But since most students are equipped with their own gadgets today, some US schools are trying to take another ____________________. Not only have they started to permit mobile phones at school, they also make use of them as powerful ________________ ________________ during lessons.

One obvious advantage of this is that by ____________________ into their students' devices, schools do not need to spend any money on new PCs. What's more, computer experts claim that using gadgets in lessons will provide students with a ________________ ________________ that will encourage them to use their mobile phones for educational purposes. Studies have also shown that such students achieve higher ________________ in exams.

2. **Short-answer questions/Sentence completion** (4)
Answer the following questions by giving the required information from the text. (paragraphs D–F)

2.1 By using electronic devices teachers can make sure that each learner has … (2)

- ______________________________
- ______________________________

2.2 Which phrase expresses that mobile devices are of extreme importance for most young people? (1)

They are almost like ______________________________

2.3 Which phrase expresses that using mobile phones during lessons is a controversial issue?

School is still a ______________________________ (1)

3. **Mediation Englisch-Deutsch** (2)

Beantworten Sie die folgende Frage auf Deutsch.

Nennen Sie die Konsequenzen, welche Schulen zu befürchten haben, wenn sie den Einsatz von Mobiltelefonen im Schulunterricht erlauben.

juristisch	
finanziell	

B Writing

Task IV: Descriptive Writing

9 credits

Choose one of the following tasks (1 or 2) and write about 100 words.

1. **Describing a cartoon:**
   Describe the situation in the cartoon and state what point the cartoon is making.

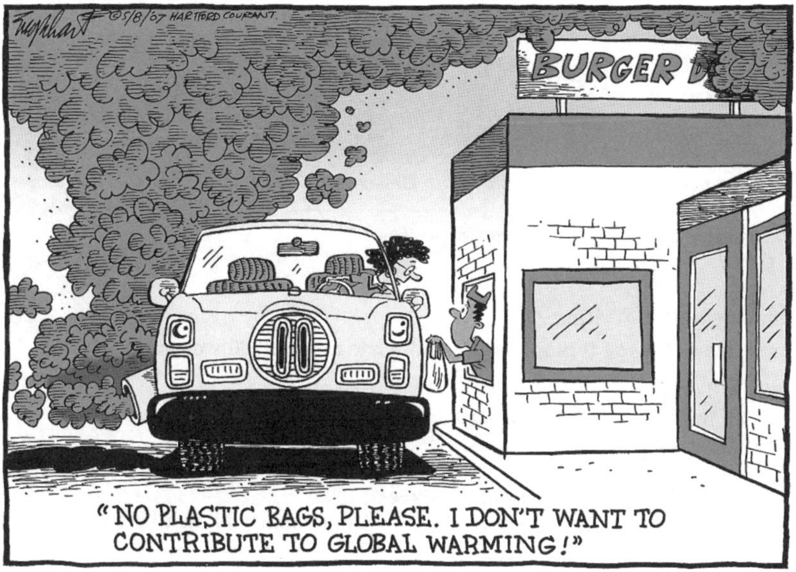

2. **Describing statistics: Youth unemployment in Europe (2007 vs. 2012)**
   Describe the following statistics and point out the main trends.

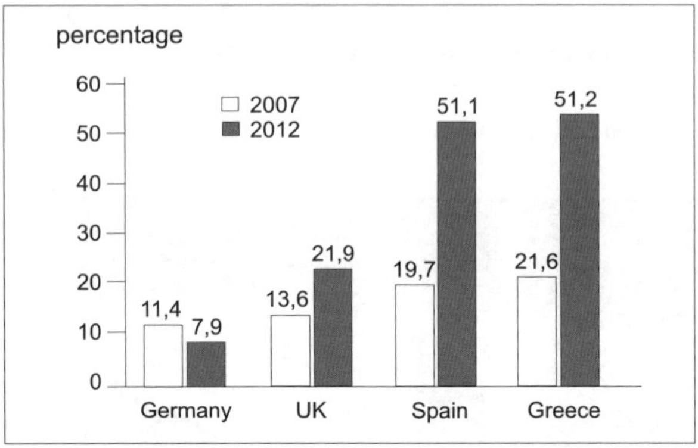

Note: Percentage of total youth labour force, 15–24.
Source: OECD

Task V: Argumentative Writing 21 credits

Choose one of the following topics (1 or 2) and write at least 200 words.

1. **Composition Topic 1: Cheap clothes**
   Shops in Western countries should no longer sell cheap clothes produced in countries like China and India. Discuss.

2. **Composition Topic 2: Alcohol in public places**
   In your opinion, should there be a general ban on drinking alcohol in all public places and means of transport? Give reasons for your point of view.

Lösungsvorschläge

A Reading Comprehension

Task I: Mixed Reading Tasks (Pedal Push)

Hinweis: *Notieren Sie sich am Rand des Textes, welche der Absätze A–H für welche Fragen relevant sind. Die Mediation Englisch-Deutsch bezieht sich auf Absatz I.*
Frage 1 und 2 der Multiple Choice-Aufgaben beziehen sich auf die Absätze A und B, in denen es um Jeff Frings geht. Frage 3 bezieht sich ausdrücklich auf den Absatz D. Frage 4 nennt das Stichwort „New York", das man in Absatz E findet. Die Fragen 5 bis 7 nennen wieder ausdrücklich die Absätze bzw. Zeilen, auf die sie sich beziehen.

1. Multiple Choice

1 D

Hinweis: *Hier geht es um die Erfahrung, die Jeff Frings nicht gemacht hat. Suchen Sie daher in Abschnitt A und B im Ausschlussverfahren zuerst nach den Erfahrungen, die er gemacht hat:*
1 A: siehe Z. 2: "He's been called unprintable names …"
1 B: siehe Z. 1: "Soda bottles have been hurled at his head …"
1 C: siehe Z. 3/4: "He's been sideswiped and rear-ended and run off the road more times than he can count."
Also stellt sich D als richtige Lösung heraus. Beachten Sie, dass „inattentive drivers" (Z. 9) sich auf die Autofahrer und natürlich nicht auf Jeff Frings bezieht.

2 A

Hinweis: *siehe Z. 8/9: "… what really stands out is the gratuitous hostility."*
gratuitous = unnecessary, uncalled-for; hostility = animosity, enmity

3 C

Hinweis: *siehe Z. 22/23: "… drivers and pedestrians ally against these rebels usurping precious traffic space."*
to ally = sich verbünden; to usurp = unrechtmäßig besetzen/in Beschlag nehmen

4 A

Hinweis: *siehe Z. 25/26: "… New Yorkers ride the nation's most extensive transit system …"; extensive = ausgedehnt*

5 C

Hinweis: *Hier müssen die Aussagen A bis D mit dem Text abgeglichen werden, um die falsche Aussage herauszufiltern.*
5 A: siehe Z. 29/30: "One way to relieve some of that congestion … is to take people out of cars and put them onto bikes."; to relieve = to ease
5 B: siehe Z. 35/36: "… bike paths … including segregated, protected lanes on major streets like Manhattan's Ninth Avenue."; siehe auch Z. 11 (Absatz C) : "… there's never been a better time to be a bicyclist in the US."
5 D: siehe Z. 41/42: "More than twice as many New Yorkers commuted to work by bike in 2011 as in 2006 …"
C ist also die richtige Lösung, da die Aussage nicht im Text vorkommt. Der Ausbau der Fahrradwege wird zwar einige Male genannt (vgl. Z. 35, 37), es wird aber nicht erwähnt, dass dadurch weniger Parkplätze für Autos benötigt werden.

6 A

Hinweis: *mercurial = unberechenbar; reckless = rücksichtslos*

7 B

Hinweis: *siehe Z. 50: "... that all these outsiders are careless ..."; Z. 51: "... that all drivers are thoughtless"; Z. 52: "... confirmation bias ..."*

2. Mediation

Hinweis: *Die Mediation bezieht sich auf Absatz I. Hier ist keine wörtliche Übersetzung verlangt, vielmehr soll die Hauptaussage wiedergegeben werden.*
2.1 siehe Z. 55–57: "In the Netherlands ... drivers are drilled early to watch out for cyclists on the road ..."; "... bikers enjoy physically separated lanes."
2.2 siehe Z. 58–60: "But more than any law, it's that sheer number of cyclists – men and women, kids and the elderly – that really makes the difference."

2.1 – Die Autofahrer lernen von Anfang an, auf Radfahrer Rücksicht zu nehmen.
– Es gibt eigene Radwege, die von den Fahrspuren der Autos getrennt sind.

2.2 Es müssten mehr Menschen in den USA mit dem Rad fahren.

Task II: Multiple Matching (Text: Good-Grade Pill)

Hinweis: *Von den vorgeschlagenen zehn Überschriften sind acht für die Absätze A–H zutreffend. Lesen Sie immer einen Absatz und gehen Sie danach die Überschriften durch. Notieren Sie sich die jeweils passende.*

A 6: *Students behaving like drug addicts*
Siehe Z. 5–7: "... he twisted open a capsule of orange powder and arranged it in a neat line on the armrest. He leaned over, closed one nostril and snorted it."

B 1: *Drugs help to concentrate*
Siehe Z. 9–11: "... an amphetamine prescribed for attention deficit hyperactivity disorder (ADHD) ... to study late into the night, focus during tests ..."

C 8: *Widespread in colleges and high schools*
Siehe Z. 16/17: "At high schools across the United States ... and competition for college admissions ..."

D 9: *Young people as potential criminals*
Siehe Z. 26/27: "So they carry high legal risks, too, as few teenagers appreciate that merely giving a friend such a pill is the same as selling it illegally and can be prosecuted as a felony."

E 2: *Negative side effects*
Siehe Z. 29–31: "But abuse of prescription stimulants can lead to depression and mood swings ..., heart irregularities and acute exhaustion or psychosis ..."

F 3: *Gateway drugs („Einstiegsdrogen")*
Siehe Z. 33/34 und 37: "... the pills eventually become an entry to the abuse of painkillers and sleeping pills. ... later became addicted to painkillers and eventually heroin."

G 10: *Drugs intended to help ill people*
Siehe Z. 40/41: "It's one thing if you have a real deficiency – the medicine is really important for those people – but not if your deficiency is not getting into the best universities."

H 4: *No exact figures available*
Siehe Z. 45–48: "But there is no reliable research on how many high school students take stimulants ... portion of students who do so ranges from 15 to 40 percent."

Die Überschriften 5 und 7 treffen auf keinen Absatz zu.

Paragraph	A	B	C	D	E	F	G	H
Heading	6	1	8	9	2	3	10	4

Task III: Mixed Reading Tasks (Gadgets to class)

Hinweis: *Zu dem Text müssen Sie verschiedene Aufgaben bearbeiten. Markieren Sie dabei immer die für die jeweilige Aufgabe relevanten Abschnitte.*

1. Gapped Summary

Hinweis: *Lesen Sie zuerst die Absätze A–C und I–K, um den Inhalt zu erfassen. Darin geht es um den Einsatz mobiler technischer Geräte (Smartphones, Tablets, etc.) im Unterricht. Lesen Sie danach den Lückentext und ergänzen Sie ihn mit Wörtern aus dem Text. Diese müssen inhaltlich und grammatikalisch in den Satz passen.*

Lücke 1: outlawing (Z. 4) = verbieten; auf „by" muss hier ein Gerund folgen

Lücke 2: approach (Z. 3) = Vorgehensweise, Ansatz

Lücke 3: hier sind 2 Wörter gesucht: learning tools (Z. 14) = „Lernwerkzeuge"

Lücke 4: tapp<u>ing</u> (Z. 11) von "to tap" = (an)zapfen; auf „by" muss hier ein Gerund folgen

Lücke 5: hier sind 2 Wörter gesucht: classroom experience (Z. 49) = in etwa „Lernerfahrung"

Lücke 6: scores (Z. 53) = Ergebnisse; für „test scores" gibt es nur einen halben Punkt, da „test" ja bereits in „exams" enthalten ist.

What is the best way of dealing with the use of mobile devices in an educational environment? So far most US schools have answered that question by **outlawing** cell phones on their premises. But since most students are equipped with their own gadgets today, some US schools are trying to take another **approach**. Not only have they started to permit mobile phones at school, they also make use of them as powerful **learning tools** during lessons.
One obvious advantage of this is that by **tapping** into their students' devices, schools do not need to spend any money on new PCs. What's more, computer experts claim that using gadgets in lessons will provide students with a **classroom experience** that will encourage them to use their mobile phones for educational purposes. Studies have also shown that such students achieve higher **scores** (test scores = 0.5 cr) in exams.

2. Short Answer Questions

Hinweis: *Für diese Aufgabe sind die Absätze D–F relevant. Hier können Sie die Lösung wörtlich aus dem Text übernehmen. Dennoch müssen Sie darauf achten, dass der vorgegebene Satzanfang grammatikalisch korrekt zu Ende geführt wird.*
Zu 2.1: siehe Z. 21 und 24
Zu 2.2: siehe Z. 26; appendage = Anhang, Anhängsel
Zu 2.3: siehe Z. 31; contested = umstritten, umkämpft

2.1 – responded to the assignment
– comprehended (the) lessons

2.2 biological appendages

2.3 contested arena

3. Mediation Englisch-Deutsch

Hinweis: *zu den juristischen Konsequenzen Z. 30–33: "Teachers look away when kids pull phones from backpacks during lunch, but the classroom remains a contested area … school officials fear getting caught up in lawsuits. 'The technology … has created huge legal issues for school districts.'"*
Zu den finanziellen Konsequenzen siehe Z. 37/38: "The law says schools can lose federal funding if they don't adequately monitor the online activities of minors."

Juristisch: Die Schulen fürchten Gerichtsverfahren (wenn die Geräte im Unterricht missbräuchlich verwendet werden).

Finanziell: Die Schulen können ihre staatliche Förderung verlieren (wenn sie die Online-Aktivitäten der minderjährigen Schüler nicht ausreichend überwachen).

B Writing

Task IV: Descriptive Writing

Hinweis: *Nur eine der beiden Aufgaben ist zu bearbeiten. Die Vergabe von 9 Punkten erfolgt im Verhältnis von 3 : 6 (Inhalt : Sprache). Halten Sie sich auch an die angegebene Länge des zu verfassenden Textes von etwa 100 Wörtern. Deutliche Unter- oder Überschreitungen können zu Punktabzügen führen.*

1. **Describing a cartoon**

Hinweis: *Sie sollen erkennen, dass es in dem Cartoon um das oft widersprüchliche Verhalten der Menschen in Sachen Umweltschutz geht.*

- *Beschreibung des Bildes:*
  - *ein Kunde fährt in einem großen Auto, das riesige Abgaswolken ausstößt, in ein Drive-in*
  - *der Verkäufer überreicht ihm das Bestellte in einer Plastiktüte*
  - *der Kunde lehnt diese ab mit der Begründung, dass er nicht zum Treibhauseffekt beitragen möchte*
- *Kernaussage: Manche Leute handeln oft widersprüchlich und nicht konsequent, wenn es um den Schutz der Umwelt geht. In dem Cartoon lehnt der Kunde zwar die Plastiktüte ab, fährt jedoch in einem die Umwelt verschmutzenden Auto vor.*

A customer at a drive-in burger restaurant has ordered a meal. The vendor is handing over the food in a plastic bag which the customer is refusing to take, not wanting to contribute to global warming. He himself, however, drives a huge car that is producing a thick, dark cloud of exhaust fumes.

The cartoonist wants to point out that, when it comes to the environment, people are often inconsistent and behave in contradictory ways. One the one hand, the customer is against plastic bags, but on the other hand he doesn't care enough to drive a vehicle which does less harm to the environment. *(105 words)*

2. **Describing Statistics:**

Hinweis:
- *Die Balkengraphiken zeigen die Prozentrate der Jugendarbeitslosigkeit in Deutschland, dem Vereinigten Königreich (UK = United Kingdom)/Großbritannien, Spanien und Griechenland in den Jahren 2007 und 2012.*
- *Entwicklung der Jugendarbeitslosigkeit: in Großbritannien, Spanien und Griechenland nahm die Jugendarbeitslosigkeit zu, in beiden letztgenannten Ländern stieg sie sogar um mehr als das doppelte. In Deutschland nahm die Zahl der arbeitslosen Jugendlichen ab.*

The bar chart compares the rates of youth unemployment in Germany, the UK, Spain, and Greece in the years 2007 and 2012.

In Germany, the youth unemployment rate fell from 11.4 percent to 7.9 percent, whereas in the UK it increased significantly from 13.6 percent to 21.9 percent. In Spain and Greece, where the rates had already been high in 2007, they even rose to more than double, from 19.7 percent to 51.1 percent and from 21.6 percent to 51.2 percent respectively.

In other words, Spain and Greece are particularly badly affected by youth unemployment, whereas the chances for young Germans to find a job improved. *(106 words)*

Task V: Argumentative Writing

Hinweis: *Hier müssen Sie sich für ein Thema entscheiden. Sie sollten nicht weniger als 200 Wörter schreiben, wenn Sie vermeiden wollen, dass Ihnen deswegen Punkte abgezogen werden. Die Punkte werden nach den Kriterien Inhalt/Sprache/Stil (jeweils 7 Punkte) verteilt (vgl. Seiten V und VI). Neben dem Einleitungs- und Schlussgedanken sollten im Hauptteil mindestens zwei Argumente ausgeführt werden. Vergleichen Sie hierzu auch die „useful phrases" im Kapitel „Hinweise und Tipps".*
Achten Sie darauf, was von Ihnen verlangt wird. Bei der Aufgabenstellung "Discuss." in Composition 1 sollen Sie das Thema kritisch von verschiedenen Seiten beleuchten. In Composition 2 lautet die Aufgabenstellung "Give reasons for your point of view". Hier sollen Sie Ihren eigenen, subjektiven Standpunkt vertreten.

1. **Composition Topic 1**

Cheap clothes
In 2013, hundreds of workers lost their lives when a clothes factory in Bangladesh collapsed. This catastrophe has a lot to do with clothes that are sold at cheap prices in Western countries.
In a very drastic way, this opened the eyes of the industrialised nations. It revealed the extent to which the workers, for the most part female, are exploited when they sew pieces of garments, e. g. T-shirts or jeans, as cheaply as possible for the Western market. Their wages are so low that they can hardly make a decent living. In addition, their working conditions are far from meeting Western standards. The factories are often in a dilapidated state and lack fire protection.
In order to raise standards, the big clothing companies in the West should make sure that working conditions in the factories are humane and that the pay is decent. They should also not hesitate to demand higher prices for the garments in their stores. Last but not least, it is up to the customers to decide whether they want to pay more for their clothes and thus improve conditions for the factory workers and increase their income.
The garment industry in developing countries provides workplaces and jobs for the people, who depend on the income they earn in the factories. The only option is, therefore, not to give up producing clothes in developing countries, but to introduce an effective system of supervision that ensures humane working conditions and a decent income. *(248 words)*

2. **Composition Topic 2**

Alcohol in public places
For some time now there have been discussions in the media about a ban on drinking alcohol in public places such as trains, buses or the underground. Some cities in Germany, e. g. Hamburg and Munich, have already introduced a ban on alcohol on public transport.
When social drinking or "binge drinking" gets out of hand, most people feel harassed by drunks in the street. Drinking too much alcohol affects the human body severely: loss of coordination and reduced self-control are the most common problems. In addition, drunks often become aggressive and even violent. They may begin to quarrel over taxis or about who should be served first at fast-food stands. All this can lead to public disturbances and escalate into fights in the streets and on buses and trains.
Furthermore, when people drink in public, the streets and pavements are often littered with smashed bottles, which not only looks ugly, but can also be a hazard. It would therefore be better if the consumption of alcohol were to be banned in public places and restricted to pubs, restaurants or, for example, the home.
To conclude, a ban on alcohol in public places could be a sensible measure because the security in social spaces and means of transport could thus be more easily maintained.

(218 words)

Berufliche Oberschulen Bayern – Englisch 12. Klasse
Fachabiturprüfung 2014

A Reading Comprehension

Text I: Royal Baby – How the Rest Of The World Covered The Story

The following is a collection of stories and quotations from around the world responding to the birth of George, son of Prince William and his wife Catherine, Duchess of Cambridge, on 23 July 2013 – an event that met with massive public interest worldwide.

United States

The *NewYorker* questioned: "Why are Americans so interested in an overseas monarchy that has virtually no power and which now functions primarily to attract tourists?"
In the *New York Times,* Lauren Apfel bemoaned a "princess culture in which girls … idolise characters distinguished mainly by their trim waistlines, their title, and their ability to wear a diadem." She called for "women who can be admired for their strength of purpose, their brains, their skills".

Australia

The royal baby's gift from the Australian government was a donation for a research project to save the Australian desert rat, the bilby.
The Northern Territory has announced it will be presenting the royal couple with baby crocodile George. He will live with crocodiles William and Kate that were given to the couple on the occasion of their engagement.

Iran

Tehran's take on the event was somewhat different from that of the rest of the world's media. *State TV* revealed that public opinion in Britain was heartily against the royal family and exposed the Queen as an iron-fisted dictator.
Press TV, aiming at an English speaking audience outside Iran, did make a sensible point: "Today, the British public – grinding under massive budget cuts, unemployment, poverty wages, social deprivations and crumbling services – are thrown scraps of feelgood comfort from the much hyped event."

Canada

The capital, Ottawa, joined the global welcome for the new Prince of Cambridge, lighting up the country's parliament in blue on Monday evening.
The Monarchist League of Canada suggested that "everyone consider holding a Canadian royal baby shower some time during this summer – a simple neighbourhood party, with guests raising a glass, giving a few dollars to a charity and signing a card".

Russia

Vladimir Zhirinovsky, leader of the Liberal Democrat Party, said: "I don't care about the heir. The British monarchy destroyed our state. The birth of another British monarch, who will suck our blood, cannot bring us any kind of happiness."
Elsewhere, the Russian newspaper *Kommersant's* website embarrassingly wrote that the baby was the "first child of Charles and Kate".

China

The royal baby's birth was preceded by earthquakes in Gansu province, so many newspapers' front covers featured the first baby born in the Gansu area after the disaster instead.

Elsewhere Chinese fortune tellers forecast George's future in a rather predictable way. Mak Ling-ling took no risks: "It's likely he will have to go overseas, perhaps representing the army or go to a boarding school." Au Chung-tak found: "He will achieve harmony with his siblings".

France

Le Monde mocked the media frenzy in the UK. But many other French newspapers bought into the hype. "Everything you need to know about this birth," read the headline in *Le Parisien.*

Le Figaro dedicated articles to "l'arbre genealogique des Windsor" *(the Windsor family tree).* One commentator suggested the French were missing their own royal family, who were rather unceremoniously ditched over 220 years ago.

India

Sudarsan Pattnaik, noted sand artist and winner of last week's international sand art competition, created a sculpture for the royal baby with the message "Welcome Baby Cambridge". Plans to exhibit it had to be put on hold, though, due to heavy rainfalls in the state of Orissa, where he sculpts.

The Indian mystic and healer, Larrah Shah, has said Prince George will run in an election for president or prime minister "and will probably win it". She predicted that he would improve international relations, particularly with Arab countries.

Pakistan

Islamabad-based *Daily BBC Record London Ltd* (no relation to the BBC) has investigated the royal baby's family tree and made this discovery: "The baby's relations will stretch from a simple Parisian actress via the Dracula princes in Romania, to even an Islamic sultan from Seville in Spain, who descended from the Muslim prophet Mohammed, experts say."

South Africa

Suretha Erasmus is a South Africa-based genetic counsellor who has created images of the royal baby as a teenager. He believes George will share many of Diana's facial features but will have his mother Catherine's dark hair.

The website *AllAfrica* published a piece about the dangers of pregnancy in Africa and whether the duchess would have survived there. "Every day, around 800 women die from causes linked to pregnancy and childbirth. And it will come as little surprise that the majority of these deaths occur in poor countries … 99 % of all maternal deaths occur in developing countries, largely in sub-Saharan Africa and South Asia." *(778 words)*

Task I: Multiple Matching (Royal Baby – How the Rest of the World Covered The Story) 10 credits

Multiple Matching

In which country's coverage of the royal birth can the following aspects be found?

	Aspects
1	a criticism of the state of affairs in Britain
2	the British royals presented as a globally branched-out family
3	a mixture of ridicule, excitement and nostalgia in the media
4	an alternative version of the young royal family
5	anger about unsuitable ideas of femininity
6	a mistake concerning the members of the royal family
7	praise for the worldwide popularity of the royal family
8	the difficulty in putting the birthday present on display
9	the focus on more pressing problems in large parts of the world
10	a whole country asked to pay tribute to the baby
11	a potentially dangerous present that arrived too late
12	the celebration of a new life born in less happy circumstances

Match each country with the correct aspect.
Note: For each country, there is just one aspect that fits.
There are two aspects in the list that don't fit any of the countries.

country	United States	Australia	Iran	Canada	Russia
aspect no.					

country	China	France	India	Pakistan	South Africa
aspect no.					

Text II: High Youth Unemployment Is A Global Time Bomb

(A) In the US and countries around the world, high youth unemployment threatens the futures of individuals and the broader economy. Youths between the ages of 15 and 24 make up 17 % of the global population but 40 % of the unemployed, a figure that doesn't include those enrolled in school. The Middle East and North Africa region has the highest youth unemployment rate, with one in four young people unemployed. Youth unemployment is even higher in some parts of Europe, such as in Greece and Spain where more than 50 % of young people are out of work. In the United Kingdom, more than 15 % of the youth population is not in education, employment or training. And in the United States, a recent analysis by the Center for American Progress concluded that more than 10 million youths are unable to find full-time work. That means the number of young Americans out of work is greater than the population of New York City.

(B) The much-criticised Millennial generation isn't lazy. They want to continue their education, receive employment training and participate productively in the workforce. But they're hampered by weak economies, discrimination and inequality of opportunity. That's what young people around the world told a United Nations work group, of which I was privileged to be a member. Although our mandate was to make recommendations for a global development agenda for the years from 2015 onwards, I firmly believe policymakers must not wait until then to address the youth unemployment crisis. Indeed, they need to act with particular urgency.

(C) High youth unemployment causes immediate and long-term economic damage. It means young adults take longer to get married, buy homes and start families. In the long run, it means slower economic growth and lower tax revenues. Things aren't necessarily better if young people do find some sort of job. Young adults entering employment in periods of economic weakness receive lower salaries and are more likely to work in lower-skilled jobs than those who begin work during better times. As a result, they can earn 10 to 15 % less than they might otherwise have done for 10 years or longer after entering the workforce. Countries with prolonged high levels of youth un- or underemployment and a large number of disaffected youths risk social unrest.

(D) For the report we released on 30 May, we sought to hear the perspectives of the global youth. Young men and women alike pointed to education as a priority, and to ensuring sexual health care and rights. They called for an end to forced child marriage. They sought equality for women and the gay and lesbian community. The voices of the world's youth can be heard in many of the goals and targets in our report. But I think it is strongest when we call for the world to "decrease the number of young people not in education, employment or training" in every country.

(E) Policymakers and businesses need to begin today to address the youth unemployment crisis by creating jobs; helping young people build skills needed for work, including technical and vocational skills and entrepreneurship, and ensuring that the youth receive an adequate education. Socially disadvantaged youths are more likely than their wealthier, and usually better-educated, peers to be unemployed, so policymakers must deliberately make efforts to reach them in particular. The European Union's new €6-billion plan to direct more resources toward countries with youth unemployment rates above 25 % will help, but should be considered only the beginning of a larger effort.

(F) It will fall to the youth to build the world that the UN work group envisions in its report. The hundreds of young people I met over the past year showed me with their passion, energy, commitment to equality and to environmental sustainability, and above all their optimism, that they are eager to take on the task.

(G) We must do everything possible today to give young people the skills, education and employment experiences they're asking for. If we do, I am confident that 2030 will see a world where environmentally sustainable economic development is the norm, a world where we've ended extreme poverty and hunger, and a world where women and men have achieved social equality everywhere. That is the world today's young people want to build. Let's give them the tools for it. *(730 words)*

Task II: Mixed Reading (High Youth Unemployment Is A Global Time Bomb) 9 credits

1. **Multiple Choice Questions** (7)

Mark the most suitable option with a cross.

1. According to paragraph A, which of the following is true?
   - A More than half of young Europeans have no work.
   - B 25 % of young people in the Middle East and North Africa region are jobless.
   - C Globally, the youth unemployment rate is 40 %.
   - D New York City has the highest number of jobless youths in the USA.

2. Which of the following reasons why it is hard for young people to find work is mentioned in paragraph B?
   - A the young people's lack of ambition
   - B the prejudices of potential employers
   - C high expectations of potential employers
   - D the young people's ideas about careers

3. Which effect of youth unemployment, or low-level employment, is **not** mentioned in paragraph C?
   - A a difficult start for young people
   - B violent reactions of disappointed youths
   - C less income for the state
   - D the gradual decline of family values

4. According to paragraphs D and F, which of the following is **not** a concern of the global youth?
   - A a healthy natural environment
   - B unlimited opportunities
   - C protection from parental power
   - D an end to sexual discrimination

5. In paragraph E, the writer says that policymakers must focus on those young people who are …
   - A underprivileged.
   - B risk-takers.
   - C slow learners.
   - D unemployable.

6. The "report" mentioned in line 29 was compiled by …
   - A the writer.
   - B business and non-profit organisations.
   - C a group of young men and women.
   - D a United Nations work group.

7. The article is a/an …
   A appeal to political and economic leaders to act now.
   B criticism of businesses for acting irresponsibly.
   C warning for young people not to rely on government help.
   D comment on the attitudes of today's young people.

2. **Sentence completion** (2)
   Complete the following two sentences with words/expressions from paragraphs F and G.

   2.1 According to the writer, the global youth is full of energy and keen ________________________ of creating their own world.

   2.2 Education, training and employment are the ________________________ that young people need for this.

Text III: The Costs Of Draconian Anti-Crime Policies

(A) I'm old enough to remember New York in the 1980s. It was violent, exciting and often depressing. As the crack epidemic laid waste to African-American neighbourhoods, in particular, the city felt like it must have in the gang-ridden New York of the 19th century. The number of murders in the city kept rising until, in 1990, a modern record of 2254 victims was marked. The city was ungovernable, we were told. And then mayor Rudy Giuliani governed it.

(B) New police tactics, attention to smaller offences such as vandalism and graffiti, and draconian minimum sentences made a big difference. By 2005, as the prison population soared, the number of murders was just 539. And the murder and crime rates kept going down. Even when the recession hit, crime did not revive. Now there are more than 100 US cities with a crime rate higher than the Big Apple's.

(C) That is the context for what's happening now. Last week, a federal judge declared a key police tactic called "stop and frisk" – the searching of young men in high-crime areas for guns and drugs – unconstitutional.

(D) Who lives in those high-crime areas? Mainly black and Hispanic New Yorkers. And that meant that black and Hispanic young men were all too easily the main target for the policy. The statistics tell the tale. One way to see whether race, rather than genuine suspicion of illegality, was the criterion for stopping someone is to see how many of those stopped were in fact carrying a gun or drugs. Between 2004 and last year, New York police stopped and frisked black New Yorkers 2.3 million times and white New Yorkers 435,000 times. The black suspects were found to be carrying drugs or guns or other weapons about 16,000 times. The whites? Also about 16,000 times. In other words, 143 innocent black New Yorkers were stopped and frisked for every 27 innocent white New Yorkers. This huge discrepancy can only be interpreted as racial profiling.

(E) More to the point, the number of people stopped and frisked rose by a staggering 600 per cent in the past decade although the crime rate was reaching record lows. If black citizens are targeted disproportionately, they understandably feel singled out only because of their race. White youngsters in the hip nightclubs of lower Manhattan routinely have ecstasy or a cannabis joint in their pockets and are almost never stopped. But a young black kid with a joint in his pocket in the Bronx is a sitting duck. If he is found guilty, his future is ruined by drug laws that give him a jail sentence and a criminal record. This unfairness causes resentment, even if it can reduce crime rates even more.

(F) My diagnosis: the anti-crime pendulum has clearly swung too far. The goal in a free society is not to get rid of crime but to get rid of crime without creating a police state. So it's good news that the turning of the tide in New York has been matched by a similar broad backtrack across the country. Many Republican southern states with very high incarceration rates have begun to cut costs by jailing fewer non-violent drug offenders. And last week the federal government announced that there would no longer be minimum sentences for first-time non-violent drug offenders in federal jails.

(G) Of course, generally, the US is still another universe when it comes to incarceration rates. There are about 720 people in jail per 100,000 Americans. But even in this hard-on-crime country there comes a point at which the social and financial costs of draconian anti-crime policies overwhelm the benefits. To be in favor of the crackdowns that the mayor of New York City ordered in the 80s and 90s does not mean you have to support them long after they have resolved the problems of their time. In that chaotic crime-ridden era, Giuliani was right. But today the cost of mass incarceration, the toll of lives ruined and the dangers of racial profiling loom larger. *(674 words)*

Task III: Mixed Reading (The Costs Of Draconian Anti-Crime Policies) 11 credits

1. **Gapped summary** (6)
   Fill in the gaps with words from the corresponding passages from paragraphs A, B and G of the text – only one word per line.
   Note: The summary does not always follow the order of the text. Please also provide the number of the line in which you have found the word/expression.

   Throughout the 1980s, the murder rate in New York City increased, mainly due to a ________________ ________________ (l.). It peaked in 1990, when more than 2000 murders were counted. To solve the crime problem, the ________________ (l.) of the city took harsh measures. For example, very strict ________________ (l.) prison terms were introduced. The consequence: rates ________________ (l.) while the number of crimes, including murders, went down. And the figures stayed low. Even during the economic downturn after 2007 crime did not increase again.

   Therefore, in his conclusion, the author says that the crime problem has been ________________ (l.). That is why he calls for a return to less draconian crime prevention policies. He says that nowadays the disadvantages of those policies are much greater than the ________________ (l.).

2. **Short-Answer Questions and Sentence Completion** (5)
   Answer the following questions with words from paragraphs D–F only.

   2.1 How does the writer support his argument that "stop and frisk" is unfair?
   with the help of ________________________________

   2.2 When people are stopped and frisked because they are black, it is called
   ________________________________.

2.3 Which expression does the author use to describe a person who is very likely to be picked on by the police?

____

2.4 Name <u>one</u> of the expressions the writer uses in paragraph F to describe the <u>radical change</u> in anti-crime policy.

____

2.5 Which group of people benefits from the new ideas concerning incarceration?

____

B Writing

Task IV: Descriptive Writing 9 credits

Choose <u>one</u> of the following tasks (1 <u>or</u> 2) and write about 100 words.

1. **Describing a picture:**
   Describe the situation in the picture. What can we learn from it?

© *gazmandhu. Shutterstock*

2. **Describing statistics**
   What do the following statistics tell you about the employment situation of black and white men and women in the USA?

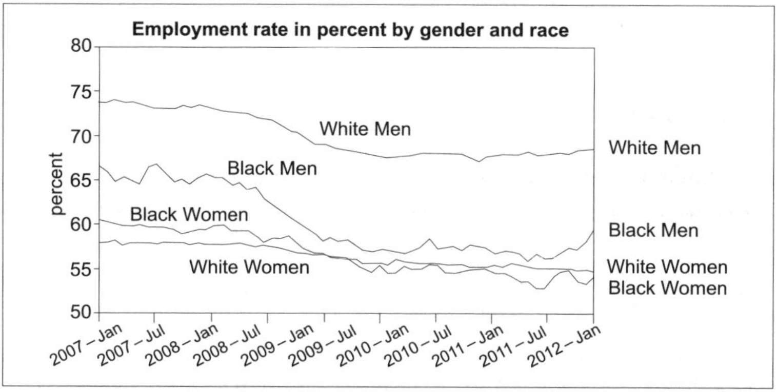

source: Bureau of Labor Statistics, Current Population Survey

Task V: Argumentative Writing 21 credits

Choose <u>one</u> of the following topics (1 <u>or</u> 2) and write at least 200 words.

1. **Topic 1**
   Why are more and more people fed up with big sport events?

2. **Topic 2**
   Playing games is just as important for adults as it is for children.
   Do you agree? Give reasons for your opinion.

Lösungsvorschläge

Hinweis: Die Aufgaben müssen nicht in der vorgesehenen Reihenfolge bearbeitet werden. Sie können so vorgehen, dass Sie die Aufgaben zuerst lösen, die Ihnen am leichtesten fallen. Halten Sie sich nicht zu lange bei einer Aufgabe auf, bei der sie nicht weiterkommen, sodass Sie noch genügend Zeit für die anderen Aufgaben haben.

A Reading Comprehension

Task I: Multiple Matching (Royal Baby – How the Rest of the World Covered the Story)

***Hinweis:** Es empfiehlt sich, jeden der zehn Textauszüge zur Berichterstattung in einzelnen Ländern für sich zu lesen und danach die zwölf genannten Aspekte zu überfliegen. Aus der Arbeitsanweisung geht hervor, dass zu jedem Textauszug nur ein Aspekt passt. Falls Sie einen Aspekt nicht gleich zuordnen können, fahren Sie erst einmal mit der Aufgabe fort und grenzen Sie die richtige Lösung dann anhand des Ausschlussverfahrens ein.*

United States: 5 – anger about unsuitable ideas of femininity

***Hinweis:** siehe Z. 7–10: "… Lauren Apfel bemoaned a "princess culture in which girls … idolise characters distinguished mainly by their trim waistlines, their title, and their ability to wear a diadem." She called for "women who can be admired for their strength of purpose, their brains, their skills".*

Australia: 4 – an alternative version of the young royal family

***Hinweis:** siehe Z. 14–16: "The Northern Territory has announced it will be presenting the royal couple with baby crocodile George. He will live with crocodiles William and Kate that were given to the couple on the occasion of their engagement."*

Iran: 1 – a criticism of the state of affairs in Britain

***Hinweis:** siehe Z. 22–24: "'Today, the British public – grinding under massive budget cuts, unemployment, poverty wages, social deprivations and crumbling services – are thrown scraps of feelgood comfort from the much hyped event.'"*

Canada: 10 – a whole country asked to pay tribute to the baby

***Hinweis:** siehe Z. 28–30: "… suggested that 'everyone consider holding a Canadian royal baby shower some time during this summer – a simple neighbourhood party, with guests raising a glass, giving a few dollars to a charity and signing a card.'"*

Russia: 6 – a mistake concerning the members of the royal family

***Hinweis:** siehe Z. 35/36: "… the Russian newspaper Kommersant's website embarrassingly wrote that the baby was the "first child of Charles and Kate".*

China: 12 – the celebration of a new life born in less happy circumstances

***Hinweis:** siehe Z. 38–40: "The royal baby's birth was preceded by earthquakes in Gansu province, so many newspapers' front covers featured the first baby born in the Gansu area after the disaster instead."*

France: 3 – a mixture of ridicule, excitement and nostalgia in the media

***Hinweis:** siehe gesamten Abschnitt: "Le Monde mocked the media frenzy in the UK. But many other French newspapers bought into the hype. "Everything you need to know about this birth," read the headline in Le Parisien.*
Le Figaro dedicated articles to 'l'arbre genealogique des Windsor' (the Windsor family

tree). One commentator suggested the French were missing their own royal family, who were rather unceremoniously ditched over 220 years ago."

India: 8 – the difficulty in putting the birthday present on display

***Hinweis:** siehe Z. 53–55: "Sudarsan Pattnaik, noted sand artist … created a sculpture for the royal baby … Plans to exhibit it had to be put on hold, though, due to heavy rainfalls …"*

Pakistan: 2 – the British royals presented as a globally branched-out family

***Hinweis:** siehe gesamten Abschnitt: "… has investigated the royal baby's family tree and made this discovery: 'The baby's relations will stretch from a simple Parisian actress via the Dracula princes in Romania, to even an Islamic sultan from Seville in Spain, who descended from the Muslim prophet Mohammed, experts say.'"*

South Africa: 9 – the focus on more pressing problems in large parts of the world

***Hinweis:** siehe Z. 70–74: "… dangers of pregnancy in Africa and whether the duchess would have survived there. 'Every day, around 800 women die from causes linked to pregnancy and childbirth. And it will come as little surprise that the majority of these deaths occur in poor countries … 99 % of all maternal deaths occur in developing countries, largely in sub-Saharan Africa and South Asia.'"*

***Hinweis:** Die Aspekte 7 und 11 passen zu keinem Textauszug.*

country	**US**	**Australia**	**Iran**	**Canada**	**Russia**
aspects	5	4	1	10	6
country	**China**	**France**	**India**	**Pakistan**	**South Africa**
aspects	12	3	8	2	9

Task II: Mixed Reading Tasks (High Youth Unemployment Is a Global Time Bomb)

1. Multiple Choice

1 B

***Hinweis:** siehe Z. 4/5: "The Middle East and North Africa region has the highest youth unemployment rate, with one in four young people unemployed."("one in four" = 25 %); Hier müssen Sie genau lesen, auf was sich die Daten beziehen.*

2 B

***Hinweis:** siehe Z. 12–14: "The much-criticised Millennial generation isn't lazy. They want to continue their education, receive employment training and participate productively in the workforce. But they're hampered by weak economies, discrimination and inequality of opportunity."*

3 D

***Hinweis:** Hier sollen Sie ankreuzen, welche Auswirkungen der Jugendarbeitslosigkeit in Abschnitt C nicht erwähnt werden. Gehen Sie nach dem Ausschlussverfahren vor:*
A siehe Z. 21: "young adults take longer to get married, buy homes and start families"
B siehe Z. 28: "risk social unrest"
C siehe Z. 22: "lower tax revenues"

4 B

Hinweis: Gehen Sie auch hier nach dem Ausschlussverfahren vor:
A siehe Z. 46: "commitment to environmental sustainability"; ("sustainability" = Nachhaltigkeit)
C siehe Z. 31: "end to forced child marriage"
D siehe Z. 32: "equality for women and the gay and lesbian community"

5 A

***Hinweis:** siehe Z. 39–41: "Socially disadvantaged youths are more likely than their wealthier, and usually better-educated, peers to be unemployed, so policymakers must deliberately make efforts to reach them in particular."*

6 D

***Hinweis:** siehe Z. 15/16 und Z. 44/45: "… young people around the world told a United Nations work group, of which I was privileged to be a member."; "… that the UN work group envisions in its report"*
Der Autor („writer") des Artikels hat den Bericht („report") nicht alleine verfasst, sondern er war Teil der Arbeitsgruppe der Vereinten Nationen, die den Bericht erstellt hat.

7 A

***Hinweis:** siehe Z. 36/37: "Policymakers and businesses need to begin today to address the youth unemployment crisis by creating jobs …"*
Auch die Überschrift versinnbildlicht eindrücklich den Ernst der Lage („time bomb").

1	2	3	4	5	6	7
B	B	D	B	A	D	A

2. **Sentence completion**

***Hinweis:** Zur Vervollständigung des jeweils Satzes sollen Wörter oder Ausdrücke aus den Absätzen F und G entnommen werden.*

2.1 According to the writer, the global youth is full of energy and keen **to take on the task** (**Z. 47**) of creating their own world.

2.2 Education, training and employment are the **tools** (**Z. 53**) that young people need for this.

Task III: Mixed Reading

Text III: The Cost of Draconian Anti-Crime Policies

1. **Gapped Summary**

***Hinweis:** Für diese Aufgabe sollen sie sich auf die Absätze A, B und G konzentrieren (markieren Sie diese am besten). Lesen Sie die Absätze genau durch, bevor Sie die Sätze vervollständigen. Schreiben Sie in jede Zeile nur ein Wort aus dem Text. Beachten Sie auch, dass der Inhalt des Lückentextes nicht immer der Reihenfolge im Text entspricht. Vergessen Sie auch nicht, jeweils die Zeilennummer anzugeben.*
Worterklärungen:
Z. 2: crack – Name einer äußerst gefährlichen Droge; epidemic – Epidemie, Seuche
Z. 9: to soar – hier: in die Höhe schnellen
Z. 40: incarceration = imprisonment
Z. 43: crackdown – hartes Vorgehen

Throughout the 1980s, the murder rate in New York City increased, mainly due to a **crack epidemic** (l. **2**). It peaked in 1990, when more than 2000 murders were counted. To solve the crime problem, the **mayor** (l. **5**) of the city took harsh measures. For example, very strict **minimum** (l. **8**) prison terms were introduced. The consequence: incarceration rates **soared** (l. **9**) while the number of crimes, including murders, went down. And the figures stayed low. Even during the economic downturn after 2007 crime did not increase again. Therefore, in his conclusion, the author says that the crime problem has been **resolved** (l. **45**). That is why he calls for a return to less draconian crime prevention policies. He says that nowadays the disadvantages of those policies are much greater than the **benefits** (l. **43**).

2. **Short Answer Questions and Sentence Completion**

Hinweis: Hier müssen Sie sich auf die Absätze D, E und F konzentrieren, die Sie am besten wieder markieren. Entnehmen Sie die Wörter nur diesen Abschnitten. Zeilen müssen Sie hier nicht angeben.
Worterklärungen:
zu 2.2.:
to frisk: to search with one's hands to see if someone hides something
racial profiling – hier: aus rein ethnischen Gründen „filzen"
zu 2.3.:
to be picked on: to treat someone repeatedly unfairly
sitting duck: someone easy to attack or to take advantage of

2.1 with the help of **statistics** (Z. 17)

2.2 When people are stopped and frisked because they are black, it is called **racial profiling**. (Z. 24)

2.3 **sitting duck** (Z. 30)

2.4 **turning of the tide** (Z. 35) / **backtrack** (Z. 36)

2.5 **non-violent drug offenders** (Z. 37, 39)

B Writing

Task IV: Descriptive Writing

Hinweis: *Nur eine der beiden Aufgaben ist zu bearbeiten. Die Vergabe von 9 Punkten erfolgt im Verhältnis von 3 : 6 für das Erfassen des Inhalts inklusive darin enthaltener Botschaft und der sprachlichen Darstellung. Halten Sie sich auch an die vorgegebene Länge von etwa 100 Wörtern. Deutliche Unter- oder Überschreitungen können zu Punktabzügen führen.*

1. **Describing a picture**

Hinweis: *Sie sollen erkennen, dass es hier um die Sicherheit im Straßenverkehr geht.*
- *Beschreibung des Bildes: Die Fahrerin des Autos liest oder sendet gerade eine SMS auf ihrem Handy. Dabei sieht sie nicht, dass vor ihr eine Frau mit zwei Kindern über die Straße geht.*
- *Kernaussage: Man darf sich beim Autofahren nie ablenken lassen, da sonst gefährliche Situationen entstehen.*

Safe driving

Inside a car, we see a young lady. She is driving with only her right hand on the steering wheel. In her left hand she is holding a mobile phone. Obviously, she is reading or typing a text message. In the rear mirror we see her face turned towards her phone, which shows she is not looking at the street, where a young woman, a child next to her and another child in her arm, is in the middle of the left lane (the photo is taken in Britain), crossing the street. A terrible accident seems to be inevitable.

We learn from this cartoon that we should never be diverted from watching the traffic as the unexpected can happen. *(119 words)*

2. **Describing Statistics:**

Hinweis:

- *Wie aus Überschrift und Einleitung ersichtlich, handelt sich bei der Statistik um die Entwicklung der Beschäftigungsrate (in %) in den USA, aufgeteilt nach Geschlecht und ethnischer Zugehörigkeit.*
- *Der Statistik ist zu entnehmen, dass die Beschäftigungszahlen der weißen Männer beträchtlich höher sind als die der schwarzen Männer, während jene für die weißen bzw. schwarzen Frauen nahe beieinander liegen. Die Linien für schwarze Männer und Frauen zeigen auch deutliche Auf- bzw. Abwärtsbewegungen.*
- *Aus der Statistik kann geschlossen werden, dass schwarze Arbeitnehmer und Arbeitnehmerinnen weitaus stärker von wirtschaftlichen Entwicklungen betroffen sind, als weiße Angestellte, und ihre Arbeitsverhältnisse weniger stabil sind. Die Kurvenverläufe könnten auch eine Benachteiligung aufgrund der Hautfarbe nahelegen.*

From 2007 to 2012, the employment rate of white men went down from 74 % to 70 %, the rate of black men from 67 % in 2007 to 61 % in 2012, showing more ups and downs. So the gap between black and white employment rates increased from 7 % to 9 %.
In contrast, the rates for white and black women were closer, with 61 % of black and about 58 % of white women employed in 2007. In 2012, 57 % of white and 56 % of black women were employed. The line for white women is quite stable, whereas that of black women shows more ups and downs – similar to that of black men. All in all, it seems that black employees are more affected by economic trends. *(132 words)*

Task V: Argumentative Writing

Hinweis: *Hier sollten Sie nicht weniger als 200 Wörter schreiben, wenn Sie Punktabzüge vermeiden wollen. Die 21 Punkte werden nach den Kriterien Inhalt, Sprache und Stil (3×7 Punkte) vergeben. Neben dem Einleitungs- und Schlussgedanken sollen dabei mindestens zwei Argumente ausgeführt werden. Vergleichen Sie hierzu auch die „useful phrases“ im Kapitel „Hinweise und Tipps“. Beachten Sie, dass Sie nur eines der beiden Topics bearbeiten müssen.*
Topic 1 fragt nach den Gründen (why?) für eine Entwicklung, wobei der wichtigste Grund zum Schluss dargelegt werden sollte. In Topic 2 wird nach der eigenen Meinung gefragt. Dabei können nur zustimmende als auch nur ablehnende Argumente gebracht werden, aber auch eine ausgewogene Sichtweise mit begründeter Entscheidung.

1. **Composition Topic 1**

Why are more and more people fed up[1] with big sport events?

More and more people are critical of huge sports events. In Brazil, for example, a great number of people were against the Football World Championships in their country. Why is that so?

In the eyes of a lot of people, the Football World Championships or the Olympic Games now only take place to make sponsors, officials and politicians richer. Mega sports events are also often misused by authoritarian governments, for example the Winter Games in Sotchi, Russia. They were a big show, but at a huge cost: the environment was destroyed and people were forced out of their homes.
The most important reason for the opposition to big sports events is that they cost a huge amount of money – which the host country's citizens (or taxpayers) have to pay. The Sotchi Games have been the most expensive Winter Games so far, and the Football World Championship in Brazil was more expensive than the World Cups in Germany and South Africa added together. In Brazil, people took to the streets to protest against the waste of money – money which could have been spent on education, social welfare and infrastructure.

To conclude, more and more people demand sustainable and more considerate sport events that don't take place at the expense of the environment and the population. *(214 words)*

1 to be fed up with sth.: to be tired / unhappy / bored of sth.

2. **Composition Topic 2**

Playing games is just as important for adults as it is for children.
Do you agree? Give reasons for your opinion.

In one of his great essays, the German poet Friedrich Schiller claimed that human beings are only at their best when they are playing. When people play they enjoy themselves and forget all their troubles and sorrows.

I agree with Schiller's statement, and I think playing can also have a positive effect on grown-ups. They can exercise their skills and expertise, and they learn that even if they lose, it isn't tragic. Furthermore, playing with others is a social activity which brings people together and can make them content and happy.

For children, however, playing is more important for two main reasons. Children follow their natural impulse of exploring the world through playing. Even when they destroy, e. g. a mechanical clock, they gain experience. While playing with others, for example, they also get to know what it means to win or to lose. In each case, they have to learn that it must be done in a gracious way. Parents and teachers should take up this natural drive and teach children the things they need to know in a way which is appropriate.

To sum up, Schiller's thesis should be embraced, the more so as far as children are concerned. *(202 words)*

Berufliche Oberschulen Bayern – Englisch 12. Klasse
Fachabiturprüfung 2015

A Reading Comprehension

Text I: Taking Control of Everest Climbers' Environmental Impact

(A) More than 3,000 people have stood atop Mount Everest since the world's highest peak was first climbed by Edmund Hillary and Tenzing Norgay 60 years ago. Climbing Mount Everest has become part of the adventure industry. In 2013, the first Saudi woman and female amputee made the summit. Other mountain records include the first wedding and the first video call. But all of these firsts come with a downside: the booming alpine tourism industry is having a big environmental impact.

(B) Nepal has eight of the 14 highest mountains in the world, including Mount Everest. Nepalese authorities say that the number of visitors has roughly tripled in the past 20 years. With the increasing number of tourists comes a growing amount of rubbish left behind on the mountains: food wrappers, climbing gear, oxygen cylinders, and even the bodies of climbers who died along the way. The frigid temperatures mean trash does not biodegrade.

(C) Over the past six decades, an estimated 50 tons of trash has been left on Mount Everest, "the world's highest garbage dump." Mountaineering associations have complained about the growing number of inexperienced climbers leaving their garbage behind to save the energy they need to reach the summit or return to base camp alive. Famous climbers such as Reinhold Messner have said Mount Everest has been trivialized, calling for Nepal to close off access to the mountain for a handful of years to allow it to recover.

(D) Now Nepal's tourism ministry has acted, deciding that from April 2014 onward, every climber going beyond base camp will be required to bring back at least eight kilograms (17.6 pounds) of their personal waste and hand it over to officials stationed there. That's the amount the government estimates an exhausted climber discards along the way. The aim is to make sure that no new trash will be left on Everest.

(E) Pasang Sherpa, general secretary of the Nepal National Guide Association, thinks this new garbage rule is a good idea, but what's lacking are clear instructions. "It's not yet clear how many days after starting the ascent of Mount Everest we have to bring back the trash. And they also didn't say how much has to be brought down from which camp. There are many different camps on different heights and we have to know from which camp we have to bring back how much," he said.

(F) If climbers don't bring back their garbage, the tourism ministry will take legal action against them, Nepalese officials said. But what exactly these legal actions entail remains unclear as well. Up to now, Everest climbers have had to pay a deposit of $4,000 (€ 2,900) that was refunded after proving that they brought back everything they took up the mountain.

(G) According to Gordon Janow, Director of Programs of *Alpine Ascents*, a United States-based mountaineering school, Mount Everest can push even the most experienced climbers to their limit and if someone doesn't pick up all of their trash, it doesn't mean that this mountaineer doesn't care about the environment or is lazy. "If someone is struggling to get down and stay alive it might be hard to think about picking up the trash," he said. "So if someone doesn't come down with eight kilos, will a Nepali attorney find the person in their home country and will a judge say they should have taken the trash down even though it might have caused them an injury?"

(H) The new rules were not implemented to limit tourism. The Nepalese tourism ministry in fact encourages the increasing number of climbers and recently cut its fees in half for individual climbers of Mount Everest and other Nepalese peaks to attract yet more tourists. There are also plans to fix additional ropes and possibly ladders to ease congestion at bottleneck areas like the Hillary Step[1]. After all, Everest's tourism industry earns Nepal $ 3.3 million a year in climbing fees. On top of that, it supports tens of thousands of trekking guides and hotel owners who depend on climbers and tourists for their livelihoods. It will take a combined effort from mountaineers, the local Sherpa people and Nepalese authorities to liberate Mount Everest from its piles of rubbish. *(697 words)*

© Anne-Sophie Brändlin, Deutsche Welle;
http://www.dw.de/taking-control-of-everest-climbers-environmental-impact/a-17502443
(March 19, 2014, adapted and abridged)

1 Hillary Step – the 12-meter-high (40 feet) final rock wall which climbers have to scale to reach the summit of Mount Everest

Task I: Mixed Reading (Taking Control of Everest Climbers' Environmental Impact) 11 credits

1. **Gapped summary** (6)

Fill the gaps in the summary with appropriate words or expressions (one word per line) from the corresponding sections of the text (B and D to G). Do not make any changes or adjustments. Please also provide the number of the line in which you have found the word/expression.

In Nepal, a growing number of mountaineers has caused masses of rubbish which will not ____________________ (l.) due to the extremely cold climate at this altitude. In the case of Mount Everest, Nepal's ministry of tourism has ordered visitors to carry down the portion of waste which each of them supposedly __________________ (l.) while climbing and descending the mountain. Despite the approval of the Nepal National Guide Association, it has been pointed out that this new regulation is ______________ (l.) clarity. Until now, mountaineers have had to make a payment which was __________ (l.) when they carried back their waste. In the future, those who do not cooperate will have to face ______________ ______________ (l.), but the exact procedure has not been established yet.

In the death zone of Mount Everest even the ___________ _____________ (l.) adventurers have to fight to survive and may therefore be unable to think about collecting waste. However, that does not mean that they are not interested in protecting the environment.

2. **Short-Answer Questions and Sentence Completion** (5)
Answer the following questions or complete the sentences with words/expressions from paragraphs A, C and H.

2.1 In recent years Mount Everest has seen a lot of unusual superlatives – however this trend is not only positive because of its

____.

2.2 Which temporary measure has been demanded by well-known mountaineers to protect Mount Everest?

____

2.3 The local authorities did not intend ______________________________ when they set up the new regulations regarding Mount Everest.

2.4 Why do local authorities plan to attach new climbing gear to certain passages?

____

2.5 Apart from the money they pay the country directly, tourists also contribute to the locals' ______________________.

Text II: How Britain got so fat

(A) In May 2012, fire engines, police and an ambulance were called to the family home of a teenager called Georgia Davis in Aberdare, South Wales, in order to get her out of it. Nobody could dream up a more horrifying and humiliating nightmare for a girl of her age. A team of more than 40 people was involved in demolishing an upstairs wall of the semi-detached house and constructing a wooden bridge to get a specially reinforced stretcher into her bedroom. Georgia weighed 400 kg, said some reports. Nobody really knew – she was too heavy to get on the scales. Georgia's rescuers extracted her through a 10 ft square hole in the brickwork and took her to hospital. She was covered by a sheet, because she could no longer get into any of her clothes.

(B) The 19-year-old was morbidly obese and her organs were failing. Her mother, Lesley, called the ambulance because Georgia could no longer stand. For months she had not moved from her bedroom, where she spent her days on her laptop and watching TV. Eventually she grew too big to get out of the door.

(C) Georgia is the extreme marker of a massive problem that has its roots in the way we live today and affects all of us. Two-thirds of us are overweight. A quarter of us are obese and in real danger of damaging our health and dying prematurely. But we are in denial. Obesity looks like Georgia, we think. It doesn't look like us.

(D) Obesity is not something to gawp at, and it is not a problem just for other people. It affects most of us. It's not about the way we look, or the size of dress or trousers we wear. This is about a very real threat to our health. Obesity is a life-shortening condition. Life expectancy in the UK, which has risen steadily since records began, may for the first time be about to fall. Moderate obesity cuts life expectancy by two to four years, and severe obesity could wipe an entire decade off your life. The costs to health services and to the world's economies of vast numbers of people becoming sick and unable to work are already huge and increasing. The National Health Service (NHS) is spending £ 5 bn a year treating the consequences of obesity, and the bill is expected to reach £ 15 bn within a few decades.

(E) Georgia was 15 when she first hit the front page of the Sun, weighing more than 200 kg and branded Britain's fattest teen. The question everybody eagerly asked was what had she been eating – how big a mountain of food? How many cakes at one sitting? Why she should want to was very much of minor interest. Georgia and her mother, who is also obese, spoke of comfort eating after Georgia's dad died when she was five. Social services discussed removing her from the family, but she resisted.

(F) We can avoid being overweight by exercising personal responsibility, politicians say, voicing the script written by the food industry. We choose what we put into our mouths. We ought to know what will make us fat and have the self-restraint to stop eating. But can you really make that judgment of Georgia at the age of seven, who even then weighed 70 kg and whom Lesley admits she fed with condensed milk as a baby?

(G) Georgia sold her story to the tabloids and TV to get the money to go to a weight-loss camp in North Carolina, where she lost half her body weight. She came back to find nothing had changed at home – her mother bought fish and chips because there was nothing to eat in the house. Georgia's own account, as told to a tabloid newspaper: "Around eight weeks after returning from camp, I drifted off the plan. I felt really alone. My mother wasn't doing it with me at home and my friends weren't doing it at college, so there was no motivation to continue. I started reverting to my old ways. I wouldn't eat for half a day, then start bingeing into the night."

(H) There has been no comprehensive plan from any political party to tackle the obesity problem. The unwillingness to talk about fatness allows politicians to avoid the issues or offer half-hearted responses; above all else, it enables them to avoid what they fear would be a damaging confrontation with the powerful economic players within the food and drink industry. Politicians are also afraid they will be accused of taxing the poor if they hike the prices of cheap foods. One government after another has opted for talks and voluntary agreements on food labelling and marketing to children. The deals that have been struck have been partial and ineffective.

(I) To reach the housing estate where Georgia was brought up, you have to climb a steep road. A lot of cars are passing, where once adults and children would have had no option but to walk. Now there is nobody on the pavement. Neither is Georgia in the yellowish-cream semi-detached house, one of many identical homes on the estate. Her mother appears at the door. "She doesn't live here any more," she says. "But she won't speak to you. She has a contract with the Sun." *(878 words)*

Task II: Multiple Choice (How Britain got so fat) 9 credits

Mark the most suitable option with a cross.

1. Georgia's rescuers …

   A were able to use already existing equipment to help her.

   B had to make special preparations to get her out of her house.

   C could not move her because she was too heavy.

   D had never seen anything more shocking before.

2. At the time Georgia was rescued, she had …

   A recently spent the whole day in her own room.

   B moderate physical problems.

   C learned a lot about media usage.

   D been off balance for some time.

3. Figures suggest that most people …
   - A don't lead a life that is beneficial to their health.
   - B realize the dangers involved in being obese.
   - C are suffering from life-threatening obesity.
   - D ignore reports about unhealthy diets.

4. In paragraph D, the author states that …
   - A obesity is a major problem for the textile industry.
   - B fat people inevitably die young.
   - C the rise in Britons' life expectancy may come to a halt.
   - D extremely obese people may die up to 10 years earlier.

5. Which of the following is **<u>not</u>** mentioned as an economic effect of obesity (paragraph D)?
   - A Losses for industry because of sick leave and early retirement.
   - B Higher spending on weight-related illnesses.
   - C Unaffordable costs for the National Health Service.
   - D A tripling of National Health Service expenditure.

6. The author tells us about Georgia's past that …
   - A her mother had welcomed the help of social services.
   - B initially she had had a rather happy childhood.
   - C the public was very interested in why she was eating so much.
   - D she had already gained nationwide attention at a younger age.

7. Paragraph F says that British politicians …
   - A have set up a plan to tackle wrong eating habits among children.
   - B often state that gaining too much weight can be prevented.
   - C regularly voice that obesity is linked to a genetic predisposition.
   - D are independent of the food industry in their view on obesity.

8. After returning from a weight-loss camp Georgia …
   - A was no longer influenced by her social environment.
   - B regained weight because she would eat all day long.
   - C didn't succeed in maintaining her new lifestyle.
   - D urged her mother to buy fast food.

9. According to paragraph H, …
   - A politicians fear being blamed for putting lower social classes at a disadvantage.
   - B there have already been well-designed political schemes to combat obesity.
   - C several British governments have had some success in fighting obesity.
   - D British politicians don't mind a clash with the food and drink industry.

Text III: This is what happened when I drove my Mercedes to pick up food stamps

(A) I grew up in a white, affluent suburb, where failure seemed harder than success. In college, I studied biology and journalism. I climbed the ladder quickly, always achieving a better title, a better salary. And my boyfriend was making good money, too.

(B) When I found out I was pregnant in February 2008, it was a shock, but nothing we couldn't handle. Two weeks later, when I discovered "it" was actually "they" (twins, as a matter of fact), I panicked a little. But not because I worried for our future. My middle-class life still seemed perfectly secure. I just wasn't sure I wanted to do that much work.

(C) The weeks flew by. My boyfriend proposed, and we bought a house. Then, just three weeks after we closed the deal, the market crashed. The house we'd paid $ 240,000 for was suddenly worth $ 150,000. It was okay, though – we were still making enough money to cover the exorbitant mortgage payments. Then we weren't. Two weeks before my children were born, my future husband found himself staring at a pink slip. The days of unemployment turned into weeks, months, and, eventually, years. In just two months, we'd gone from making a combined $ 120,000 a year to making just $ 25,000. Our savings dwindled, then disappeared.

(D) So I did what I had to do. I signed up for Medicaid and the Special Supplemental Nutrition Program for Women, Infants and Children (WIC). It's not easy. To qualify, you must be pregnant or up to six months postpartum[1]. I had to fill out at least six forms and show my Social Security card, birth certificate and marriage license. I sat through exams, meetings and screenings. They had a lot of questions about the house: Wasn't it an asset? Hadn't we just bought it? They questioned every last cent we'd ever made. On top of this, I had to get my health checked and blood work taken to determine whether I was at risk of improper nourishment without the program. It's not very bourgeois. But I did it.

(E) Driving to the WIC office the first time was scary. It wasn't an office, like I'd thought it would be. It was the basement of a dreary church. We sat in disused pews, waiting to be called for our coupons, which would get us some tuna, a gallon of milk, baby formula. To this day, it is the single most embarrassing thing I've ever done. No one spoke to me, but they did stare. Mouths agape, the poor mothers struggling with infant car seats, paperwork and their toddlers never took their eyes off me, the tall blond girl, walking with purpose on high heels from her Mercedes to their grungy den. I didn't feel animosity coming from them, more wonderment, maybe a bit of resentment. The most embarrassing part was how I felt about myself; that I felt ashamed to be there, with that car, getting food.

(F) Using the coupons was even worse. The stares, the pity, the outrage – I hated it. Once, a girl at the register actually stood up for me when an older mother of three saw the coupons and started criticizing my purchase of root beer. "Surely, you don't need those," she said. "WIC pays for juice for you people." The girl saw my grimace. "Who are you, the soda police?" she asked the woman loudly. "Anyone bother you about the pound of candy you're buying?" Later, I thanked the girl profusely. "I've got a son," she said, softly. "I know what it's like."

(G) That's the funny thing about being poor. Everyone has an opinion on it, and everyone feels entitled to share. That was especially true about my husband's Mercedes. Over and over again, people asked why we kept that car, offering to sell it in their yards or on the Internet for us. But it was paid off. My husband bought that car in full long before we met. Were we supposed to trade it in for a crappier car we'd have to make payments on? Only to have that less reliable car break down on us? And even if we had wanted to do that, here's what people don't understand: when you're struggling, you hang on to the things that work, that bring you some comfort. That Mercedes was the one reliable, trustworthy thing in our lives.

(H) We've now sold the house. My husband found a job that pays well, and President Obama's extended unemployment benefits allowed us to crawl our way out of the hole. But what I learned there will never leave me. We didn't deserve to be poor, any more than we deserved to be rich. I still have to remind myself sometimes that I was my harshest critic. That the judgment of the disadvantaged comes not just from conservative politicians and Internet trolls. It came from me, even as I was living it.

We still have the Mercedes. *(822 words)*

© Darlena Cunha: This is what happened when I drove my Mercedes to pick up food stamps, The Washington Post, July 08, 2014 (adapted and abridged), see also: darlenacunha.com

1 Period after the birth of a child

Task III: Mixed Reading (This is what happened when I drove my Mercedes to pick up food stamps) 10 credits

1. **Multiple Matching** (6)
Match paragraphs A to F of the text with the most suitable heading (1 to 8). Fill in one number per box. Please note: There are two more headings than needed.

Paragraph	A	B	C	D	E	F
Heading						

Headings	
1	Ambivalent feelings but secure livelihood
2	Accomplishment takes great effort
3	Being judged and defended
4	Everything worked out as expected
5	Forced to reveal everything
6	Existence under threat
7	Too rich to belong there
8	Standing out from the crowd

2. **Mediation Englisch – Deutsch** (4)
Beantworten Sie die folgenden Fragen auf Deutsch. Beziehen Sie sich auf die Absätze G und H.

2.1 Aus welchen Gründen wollten die Autorin und ihr Mann ihren Mercedes in dieser schweren Zeit nicht verkaufen? (3)

- ____
- ____
- ____

2.2 Welche Maßnahme der Regierung half ihrer Familie, sich aus ihrer finanziellen Krise zu befreien? (1)

____

B Writing

Task IV: Descriptive Writing 9 credits

Choose one of the following tasks (1 or 2) and write about 100 words.

1. **Describing a cartoon**
   Describe and interpret the situation in the cartoon.

© *Randy Bish / politicalcartoons.com*

Annotation: *dt. Schneeschaufel* – engl. snow shovel

2. **Describing statistics**
   Describe the following chart. What does it tell you about murder rates in US states with and without the death penalty?

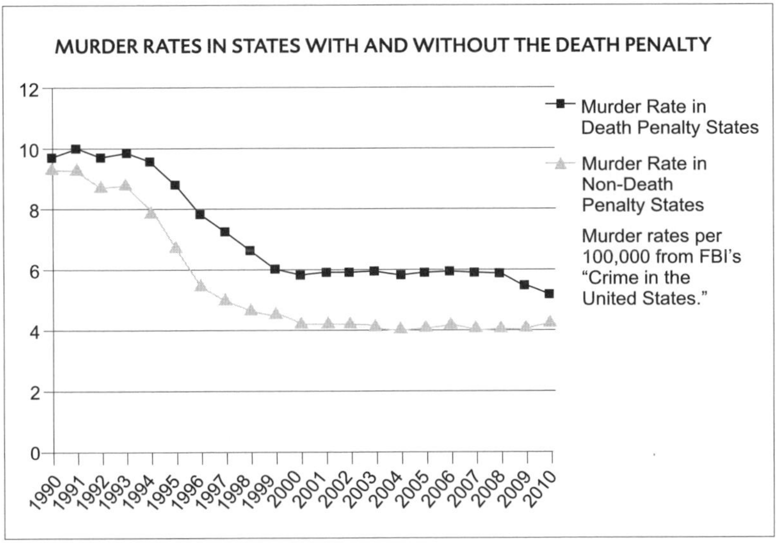

Source: Death Penalty Information Center, www.deathpenaltyinfo.org

Task V: Argumentative Writing 21 credits

Choose <u>one</u> of the following topics (1 <u>or</u> 2) and write at least 200 words.

1. **Composition Topic 1**
   Cheap fashion labels and continuous innovation in electronics have contributed to a throw-away mentality in society.
   What is problematic about this trend?

2. **Composition Topic 2**
   Modern technology makes it possible for us to be in permanent contact with employers, family and friends.
   Discuss the pros and cons.

Lösungsvorschläge

Hinweis: *Die Aufgaben müssen natürlich nicht in der vorgesehenen Reihenfolge bearbeitet werden. Vielmehr ist es empfehlenswert, so vorzugehen, dass Sie zuerst die Aufgaben lösen, die Ihnen leicht fallen. Verwenden Sie nicht zu viel Zeit für Aufgaben, bei denen Sie nicht weiterkommen, damit noch genügend Zeit für die übrigen bleibt.*

A Reading Comprehension

Task I: Mixed Reading (Taking Control of Everest Climber's Environmental Impact)

Hinweis: *Zu diesem Text müssen Sie verschiedene Aufgaben bearbeiten. Markieren Sie dabei immer die für die jeweilige Aufgabe relevanten Abschnitte.*

1. **Gapped Summary**

Hinweis: *Es ist wichtig, die Aufgabenstellung genau zu lesen. Für diese Aufgabe kommen nur die Absätze B und D bis G infrage. Zudem sollen die Antworten wortwörtlich übernommen werden, wobei für jedes Wort eine Schreiblinie vorgesehen ist. Sie sollen auch die jeweilige Zeile angeben, in der die entsprechende Wendung zu finden ist. Beachten Sie ferner, dass die Informationen hier nicht immer der Reihenfolge des Textes folgen.*
Sie sollten in jedem Fall die Absätze zum Verständnis gründlich lesen.

Worterklärungen:
Z. 12: to biodegrade – to break down or decay without any special treatment, and does not cause pollution in the process
Z. 22: to discard – to get rid of something you no longer want or need
Z. 25: to lack – to be absent/to miss
Z. 33: to refund – to have a sum of money being returned to you

In Nepal a growing number of mountaineers has caused masses of rubbish which will not **biodegrade** (**l. 12**) due to the extremely cold climate at this altitude.
In the case of Mount Everest, Nepal's ministry of tourism has ordered visitors to carry down the portion of waste which each of them supposedly **discards** (**l. 22**) while climbing and descending the mountain. Despite the approval of the Nepal National Guide Association, it has been pointed out that this new regulation is **lacking** (**l. 25**) clarity.
Until now, mountaineers have had to make a payment which was **refunded** (**l. 33**) when they carried back their waste. In the future, those who do not cooperate will have to face **legal action** (**l. 30**), but the exact procedure has not been established yet.
In the death zone of Mount Everest even the **most experienced** (**l. 36**) adventurers have to fight to survive and may therefore be unable to think about collecting waste. However, that does not mean that they are not interested in protecting the environment.

2. **Short Answer Questions and Sentence Completion**

Hinweis: *Für diese Aufgaben sind die Absätze A, C und H heranzuziehen. Die Lösungen sind wörtlich aus dem Text zu übernehmen, müssen aber den Satz grammatikalisch und/bzw. idiomatisch korrekt zu Ende führen. Zeilenangaben sind nicht verlangt, werden hier aber als Hilfestellung angegeben.*
zu 2.1: Für die „unusual superlatives" siehe Z. 3–5: "the first Saudi woman and female amputee […] the first wedding and the first video call. But all of these firsts come with a downside"
(a downside = an aspect less positive, pleasant or useful)
(an impact on sth = an impression on sb/sth)

zu 2.2: Für die „temporary measure" (hier: zeitlich begrenzte Maßnahme) siehe Z. 17/18: „to close off access to the mountain for a handful of years to allow it to recover."; (access to = entry, approach, entrance)
zu 2.3: „The local authorities did not intend", siehe hierzu Z. 43: "The new rules were not implemented" (to implement = to apply; to introduce to be used)
zu 2.4: Der Ausdruck „climbing gear" bezieht sich hier auf Z. 46: „additional ropes and possibly ladders" (congestion = accumulation, cluster) (bottleneck = very narrow, causing traffic jams/congestions)
zu 2.5: Für „contribute to the locals'" siehe Z. 48/49: "it supports tens of thousands of trekking guides and hotel owners who depend on climbers and tourists"; (livelihood = living, maintenance, subsistence)

2.1 **environmental impact** (l. 6)

2.2 **to close off access to the mountain** (ll. 17/18)

2.3 **to limit tourism** (l. 43)

2.4 **to ease congestion at bottleneck areas** (ll. 46/47)

2.5 **livelihoods** (l. 49)

Task II: Multiple Choice (How Britain got so fat)

***Hinweis:** Die Fragen folgen chronologisch dem Textverlauf. Beachten Sie darüber hinaus die Angabe der relevanten Absätze in einigen Fragen (4., 5., 7. und 9.).*

1 B

***Hinweis:** siehe Z. 4–6: „demolishing an upstairs wall of the semi-detached house and constructing a wooden bridge to get a specially reinforced stretcher into her bedroom."*

2 A

***Hinweis:** siehe Z. 11/12: "For months she had not moved from her bedroom, where she spent her days"*

3 A

***Hinweis:** siehe Z. 15: "Two-thirds of us are overweight."*
Beachten Sie hier auch Z. 15/16: "A quarter of us are obese and in real danger of damaging our health and dying prematurely." Option C kommt daher nicht infrage.

4 D

***Hinweis:** siehe Z. 22/23: "severe obesity could wipe an entire decade [= 10 years] off your life."*

5 C

***Hinweis:** Hier empfiehlt es sich, nach dem Ausschlussverfahren vorzugehen, um die Option zu finden, die nicht den Informationen im Text entspricht:*
Zu Option A siehe Z. 23–25: "The costs […] to the world's economies […] of people becoming sick and unable to work are already huge and increasing."
Zu B siehe Z. 25/26: "The National Health Service (NHS) is spending £ 5 bn a year treating the consequences of obesity"
Zu D siehe Z. 25/26: "The National Health Service (NHS) is spending £ 5 bn a year […] and the bill is expected to reach £ 15 bn"
Zu Option C findet man keinen Textbeleg, sie ist somit die richtige Lösung.

6 D

Hinweis: *siehe Z. 28: "Georgia was 15 when she first hit the front page of the Sun [= sehr bekannte engl. Boulevardzeitung]"*

7 B

Hinweis: *siehe Z. 34: "We can avoid being overweight […], politicians say"*

8 C

Hinweis: *siehe Z. 43–45: "after returning from camp, I drifted off the plan. […] I started reverting to my old ways." (to revert to sth = hier: in etw. zurückfallen)*

9 A

Hinweis: *siehe Z. 51/52: "Politicians are also afraid they will be accused of taxing the poor if they hike the prices of cheap foods."*

1	2	3	4	5	6	7	8	9
B	A	A	D	C	D	B	C	A

Task III: Mixed Reading (This is what happened when I drove my Mercedes to pick up food stamps)

1. **Multiple Matching**

Hinweis: *Die Absätze A bis F sind hier gefragt. Zu jedem Absatz ist die passende Überschrift zu finden. Beachten Sie, dass zwei der acht Überschriften nicht zutreffen.*
Nachdem Sie die Absätze A bis F im Zusammenhang gelesen haben, gehen Sie Absatz für Absatz vor. Falls Sie sich nicht sicher sind, dann gehen Sie zum nächsten Absatz weiter, um die Auswahlmöglichkeiten immer weiter einschränken zu können.

***A 4**: Everything worked out as expected*
Siehe Z. 2/3: "I climbed the ladder quickly, always achieving a better title, a better salary."

***B 1**: Ambivalent feelings but secure livelihood*
Siehe Z. 4–7: "it was a shock […] I panicked a little. But not because I worried for our future. My middle-class life still seemed perfectly secure."

***C 6**: Existence under threat*
Siehe Z. 10–15: "we were still making enough money to cover the exorbitant mortgage payments. Then we weren't. […] The days of unemployment turned into weeks, months, and, eventually, years. […] Our savings dwindled, then disappeared."

***D 5**: Forced to reveal everything*
Siehe Z. 18–21: "I had to fill out at least six forms and show my Social Security card, birth certificate and marriage license. […] They questioned every last cent we'd ever made."

***E 8**: Standing out from the crowd*
Siehe Z. 27–32: "No one spoke to me, but they did stare. […] the tall blond girl, walking with purpose on high heels from her Mercedes to their grungy den. […] I felt ashamed to be there, with that car, getting food."

***F 3**: Being judged and defended*
Siehe Z. 34/35: "a girl at the register actually stood up for me when an older mother of three saw the coupons and started criticizing my purchase of root beer."

Paragraph	A	B	C	D	E	F
Heading	4	1	6	5	8	3

2. **Mediation Englisch – Deutsch**

Hinweis: Beachten Sie, dass sich die Fragen auf die Absätze G und H beziehen. Eine wörtliche Übersetzung ist hier nicht verlangt, vielmehr genügen kurze Stichpunkte. Jede Zeile ist für ein Argument vorgesehen.
zu 2.1: siehe Z. 43–48: "But it was paid off. [...] Were we supposed to trade it in for a crappier car we'd have to make payments on?" (erster Grund); "Only to have that less reliable car" (zweiter Grund); "you hang on to the things that work, that bring you some comfort. That Mercedes was the one reliable, trustworthy thing in our lives." (dritter Grund)
zu 2.2: siehe Z. 49/50 : "President Obama's extended unemployment benefits allowed us to crawl our way out of the hole."

2.1
- er war abbezahlt / ein anderes Auto müsste noch abbezahlt werden
- ein anderes Auto wäre weniger verlässlich
- sie haben eine gefühlsbeladene Beziehung zum Mercedes / er gibt ihnen emotionalen Halt/Trost

2.2 das erweiterte Arbeitslosengeld / die erweiterte Arbeitslosenunterstützung

B Writing

Task IV: Descriptive Writing

Hinweis: Nur eine der beiden Aufgaben ist zu bearbeiten. Die Vergabe von 9 Punkten erfolgt im Verhältnis von 3 : 6 (Inhalt : Sprache). Es wird also sowohl das Erfassen des Inhalts inklusive der damit verknüpften Botschaft als auch die sprachliche Darstellung bewertet. Halten Sie sich auch an die empfohlene Länge des zu verfassenden Textes von etwa 100 Wörtern. Deutliche Unter- oder Überschreitungen können zu Punktabzügen führen.

1. **Describing a cartoon**

Hinweis: Thematisch sollten Sie erkennen, dass es sich um einen Generationenkonflikt handelt. Gegenstand des Konflikts ist der unterschiedliche Umgang mit den digitalen Medien.
- *Inhaltlich: In einer tief verschneiten Winterlandschaft – Vater und Sohn tragen warme Winterkleidung – händigt der Vater dem etwas verloren danebenstehenden Sohn die Schneeschaufel aus mit der Bemerkung, für das Schneeschaufeln gebe es keine App.*
- *Kernaussage: Kritik an der jungen Generation, die Gefahr läuft, nicht mehr zwischen virtueller und realer Welt unterscheiden zu können.*

The subject of this cartoon addresses the issue of gender gap.

It is winter, and there is heavy snowfall. A thick blanket of snow covers the car and the surroundings. Father and son are wearing warm winter clothes.

The father is handing his son a snow shovel while telling him that sadly, there's no app for shovelling snow. His son is just standing there looking a bit perplexed.

The author's intention is apparently to criticize young people who cannot distinguish between the virtual and the real world anymore because today, a lot of things can be done using apps. Obviously, shovelling snow is not one of them. *(107 words)*

2. **Describing statistics**

Hinweis: Thematisch geht es um einen Vergleich hinsichtlich der Mordrate zwischen US-Staaten, die die Todesstrafe anwenden, und denen, die es nicht tun.

- *Inhaltlich zeigt das Liniendiagramm die Mordraten in den Jahren zwischen 1990 und 2010, bezogen auf 100 000 Einwohner. In den 1990er-Jahren halbierte sich die Quote generell und blieb dann relativ konstant bis 2010. In den Staaten mit Todesstrafe ist die Mordrate sichtlich höher als in den anderen Staaten.*
- *Kernaussage: Die Todesstrafe ist kein geeignetes Mittel der Abschreckung.*

The chart shows in two lines respectively the murder rates between states with and without the death penalty in the USA.

The two line graphs indicate the murder rates per 100,000 inhabitants from 1990 to 2010. In the years from 1990 to 2000, the rates went down by half and then remained comparatively steady until 2010.

The statistics clearly reveal that the murder rate in states with capital punishment is visibly higher than in states where there is no death penalty.

The conclusion that can be drawn from this comparison is that capital punishment does not work as a discouragement for committing murder. *(103 words)*

Task V: Argumentative Writing

***Hinweis:** Topic 1 fragt nach der Problematik einer Wegwerfgesellschaft hinsichtlich billiger Modemarken und ständiger elektronischer Neuentwicklungen. Sie sollten also eine steigernde Darstellungsform wählen mit dem für Sie wichtigsten Argument am Ende, bevor ein zusammenfassender Schlussgedanke formuliert oder ein weiterer Ausblick gegeben wird.*
Topic 2 ist hingegen dialektisch (d. h. pro und kontra) anzugehen, wobei Sie wenigstens ein Argument für und wenigstens eines gegen die These anführen sollten. Setzen Sie auch hier den Standpunkt, dem Sie eher zuneigen, ans Ende. Als Schlussgedanke bietet sich ein eigener Vorschlag oder Kompromiss zur Lösung der Problematik an.
Weniger als 200 Wörter sollten Sie nicht schreiben, wenn Sie Punktabzüge vermeiden wollen. Die 21 Bewertungspunkte werden nach den Kriterien Inhalt/Sprache/Stil (3 × 7 Punkte) verteilt (vgl. hierzu die Bewertungstabelle im Kapitel „Hinweise und Tipps"). Grundsätzlich sollten neben dem Einleitungs- und Schlussgedanken wenigstens zwei Argumente dargestellt werden. Vergleichen Sie auch hierzu die „useful phrases" im Kapitel „Hinweise und Tipps".

1. **Composition Topic 1**

More and more people nowadays are becoming aware of a throw-away mentality in our society. These problematic consequences affect us all.

To begin with, cheap fashion labels induce people to buy garments like T-shirts, jeans, or shoes of any kind just because they look so trendy and are inexpensive, although consumers don't really need them. In order to make room in their wardrobe they discard their supposedly old-fashioned clothing. Thus valuable resources of wool, cotton or synthetic materials are wasted as only few people donate them to people in need or give them away to be recycled.

This waste of basic resources is even more the case with continuous innovations of electronics like tablets, smartphones, mobile phones etc. Younger and older people alike want to have them to be "fashionable", and the outmoded ones end up in some forgotten drawer. In the meantime, it has become widely known that in order to produce them, rare and scarce materials like platinum or certain raw materials are necessary. They have to be imported at high costs and therefore lead to dependence on foreign manufacturers.

Coming to a conclusion, we all need to be more conscious of the aforementioned problems and change our lifestyle to a more sustainable attitude leading to a more careful use of limited resources. *(215 words)*

2. **Composition Topic 2**

It is a common sight: in streets, on public transportation, while waiting for their buses – even while driving – people are constantly using their smartphones, tablets etc.

On the one hand, it is obviously an advantage to be closely linked with your friends, to exchange opinions, arrange dates, or as parents, have some information on the whereabouts of your children. Even a business connection makes it possible to work from home or to receive instructions from your boss.

On the other hand, in the course of time more and more people are beginning to feel permanently "occupied" – even haunted – by calls and demands. Many youngsters feel supervised by parents or friends since their online status or the locations they are currently visiting are broadcast, and they are constantly being asked what they are doing or why they aren't replying. Many cases have been reported of employers who don't hesitate to call after work – while you are trying to enjoy a quiet evening – demanding something to be settled at once. Carried on to an extreme, this can be reason for exhaustion or even burnout.

In my opinion, people should make up their minds to become aware of how they can maintain their privacy by simply switching off their connections or giving people a deadline after which only very urgent cases should be put through. *(222 words)*